MUSIC IS A GIFT: PASS IT ON

Rita Simó and The People's Music School

Cynthia Willis Pinkerton

ISBN: 10-1497562260
ISBN-13: 978-1497562264

DEDICATION

This book is dedicated to all the people who shared in the dream, the creation, and the continuing growth of The People's Music School: the friends, the teachers, the students, the parents, and many, many others who played a role in making the school a significant force in the Uptown community and the city of Chicago.

The meaning of life is to find your gift.
The purpose of life is to give it away.

Pablo Picasso

CONTENTS

CHAPTER 1

A Discovery

"¿Qué estás haciendo con mi bella mesa de caoba?" ("What are you doing to my beautiful mahogany table?")

Ana Isidra Rodríguez, who was twenty-seven years younger than her husband, did not often question his actions, but this was most unusual and disturbing. On her mahogany dining room table, Teodoro Simó was painting a full piano keyboard, which he was copying from a paper prototype he had drawn.

"Don't worry about it, Ana. The benefits will be worth it."

It was spring of 1939. A few weeks earlier, the family, including four-year old daughter Rita, had traveled several hours to visit one of Teodoro's many relatives, his niece Aura Celeste, daughter of his sister Beatriz. Growing tired of adult conversation, young Rita had made a wonderful discovery in a nearby room, a large piece of furniture on which she could make musical sounds. It was her first experience with a piano, and she was fascinated. She pushed some notes, then some other notes. Soon she was putting the notes together in a pattern she knew. From the other room the adults heard the melody "La Cucaracha," a traditional Mexican folk song about a cockroach. Aura, who was a piano teacher, came rushing in to investigate.

"Where did you learn how to play that?" she inquired.

"Nowhere. I just pushed these keys and figured it out," responded Rita.

Since she was still uncertain how to interpret this discovery, Aura asked Rita to play the song again. When she did, Aura pointed to a different starting note on the piano and asked Rita to play the song again beginning with the new note. The song rang out just as correctly as it had in the first key.

Aura went back to the gathering of adults looking for Rita's father, "Teodoro, this girl clearly has an innate musical sense. With such a fine musical ear, she must take piano lessons, and I know just the right teacher, Aurora Betances."

Aurora Betances Ricart lived a few blocks from Rita's paternal grandmother in the city of San Francisco de Marcorís, Dominican Republic. Later she would move to San Juan, about eighty miles away, and found a highly regarded music academy. But during these years, she was still in San Francisco de Marcorís, which was home to many in the Simó family including Rita. Aura Celeste knew Aurora well, as she was married to Aurora's brother, Luis Eduardo.

Though Teodoro was not a musician himself, the large Simó family was well known for their musical gifts. Rita's oldest brother, Francisco, was beginning to achieve acclaim as an exponent of merengue, the Latin music form created by musicians of the Dominican Republic. In addition, an older cousin of Rita's, Manuel Simó, son of Teodoro's brother Luis, was developing a highly respected career as a performer, classical composer, and conductor in the capital city of Santo Domingo. Many other family members were also known for their musical abilities. Even Teodoro had at one time enjoyed playing a guitar, according to Ana, though Rita never heard him play.

Arrangements were made for music lessons and the search began for a piano for the Simó home. For a number of weeks Teodoro searched diligently for a piano to buy, posting notices throughout the town and inquiring of every one he knew. But his search came up empty.

In the meantime, Rita's piano teacher was beginning to explore ear training and theory with her young pupil, and she confirmed that Rita's musical ear allowed her to hear the correct sounds in her head just by looking at a piano keyboard and thinking the notes without playing them. This was the beginning of the idea of making a fake piano keyboard of the correct size, so that Rita could practice placing her fingers on the correct locations and could begin strengthening her young fingers. Thus, the piano keyboard painted on the dining room table. Rita would look at the music propped up in back of the painted keyboard, hear the music in her head, and push the painted keys, singing the sounds as she played.

This continued for quite a while. In fact, it was a year and a half later before the family finally found an old upright piano to buy. Old it was and also full of termites! For several months, Teodoro worked diligently to rid the piano of termites and to restore it to a playable condition.

By the late 1940s, new and better utility systems had been developed in San Francisco de Marcorís. During the spring and summer of Rita's fifteenth birthday year, the family built a beautiful new house on land they owned next to their former home. This big, new, two-story home had all of the modern conveniences of indoor plumbing and reliable electricity and even telephones. The family continued living there until the mid-1950s, after Teodoro's death and Rita's departure for the United States. Then, since she was now alone, Ana had a new much smaller house built on another part of the same large family property. The rental from her former "big house" provided a good income as she aged.

Music has always been a part of the lives of the citizens of San Francisco de Macorís. The Simó family would often go to the central town square, where a community band gave free concerts every Sunday. The band usually included one or another member of the extended Simó family. Citizens either sat and listened or circled around the square looking for friends with whom to visit. Many of the members of the band were local music teachers, so joining the band provided an opportunity for additional free music instruction. Rita found special enjoyment in these musical evenings, as well as in the community spirit that was created.

San Francisco de Macorís also has a long history as a center of political activism, and it was therefore an area deeply affected by the turmoil of the years during which Rafael Trujillo held political power. In fact, Trujillo at one point withheld road-building funds from the town because of its significant resistance to his regime. The Simó family was no stranger to the vicissitudes of Trujillo's government. Rita remembers a frightening story from her childhood of a cousin, Juan de Dios Ventura Simó, son of Manuel Simó's sister, who was in the Dominican Air Force. On one of his flights, Juan threw flyers out of the plane criticizing the government of Rafael Trujillo. When he was exposed, he was arrested and taken to a special cell where he was slowly hacked to death, starting with his fingers and toes, followed by his hands and feet, and finally his arms and legs. When his body was reduced to a torso, it was put in a large sugar sack and deposited on the front door of his mother's home.

Rita's family also had a connection to the more widely-known story of the Mirabal sisters, whose story of resistance to Trujillo and subsequent dramatic deaths has been told in the semi-fictionalized novel *In the Time of the Butterflies*. One of the sisters was married to a close friend of the Simó family.

Some historians point to the fact that Trujillo was a major force in the modernization of the Dominican Republic, building many roads, schools, and hospitals. Ironically, it was his support of the National Conservatory of the Arts that made possible the free lessons available to gifted students like Rita Simó.

Yet those benefits were greatly overshadowed by the dark cloud of the atrocities that occurred under Trujillo, which he used as an ever-present threat in maintaining control over the people of the Dominican Republic during those years. Citizens had to be vigilant regarding both conversations and actions, and the lives of children, especially the lives of girls like Rita, were closely monitored and their freedoms curtailed out of concern for their safety.

In a 2011 return trip to Santo Domingo, Rita Simó visited the newly opened Memorial Museum of Dominican Resistance, a testament to the historical political struggles of the Dominican Republic and especially the atrocities of the Trujillo years (1930-1961). It was a deeply moving experience for Rita, as she recalled the old evils and revisited the instruments of torture that had lurked so ominously over her early years.

CHAPTER 3

Growing Up in San Francisco de Marcorís

While the shadow of Trujillo was ever present, Rita Simó's early years were still full of the fun, exploration, and sometimes mischief, of childhood. Though the family had no domestic pets, there were various animals on the family farm, and Rita enjoyed traveling to the farm with her father and riding the horses that were kept there. Teodoro was pleased that his daughter enjoyed visits to the farm, but he was distressed that she did not like the milk that was the primary product of his farming. In fact, drinking milk seemed to make her ill. It was only many years later that it was discovered that Rita suffered from lactose intolerance.

Like most young girls, Rita periodically enjoyed escaping into a world of fantasy, where she imagined herself mingling with the fascinating figures she learned about through her reading or her visits to the local movie theater. She was especially captivated by the flamboyant samba dancer and singer Carmen Miranda, and she had her mother make her a Carmen Miranda outfit, in which she dramatically paraded around the house on Salomé Ureña Street.

Rita also loved riding her bicycle around the neighborhood. When brother Alfredo starting spending time with a girlfriend, Rita at first resented the intrusion of this new person. Then she came up with a plan to recapture his attention. She would quietly ride her bicycle up to the place where Alfredo was talking with the girlfriend, then suddenly sound her loud bicycle bell, laugh, and pedal away.

Another time, Rita knew Alfredo had invited his girlfriend to go on a date to the beach. Pretending she didn't know, Rita begged him to follow up on his promise to take her to the beach and demanded to go at precisely the time of the planned date. Alfredo caught on to the game, however, and laughingly promised Rita another time for a beach visit.

In spite of his little sister's constant teasing, Alfredo continued to be a kind and considerate brother, and the two have remained intimate friends throughout their lives. Even after the death of her mother in 1992, Rita has continued to make yearly trips to the Dominican Republic, trips which always include visits with brother Alfredo.

Rita also had a special neighborhood friend with whom she shared many adventures. Gladys Chabebe was eight months older than Rita and lived next door. Their mothers were best friends and so were the two girls. Rita rarely spent time in the family kitchen and was never taught to cook, but one day she and Gladys decided to make some special treats. They found some lovely squashy mud that felt like dough, and proceeded to take it into the kitchen planning to make all kinds of pretend pastries. Before long, the room was a muddy mess. When the family cook appeared, the cooking adventure was over, and Rita was banned from the kitchen from then on. But that was all right with her. She found she really didn't like to cook after all, an attitude that has continued throughout her life.

Rita's piano playing was not restricted to her private lessons. As soon as the local public elementary school she attended through the sixth grade learned of her talent, she often served as accompanist for her class's daily singing exercises. Because she was so often the accompanist for communal singing, she never did much singing herself, outside of the ear training courses she took along the way, and, of course, the quiet singing that took place in her head whenever she looked at a musical score or imagined patterns on a piano keyboard.

The Simó home in San Francisco de Macorís had a large back yard dominated by two fruit trees, a mango tree and a guava tree. Rita loved poking with a long stick at the mango tree to dislodge the delicious sweet fruit. But it was the guava tree that held special magic for her.

One day while climbing the guava tree, Rita noticed a large procession of ants which had been attracted by the tree's sweet sap. As she watched, the ants broke into different groups, pursuing different secret chores. The patterns and the constant activity fascinated her, and she began to make up stories to go with their motions. It was too early for television, but Rita had been treated from time to time to shows at the local movie houses. To her, these ants were actors in a movie that she was creating in her head.

After spending many hours in this "ant movie" world, she began sharing the stories with her friends. When they wanted to come and see what she was talking about, she decided to take advantage of the opportunity and charge one cent per person to see her "movie." It was not long before her mother learned of her plan, and she was furious!

"How could you?" she admonished her daughter. "Are those ants yours?"

"But they are in my tree," Rita responded.

"No, Rita, they are not yours. Those ants are free. They are free to come and go, even if we cut down the tree. You have no right to charge money for something that is already free. If you do, we may have to cut the tree down so the ants can go somewhere else. When you experience such a free blessing, you must share it with others, not make them pay for it."

Ana Isidra was a kind and loving mother, but she could also be very tough when standing up for the important things in which she believed. Her deeper message was not lost on her young daughter. Rita Simó learned a lesson that day that would remain with her from that point on. Our blessings present us with unique opportunities. While one must be grateful for special gifts, it is important to know that they are given so that they can be shared.

CHAPTER 4

Leaving Home to Study in the Capital

Rita was ten years old in the spring of 1945 when she finished sixth grade in her local public school. Her piano teacher recommended that she now go to the capital city of Santo Domingo for more advanced piano study at the Conservatorio Nacional de Música. Students who showed interest and talent could receive excellent music instruction free of charge at the conservatory, supported by the Dominican government. Rita's family readily agreed and made arrangements for her to attend the Catholic Colegio Serafin de Asis for her seventh and eighth grade years. The nuns at this Franciscan boarding school made sure that Rita and several other students enrolled at the conservatory were transported to their various music lessons and classes following their academic work at the colegio.

Though leaving her family shortly after becoming eleven years old was a big change for Rita, she was excited to pursue the new adventure. The fact that there were a number of Simó relatives in the capital helped her avoid homesickness. Equally important was the fact that several years earlier her friend Gladys Chabebe had moved to the capital, and Rita could now renew her friendship with Gladys and her family.

Dominicans have long been proud of the fact that their capital city is the oldest European city in the Western hemisphere. Founded by Christopher Columbus's brother, Bartholomew, following two unsuccessful attempts to establish settlements in territory now part of Haiti, the city has had a long, dramatic history. In 1945, when Rita entered middle school, the capital had been re-named Ciudad Trujillo by the Trujillo regime, though in the minds of most citizens, it was still Santo Domingo. After Trujillo's death, one of the first acts of the new government was the official return of the city's name to Santo Domingo.

In her boarding school, Rita regularly played piano for church services and other events. Organ playing was another story, however. Though she had become familiar with the organ through her studies, she was much less interested in organ playing and avoided it when possible.

Rita found many of the courses at the boarding school to be repetitious of material she had already learned, so she looked forward to her afternoons at the conservatory. On days when she was not at the conservatory, she found a welcome diversion in the late afternoon sewing and embroidery classes at the boarding school. Watching the transformation of the plain fabrics and colorful threads into beautiful designs pleased her.

While the girls sewed, they were also expected to engage in saying their rosaries. The group was divided into two parts, which alternated in the recitation. After a full day of concentrating on studies, the girls were often tempted to have a little fun and would teasingly alter the words of the recitation, adding silly words that they muttered quietly.

In time, the presiding Sister caught on to the game, and the girls had to become more clever in hiding their silliness. There was a corner of the room where those not paying attention or causing mischief had to sit. Rita took turns there along with most of the rest of the girls.

Another break in Rita's routine was provided by the frequent presence in the capital of her half-brother, Francisco. Francisco Simó Damirón was an international pioneer in the writing and performing of merengue, the Dominican Republic's national music and dance style, which was much loved by the Dominican people.

As a young man, Francisco's musical ambitions had been discouraged by his father, who preferred that he study engineering, believing that it would provide a more dependable livelihood. But while Francisco was studying engineering, he was also quietly continuing with his music.

During the American occupation of the country, from 1916 to 1924, the U.S. military had introduced radio to the Dominican Republic. Francisco was among the first Dominican artists to make use of the new technology, and by the early 1930s, he was beaming his merengue music to foreign shores.

One day Teodoro Simó was listening to a radio broadcast from Venezuela when he heard his son's name given as the artist who would be performing the live music that followed. At first, Teodoro was livid. He had thought Francisco was pursuing his engineering studies in Santo Domingo. Following a serious conversation, Teodoro reluctantly agreed to let his son follow his love of music.

In 1945, Francisco formed a trio, Los Alegres Tres, with Negrito Chapeuseaux and Silvia de Grasse. In addition to performing in Santo Domingo, the group often toured throughout Latin America, including to Cuba, Panama, Venezuela, Puerto Rico, and Mexico, where they performed on local radio and television, as well as in clubs and other venues.

By the time Rita was studying in Santo Domingo, Francisco owned a house in the capital city. Between out-of-town engagements, he would perform in various locations in Santo Domingo, including some of the finest hotels. Sometimes on weekends he invited Rita to visit him at his home, outings which she enjoyed tremendously.

At the conservatory, Rita was assigned the premier piano teacher, Maria Blanca Lamarche. In addition, she attended regular classes in ear training, theory, and music history. It was under Señora Lamarche that Rita first learned to love the compositions of Johann Sebastian Bach.

At first she had not cared for the Bach compositions that her teachers had given her to learn. They all sounded the same to her, and she found them boring. As a result, she began "forgetting" her Bach book when she went to her lessons with Lamarche, hoping her teacher would forget to ask her about it. But Señora Lamarche wasn't so easily fooled. After the second or third time that the book had been left behind, she confronted her young student.

When Rita confessed that she was not fond of playing Bach, Maria Blanca Lamarche said to her kindly, but firmly, "Rita, you must bring your Bach book to every lesson, because beginning now, you are going to learn all the two-part and three-part inventions. If you are serious about piano, it is important that you know all of them."

Before long, Rita did become very fond of Bach's compositions, marveling at the brilliant designs by which they fit together. In fact, in the years to come, works by Bach were often included in her concerts.

Another composer who found a special place in Rita's heart was Beethoven. Early in her music studies, she found Beethoven's music exciting, partly because of its brilliant construction and melodies and partly because it was so unpredictable.

As Rita later commented, "Just as you learn one of Beethoven's works, you find that in the next one, he is taking off in a completely new direction."

Señora Lamarche expected great things of her young pupil, but she also proved to be a great inspiration to Rita. She had a wonderful ability to make the composers come alive as real people who were passionate about communicating with the world through their music.

As Rita worked on a composition new to her, Señora Lamarche would often say, "Let's listen carefully to what the composer is trying to tell us." Later in her career as a teacher, Rita often found herself saying the same thing to her students.

While no major hurricanes struck the island during Rita's years studying in the capital, there were several hurricane threats and lesser storms. Rita and her fellow students were always excited when the hurricane warnings were sounded. It meant a break from classes and a time to gather with everyone in a communal room and enjoy treats.

Rita does remember an earthquake that struck in 1946, however. It occurred when she was in San Francisco de Macorís, on summer break from school, and it happened on August 4, the day before her 12th birthday. The family had been away from home at the time. They anxiously returned to their house to find that the upright piano had moved about ten feet across the room.

But the damage at the Simó household was minor compared to that suffered by many others. The category-8 earthquake killed many Dominicans and left thousands homeless. It also resulted in a tsunami with huge waves, which added to the death toll and which mostly destroyed the beaches on the northern part of the island, beaches that had been so much enjoyed by Rita and her family.

CHAPTER 5

Maturation as an Artist

Once Rita graduated from eighth grade in 1947, she was enrolled in a new school, the Liceo Secundario Salomé Ureña, for her high school classes, as the colegios only went up to the eighth grade. Since the high school was not a boarding school and since it was far away from the Colegio Serafín de Asís, Rita went to live at a different boarding school, Colegio Quisqueya, associated with the Iglesia de Santa Clara and located nearer the high school.

The dormitory in which Rita stayed at Colegio Quisqueya was located directly across the street from the Fortalesa Ozama military prison, where many of the Trujillo regime's political prisoners were housed on the top floors. On warm summer nights, when Rita and her classmates opened the windows of their second story rooms for fresh air, the moans, crying, and occasional shrieks of the prisoners as they received unspeakable torture rang through the night air. Those sounds continued to reverberate in Rita's nighttime dreams for many years after.

There were times, however, when Rita's experiences and desires were those of a normal teenager. When she was fifteen, she admired the lovely long fingernails of some of her school friends and decided to grow longer nails of her own. During a break in her piano studies, she let her nails grow longer, tending to them carefully and admiring them as they grew. While the nails needed to be trimmed to a much shorter length once her piano studies resumed in earnest, she still cherished the experience and the memories of her longer fingernails. In time, she realized that having short fingernails was a small price to pay for her music. It is a sacrifice all pianists must make.

During her years at the conservatory Rita was expected to choose a second instrument to study. She chose trombone because she liked the sounds it could make, and she thought moving the slide up and down looked like fun. She laughs as she recalls that she never developed much proficiency on the instrument.

It was while Rita was attending the Liceo Secundario Salomé Ureña that she was assigned to a new piano teacher, Pedro Lerma. Señor Lerma was a highly respected teacher from Spain who was teaching at the conservatory through an exchange program. Under his guidance, Rita's knowledge and love of the piano repertoire continued to grow. She also became very fond of this kind and gentle man and was sad when it was time for him to return to Spain. Many years later, while Lerma was teaching at the Madrid Royal Conservatory, Rita spent a wonderful afternoon visiting with him during a trip to Spain.

Late in her high school years, Rita had another change of piano teacher at the conservatory. Her new teacher, Manuel Rueda, was very demanding of his pupils. He was also a man of many talents. In addition to musical accomplishments, he was renowned as an award-winning poet and playwright. Rita continued her lessons with Manuel Rueda up until the time she left the Dominican Republic for the United States of America.

In the spring of 1951, a few months before her seventeenth birthday, Rita graduated from the Liceo Secundario Salomé Ureña, but she stayed on in the capital to continue her music studies toward a performance diploma at the conservatory. The next three years were filled with deep concentration as she refined her piano skills and broadened her repertoire. It was also during this time that her father died, in April 1953, drawing her back to San Francisco de Macorís and family concerns there.

In 1954, Rita received her diploma from the Conservatorio Nacional de Música and then continued on with post-graduate study at the institution. Her 1954 graduation concert included compositions by Bach, Shubert, Chopin, Bartok, Prokofiev, and her cousin Manuel Simó, one of the most influential figures in her life.

Born in 1916, a son of Teodoro's brother, Luis, and Mary Rojas, Manuel Simó proved at an early age to be very musically talented. As a young child he was fond of making musical instruments out of plant stems and bones from his father's butcher shop. His family enrolled him in the local music academy, where he mastered several instruments and became a central figure in the local municipal band.

As a young man, he moved to the capital where he became a member of the national Army Band, led by José Dolores Cerón, who encouraged Manuel to take up conducting. In 1941, with the founding of the National Symphony Orchestra (Orquesta Sinfónica Nacional), Manuel entered the orchestra as both an English horn player and a percussionist. He also became assistant director of the orchestra, under its first director, Casal Chapi.

In 1952, Manuel Simó was appointed the interim director of the National Symphony, and in 1959, became its full-time director, a position he held until 1981. In 1955, he was named Director of the Conservatorio Nacional de Música. Manuel also composed a wide range of music, including symphonies, concertos, cantatas and chamber works. A number of his piano compositions were written for his friend and colleague, Manuel Rueda, and they performed them together with the orchestra, Simó as conductor and Rueda as piano soloist. Rueda also followed Manuel Simó as the director of the conservatory.

As one of the most accomplished students at the conservatory, Rita performed on various occasions with the orchestra, sometimes under the baton of her cousin. One concert in particular stands out in her mind. She was performing a concerto with the orchestra, when part way through the last movement of the composition, a member of the audience took a flash photograph of the stage. Rita became totally disoriented and lost her place in the music. Manuel glanced quickly at her from the conductor's podium, and she nodded to him to go ahead, indicating that she would work her way back in, which she did after a few measures. When the piece ended, and Rita was supposed to rise for her bow, she remained glued to her seat in fright. Manuel Simó had to come over and help her up.

At her next piano lesson, Manuel Rueda asked her to explain what had happened. She told him, "When the flashbulb went off, I lost my place."

"But, Rita, you were performing by memory, with no musical score."

"Yes, but I was seeing the image of the score in my head."

"Ah," Senor Rueda replied, "clearly you not only have perfect pitch, but you also have perfect sight memory. You see a score and it is imprinted on your mind. But, Rita, it is the music itself you must memorize, not a picture of a musical score. There is only one solution for that. From now on, every time you learn a new piece, you must have two different editions of it, and you must alternate your practicing from one to the other." From that point on, Rita has learned every important new composition alternating between two editions.

Because she was receiving her music instruction free of cost, one thing that was expected of Rita by the Trujillo government was that she preform for special occasions designated by the political leaders, especially during the visits of foreign dignitaries. In March 1955, the Vice President of the United States, Richard Nixon, visited Ciudad Trujillo on the next-to-last stage of his "Good Will Tour" of Latin America. The government had arranged for an official motorcade through the flag-decked streets of the city and positioned thousands of school children to cheer the dignitaries as they passed.

As part of a reception following the meeting between Nixon and Trujillo, Rita was asked to perform. She chose Beethoven's Sonata #24, Opus 78, in F-sharp Major, consisting of two movements. As the crowd began mingling and looking for drink and hors d'oeuvres, Rita began the first movement, first the exposition, then the development.

While she played, the conversation in the background grew louder and louder. No one was paying any attention to her playing, and Rita grew irritated. She might as well have been playing soft background music. To her, it was clear that attempting a serious performance of music by Beethoven was a waste of time. And, besides, from what she had heard about Mr. Nixon, she didn't think much of him, anyway.

Approaching the end of the first movement, Rita decided to modulate instead to the key in which the second movement ended. She proceeded to play the ending of the second movement, got up, and left the stage. There was a small bit of scattered polite applause, but no one realized that they had heard a very abbreviated version of the Beethoven sonata.

CHAPTER 6

Inauguration of the Palacio de Bellas Artes

In 1956, many festivities were planned in celebration of the inauguration of the new Palacio de Bellas Artes in the capital city. As part of the festivities, the four top piano students at the conservatory were asked to participate in several inaugural concerts in which they were required to perform works by Bach with the National Symphony. Rita was one of them.

Each pianist was required to perform one Bach concerto for solo piano and one Bach two-piano concerto. All four students were then to join in a performance of the Bach four-piano concerto. The concerts were to take place in February 1956 at the new hall and would be broadcast throughout the country on radio. The Bach compositions Rita was to perform, in addition to the Concerto in a minor for four pianos, included the Concerto in d minor for solo piano and orchestra and the Concerto in C Major for two pianos.

During the summer of 1955, before she began a period of intense practice for the concerts, Rita made plans to visit her brother Francisco, who by the mid-1950s was living in the United States on Long Island and performing at leading nightclubs in the greater New York area. It would be Rita's first trip out of the Dominican Republic and her first airplane ride.

Rita's mother was hesitant about her traveling alone, but finally agreed when Francisco assured her that he would meet his sister at the airport and see that she was accompanied by family members at all times during the visit. Aura Celeste, the cousin who had first discovered Rita's musical talent, also was now living in New York City with her family, and Rita looked forward to spending time with her.

Once in New York, Rita spent a few days with her brother, but soon she was staying with Aura's family, which included two young adult sons, Roberto and Luis. One was the proud owner of a motorcycle and offered to ride Rita around the city on his bike. She eagerly accepted, and her first explorations of the great city of New York were from the passenger seat of the motorcycle. It was an adventure she never shared with her mother, who would probably have been horrified.

Before Rita had left Santo Domingo, a teacher at the Conservatorio Nacional de Musíca had given her the name of a Puerto Rican professor at the Juilliard School of Music and recommended that she make contact and learn about this prestigious music institution while she was in New York. She made arrangements to meet with the professor at his studio.

Initially he was reluctant to spend much time with her, but when he heard Rita perform, he grew more interested, and he enthusiastically encouraged her to consider Juilliard for her future music study. He even suggested she take the proper application forms she would need home with her, just in case. Though it seemed like a distant dream, Rita picked up the forms, thinking how wonderful it would be if she could escape the cloud of Trujillo's rule and come to this exciting place to study.

Back in the Dominican Republic, Rita's lessons and practicing for the inauguration continued. Nervous energy filled the air as the four pianists anticipated the performances that lay ahead. They knew the whole country would be listening. Finally, the February inaugural concert dates arrived, and the hard work that had gone into the preparation was evident as the performers, dressed in concert black, took their turns over several days, performing with the National Symphony.

When the concerts were over, the performers thought that their part in the festivities had concluded. But they were wrong. Several weeks later, an exciting announcement was made. In appreciation for the hard work and outstanding performances of the pianists at the inauguration, prizes would be awarded to the top two performers, who could take their pick between two alternatives: a major teaching position with title of "professor" at the Conservatorio Nacional de Música or a stipend for $200 a month to be used for piano study in a degree program anywhere in the world, a stipend which would last through the length of the program. The two winners were Rita and a fellow student named Florencia Pierret. Florencia was already teaching at the conservatory and chose the post of professor there. For Rita, there was no hesitation. Here was her chance to leave the country and study at a top international music school, maybe Juilliard.

First, however, there were many issues to resolve. Her teachers and friends at the conservatory kept telling Rita that Juilliard was the school she should attend. But so far she only had a set of application forms. Even if she were admitted to the school, $200 per month would not provide both living expenses and tuition. She would need some additional financial aid.

There was another even more difficult issue. Ana Isidra was very much against Rita's living outside the Dominican Republic, where she could no longer provide for her daughter's safety. The thought of Rita living in a big foreign city like New York frightened her, and she envisioned Trujillo extending his influence and causing Rita harm there. At that time in the Dominican Republic, any "gift of Trujillo" was understood to imply the possibility of a demand for reciprocal sexual favors for the dictator or his supporters.

At this point, Manuel Simó came to his cousin's aid. First he pointed out the importance of the wonderful opportunity for Rita, and then he assured Ana that Rita's award was not technically a "gift of Trujillo," and the dictator would have no influence over her in New York. Also, he pointed out that she would be close to family members who lived in the New York area. Manuel was certain that Rita would be fine. For several months, Ana stubbornly resisted, but Manuel's arguments finally persuaded her, and she reluctantly gave her blessing.

CHAPTER 7

Applying to Juilliard

In the summer of 1956, Rita once again flew to New York City to stay with her brother and pursue the application process for Juilliard. Excited about the possibilities ahead for his little sister, Francisco willingly drove her back and forth to Juilliard, where she began the many steps toward admission to the school. At this time, before the building of Lincoln Center, Juilliard was located at 132 Claremont Avenue in the Morningside Heights area of New York, near Columbia University. Later, after Juilliard moved to Lincoln Center, the building on Claremont became part of the Manhatten School of Music.

The first step for Rita at Juilliard was an audition to determine whether she would be admitted to the piano diploma program. Her audition panel of three judges included two of the most illustrious piano instructors in the history of Juilliard, Joseph Bloch, whose students had included Van Cliburn, and Emanuel Ax, and Katherine Bacon, who would become Rita's piano teacher and remain her teacher throughout her studies at Juilliard.

Rita was also required to take entry tests in ear training and music theory. Those tests were taken under the direction of composer and pianist, Vincent Persichetti. Rita was confident that she was performing well on the tests until she was asked to write out the "Star Spangled Banner" in the key of G. She was baffled, because she was unfamiliar with the song.

Rita wasn't alone in her confusion. A young German student was having a similar problem. Mr. Persichetti saw the difficulty, and took the two of them aside for a different assignment. First he played an extended musical segment, and then he had Rita and the German student repeat the music. Rita not only repeated the music perfectly but also in the same key.

"You have perfect pitch!" Mr. Persichetti exclaimed. Rita was perplexed that this surprised him. She had always assumed that all musicians had the same sense of pitch that she had.

Rita's audition and other entry tests for Juilliard went very well, and she was admitted to the music diploma program on a full scholarship. She was also immediately advanced to the third level of music theory, where she was delighted to find that her professor in the course would be Vincent Persichetti. From the beginning, Rita was very fond of Mr. Persichetti, finding him to be a kindly Italian man who went out of his way to help her overcome language difficulties. During her first months at Juilliard, he regularly offered to give her oral tests, assuming his Italian would be close enough to her Spanish to allow them to understand each other.

Rita also fondly remembers one rainy day when Persichetti stopped to pick her up at a bus stop as both of them were headed to the school. Though at first she had not realized Vincent Persichetti's world stature, she soon learned that in addition to being an excellent educator, he was a famous composer and an eminent pianist. Many years later, when Persichetti came to Chicago to present a concert as part of the William Ferris Chorale Society concert series at Our Lady of Mount Carmel Church, Rita arranged to sit on the front row. At one point shortly before he was to perform, he spotted her. "Rita," he exclaimed. "How wonderful to see you again!"

With her stipend from the Dominican Republic, Rita was able to pay her modest living expenses in New York and purchase the music she needed. Her only other requirement came from her mother, who insisted that Rita must live with a Dominican family. Arrangements were made for Rita to stay with the Ariza family living on 105th Street at Western Avenue. Rita was the Arizas's second boarder. The other was a young woman from Puerto Rico.

Several years earlier, the Arizas had immigrated to the United States from Santo Domingo, joining a continually expanding group of native Dominicans living in New York. In fact, during the 1950s, Dominicans had become one of New York City's largest new immigrant groups.

CHAPTER 8

New York City

In many ways, music study was the least of Rita's challenges during her first months in New York City. The city frightened her with its huge population, massive buildings, confusing transportation systems, and unfamiliar language, which everyone spoke so quickly.

Rita struggled with English, as her earlier study of the language had been minimal. She enrolled in an ESL (English as a Second Language) class at Columbia University, which helped. Her ESL teacher recommended that she buy a daily newspaper and practice her English by reading it out loud. This would help her get used to the sound of her voice and would give her confidence to speak out in public situations.

But Rita also realized that living with the Arizas added to her difficulties in learning English. In their home, only Spanish was spoken, so Rita had no chance to practice her English there. After a few months, a Juilliard violin student named Sonya, with whom Rita had developed a friendship, suggested Rita move to a newly vacated room in the apartment where she was renting a room. Mrs. Hamm, Rita's new landlord, was an eighty-year-old woman who lived alone. By renting rooms to Juilliard students, she could afford to continue living in her fairly large apartment.

Located on Riverside Drive, Mrs. Hamm's apartment was much closer to Juilliard than the Arizas's, which helped convince Ana Isidra of the wisdom of the move, but for Rita there were other equally important benefits. First, Mrs. Hamm had a piano on which Rita was welcome to practice. Also, Mrs. Hamm loved talking with her student renters and was patient in helping Rita work on her English. Mrs. Hamm's apartment continued to be Rita's home at Juilliard until the fall of 1959, when she began work on her post-graduate diploma.

Figuring out meal arrangements was also a problem. In the apartments in which she lived, Rita had access to the kitchens for food preparation, but she had never learned how to cook. American grocery stores and products, as well as American cooking utensils, were puzzling to her.

Within the first few weeks at Juilliard, however, Rita discovered a restaurant run by a friendly Puerto Rican lady who cooked delicious Latin food. Unfortunately, it was not nearby. Every Saturday Rita would take a two-bus ride to the restaurant, stock up on meals for the week, which the owner would pack up for her, and then make the two-bus ride back home.

At other times, to tide her over until her next visit to the Puerto Rican restaurant, Rita would visit a small food mart nearby that had samples of sandwiches displayed behind glass. Because of her limited English, it was very helpful to be able to see and point to what she wanted to order.

As a newcomer to New York, Rita was naïve about its various neighborhoods, but she was also curious and eager to explore. One beautiful day, she decided to take a long exploratory walk and ended up in Harlem, an area she knew to have a unique place in the history of American popular music. Feeling hungry, she entered a local restaurant, and was in the process of ordering when a policeman came into the store and rapidly approached her.

"What are you doing here?" he demanded.
When she explained that she was new to the city and wanted to explore this area, hoping to experience some of its legendary music, he shook his head. "You better leave right now. You have to realize that you look and sound different around here."

Puzzled, but also frightened by his insistence, Rita rose and headed for a nearby bus stop and a return trip to her home neighborhood. But this experience was adding to a growing awareness for Rita. She had thought that the United States was supposed to be the most democratic of nations, and she assumed that "democracy" meant that all people lived more or less harmoniously and were treated equally. She soon learned that in New York, at least, this wasn't the case. Judgments were often made at first glance. Discrimination often occurred on the basis of color or national background. Latinos and African Americans were more likely to be suspected of wrongdoing and were often regarded as inferior by everyone from shop clerks to medical providers. She could see that the struggle to succeed was often more difficult for these people.

Good times were also part of Rita's experience in her new country. At Juilliard she developed several special friendships. Because their last names were alphabetically close to hers, two other piano students, Lily Siao and Judy Rosen, were often seated next to her in classes or during testing. Both had been students in the Juilliard Preparatory School before they entered as college students, so they were very familiar with the institution and helped Rita get acclimated. Though they came from three very different cultures, Lily was Chinese and Judy was Jewish, the three girls became best friends and did many things together.

Since Rita was unable to make frequent trips home, she was often invited to share short holiday breaks with Judy and her family. Through Judy, Rita was introduced to many Jewish holidays and traditions, some of which, like the Seder, she continues to celebrate.

Another highlight during Rita's years as a diploma student at Juilliard was a trip she made with friends to visit Niagara Falls, an experience that left her "breathless."

CHAPTER 9

Studying at Juilliard

While Rita's scholarship and stipend from the Dominican Republic took care of her everyday needs, it didn't provide extra spending money, so she decided she needed a part time job. She found one working several afternoons a week for Schirmer Music Company at their Juilliard branch. When there were no customers to wait on, Rita loved browsing through the stacks of music.

At Juilliard, one of Rita's favorite courses was a keyboard harmony course taught by Frances Goldstein. Rita's piano study to this point had followed a mostly traditional pedagogical path, which meant she had very little experience with musical improvisation. But Frances Goldstein's classes gave her some new perspectives on the spectrum of possibilities for music making, and Rita enjoyed developing these new skills.

It was common for Professor Goldstein to begin one of her classes with a statement such as: "Look at this series of chords I have written out. Improvise a minuet from these chords." Or perhaps, "I want you to start with a well-known melody and after playing it like you know it, play it again in a baroque style, then a classical style, a romantic style, a 12-tone style, a jazz style." In later years, Rita would use these improvisational skills in numerous circumstances ranging from providing music for church services to amusing herself and entertaining others at informal gatherings.

Both academic and performance studies continued to go well for Rita at Juilliard. Katherine Bacon was a strict but inspiring teacher. As Rita's piano studies advanced, however, Ms. Bacon became more and more demanding of her student.

For many months, Rita worked to perfect Beethoven's Sonata in E-flat Major, Opus 81a. One day, not long after Rita had begun working on the piece, Ms. Bacon asked her to repeat the first few slow measures of the introduction over and over, suggesting one and then another subtle modification. After an hour spent working on only those few measures, Rita was exhausted and discouraged. During the next week, she agonized over those measures and wondered if she would ever be able to play them in a manner that would please her teacher.

By the time she came to her lesson the following week, Rita had become completely disheartened. "I have thought about it, and I have concluded that I really shouldn't be here," she said, head bowed.

"Who told you that?" demanded her teacher.

"I say that. I'll never be able to play this whole piece right if I can't even get the first few measures right." Now Rita was close to tears. "I'm not good enough to study with you."

"Rita, why do you think I would keep working with you, that I would spend so much of my time if I didn't think you could succeed, if I didn't think you had an important talent? I'm tough on you, because I believe you can become a first-class pianist."

By now Rita could no longer hold back the tears.

"Rita, you are not a little girl any more. If you are going to make full use of the talent you have been given, you have to get tough. You must convince yourself that you can succeed as a performing artist."

Remembering that day, Rita has often found herself in the same position with her own students. When she does, she makes a special effort to say to them, "Yes, I am asking you to keep repeating that part until you get it right. But that is because I know that you can get it right. Otherwise, I wouldn't spend the time."

In the spring of 1959, Rita received her piano diploma from Juilliard, and the following fall she entered the post-graduate diploma program. It was at this time that she decided to find her own apartment. She had become more comfortable living in New York and was eager to become more independent. Her new apartment was at 121st and Amsterdam. It was small, but it was hers, and it was well located for her studies at Juilliard.

In the post-diploma program at Juilliard, Rita continued to study with Katherine Bacon. While she was not introduced to many new composers at this point in her piano study, she greatly expanded her repertoire of works of the masters she had grown to know and love, and she refined her technique and musicality.

One thing that concerned her, however, was that she and the other piano students were rarely assigned compositions by Latin American composers. When she mentioned this to various faculty members, she was told that few Juilliard instructors had much knowledge of Latin music.

There also was very little published music available by Latin composers. Rita silently vowed to do something to correct that situation if she ever had a chance.

Through her diploma and post-diploma years at Juilliard, Rita continued to receive monthly stipends from the Dominican Republic. Once a month she visited the Dominican Consulate to pick up her check. On May 31, 1961, as she was approaching the end of her post-graduate diploma studies, she received a phone call from the people with whom she had become friendly at the consulate telling her to come over immediately. Knowing it was a little early to pick up her check, she asked what was going on, but they refused to say anything further on the phone.

When she arrived at the Dominican Consulate in the late morning, Rita sensed great electricity in the air and knew that something very unusual had happened. Her friends soon gave her the news. Reliable sources had informed them that Trujillo had been killed in an ambush late the prior evening. Rita was told to keep it quiet until there was official confirmation. Several times in former years, premature rumors had circulated of Trujillo's death, and some who celebrated too early came to harm. Even if this time the rumors were true, there was still uncertainty about which political forces would be assuming power. Rita was invited to return to the Embassy after five o'clock that afternoon for a "quiet" celebration party. By then, the word was official. "El Jefe" was dead.

Once Trujillo's key supporters had been subdued by opposition forces, celebrations were widespread, both in the Dominican Republic and among Dominican ex-patriots living in New York. Optimism for a better life prevailed. But with no organized plan for succession, Trujillo's death left a large power vacuum, and democracy was something with which Dominicans of a whole generation had had no experience. An election was held, which was won by socialist leader Juan Bosch, but his government did not last long and was soon overthrown by the military.

By 1965, the situation had become so politically unstable that it prompted a second invasion of the country by the U.S. Marines. This proved to be a highly contentious occupation, but it continued until free elections once again took place in June 1966, at which time Joquín Antonio Balaguer, leader of the Reformist Party, was elected to lead the country. Though Balaguer had held positions of power under Trujillo, he vowed that his leadership would be more humane and free of political oppression, a pledge that proved not entirely true. By the time all of this had occurred, however, Rita Simó's life was following a very different track.

CHAPTER 10

The Beginning of a Dream

With her diploma studies at Juilliard completed and no longer receiving monthly checks from the Dominican Republic, Rita still was determined to stay in the United States, where she could find the most opportunities for a meaningful career in music. Through her Juilliard connections, she acquired an agent and began a schedule of traveling and performing. During the summer of 1961, she traveled as a performing pianist on the ocean liner S. S. Independence as it cruised from New York to the Mediterranean area and back.

In the fall she began a concert tour through the eastern part of the United States. At first these concerts excited her. She looked forward to sharing her musical gifts with many audiences and hoped she could serve as an inspiration to young musicians she would meet along the way. But very quickly she learned that the life of a traveling artist was a grueling one.

Among the many problems, Rita found that she could never depend on pianos in concert venues to be in good working order. She remembers one concert in West Virginia at which she was scheduled to perform a work by Robert Schumann requiring use of the sostenuto pedal. When she arrived on the afternoon of the concert to practice, she discovered that the sostenuto pedal on the piano in the concert hall was inoperable. At the last minute, she had to make a substitution and perform a work she was less prepared to play. Fortunately, all went well. But it was still an unsettling experience.

Something else bothered Rita as well. Often in connection with her concerts, she would remain after the performance to talk with members of the audience. In fact, it was that part of the experience which she gradually found she enjoyed the most. When she was on stage, she felt a distance between herself and her audience. But as she conversed with audience members after the concerts, answering their questions and often asking questions in return, these people became interesting individuals to her.

She especially enjoyed her discussions with younger people. She would ask them about their musical interests and whether they were studying music. Too often she found that the musical instruction in their schools was limited, and that private instruction was too expensive for many of them.

As these experiences continued, Rita came to realize that what she really enjoyed was this more intimate, person-to-person, sharing of her musical knowledge and gifts. She began to wonder if her real calling in music might be as a teacher rather than a traveling performer. If she could interact with children whose opportunities for meaningful music study were limited, she might find her life much more rewarding.

Back at her apartment in New York, she made some inquiries and learned of two elementary school music teacher positions that were open in area public schools. One was in Harlem, the other on West 23rd street. Each was for one teaching day a week. This schedule provided Rita with a steady income while allowing her to continue her piano practicing five or six hours most days. It also gave her the freedom to choose which concert engagements she wanted to accept.

Rita enthusiastically began her new teaching role, but it wasn't long before she realized that while some of her students were eager to apply themselves to music and very much enjoyed her classes, others were disinterested and saw music class as a time to either goof off or tune out. The problem was clear. They were in the classes because they had to be there, not because they chose to be there.

She began to dream of a special school where children chose to study music because they felt that music was important in their lives. In the United States, children from well-to-do families often had such schools available to them, or at least good private instruction, but what about those children with a love of music and a desire to learn whose families did not have the money? In the Dominican Republic, young people who wanted to study music were provided with free private study, even those with only modest talent. Why couldn't the same thing happen in this wonderful land of democracy?

The dream of creating a school for these children began to grow in Rita's mind. But she realized that such a dream would need a plan. She began sharing her idea with those around her. One of the people in whom she confided was her former Juilliard friend and classmate, Lily Siao Owyang. Now a music professor, Lily was also a strong advocate for music study outside the traditional framework. Lily supported the educational vision of her friend, but advised Rita that she first would need to develop a strong base of support for such an ambitious project.

Again and again Rita was told that the only way to realize her goal for a free music school was in cooperation with a large organization, one with the resources and structure to support such a school, and also one known to be interested in education and charitable works. She could think of only one organization fitting that description: the Catholic Church. Rita and her family had not been particularly devout supporters of their local Catholic church in San Francisco de Marcorís; however, beginning with her years in the boarding schools in Santo Domingo and during her years at Juilliard, Rita had come to know quite a bit about the institution. She also had developed a friendship with Father Dermot Brennan, a young Catholic priest who served as a chaplain to Juilliard students. She saw the Church as a strong supporter of both education and service to the poor. This had to be the path for realizing her goal.

Rita approached Father Brennan with her story and asked his advice on finding a Catholic organization that would best help her realize her dream. He recommended some books for her to read and introduced her to several Catholic nuns living in the area with whom she could discuss her options. After a number of conversations with these women, followed by much self-reflection, Rita reached the decision that to make her free school a reality she would become a nun and work through the Catholic Church.

An examination of various alternatives led her to the conclusion that the best place to go in order to pursue her goal was an institution in the middle of the United States near the Mississippi River called the Sinsinawa Mound Center. A Dominican educational complex in the far southwestern corner of the state of Wisconsin, Sinsinawa was well known for its strong focus on education and its tradition of outstanding programs in the arts, including music. Rita felt that in this place she would find kindred spirits who would support her plan for a free music school. Father Brennan had attended a New York parochial school run by nuns from Sinsinawa, and he agreed that this would be a good place for Rita to pursue her dream.

Contacts were made, and Rita was admitted as a postulant at Sinsinawa Mound beginning with the 1963 fall term. In the meantime, her commitment required that she give up her apartment and live with the Sinsinawa nuns in New York until it was time for her to travel to the convent.

The reactions of those closest to her were quick and mostly negative. "How could you waste your talent like this?" demanded Katherine Bacon.

Ana Isidra was equally distressed. Thinking that a change of scenery might help clear Rita's mind of this "silly notion," she arranged for a trip to Europe with her daughter in August of 1963. During the three-week tour, Rita and her mother visited many sites in Germany, Austria, and Italy.

31

While their tour did not focus on music, there were plenty of opportunities to visit sites associated with great composers, especially Beethoven and Mozart, and Rita took advantage of those whenever she could. Little did Rita realize that at the very same time she and her mother were on their tour, her future husband was traveling much the same path through Europe. In fact, at that time in her life, the idea of a husband was the last thing on Rita's mind.

Before her trip to Europe, Rita had realized that to remain in the United States and proceed with her goal of achieving U.S. citizenship, she first needed to apply for a green card, as her previous employment visa was expiring. She found the process confusing, however, so she contacted a friend, Wayne Liebst, for advice. Wayne gave her suggestions on how to proceed and happily agreed to write a letter of recommendation. Rita also located an attorney who helped her process the papers. Even then, she kept fearing that something would go wrong. Finally, Rita's friend Wayne assured her that everything was in order, and as soon as Rita returned from Europe, she made arrangements to travel to Toronto in early September, as it was necessary first to leave the country and present her application to a foreign Embassy before being accepted back into the United States.

Once in Toronto, her fears were further raised when, upon completing the filings with the Embassy, she was left with none of the papers she had taken with her. She was convinced this would be an issue as she attempted to re-enter the United States. After many tense moments, she was relieved when everything went smoothly, and she was once again in New York for a final farewell with her mother, who had been staying with relatives.

Ana Isidra's displeasure over her daughter's plan to enter Sinsinawa was still apparent. "I don't want to hear about it," she sighed. "You know I am not a strongly religious person, so I don't understand why you are doing this. When will I be able to see you again?"

When Rita repeated her reasons for her decision and explained her plans for the future, her mother could only shake her head, "Then do what you must. Just remember that if this doesn't work out, I will always be there to support you."

Rita was touched by her mother's affection and concern, but she was not to be dissuaded. A few weeks later, she flew to Chicago, where she changed to a train that took her to East Dubuque, Illinois.

CHAPTER 11

Sinsinawa Mound

To prepare for her trip to Sinsinawa and the life ahead, Rita had disposed of most of her clothing and other personal belongings. But she had kept a pink suit she especially liked and a pair of high-heeled shoes for traveling. In mid-September of 1963, the train from Chicago pulled into the station at East Dubuque, Illinois, after a trip through endless Midwest farm fields. It was becoming apparent to Rita that she was not only entering a very different new life but also a geographical part of the United States far different from New York City.

At the station she looked for a man named Mr. Francis, who was to meet her and escort her to the convent. When, after some time of waiting, there seemed to be no one looking for her, she decided to explore the area. She was also thirsty after her long ride, so she entered a nearby eating establishment. She found it was a bar, serving only alcoholic beverages, so she ordered a beer. Then she moved on to see what else of interest might be nearby. All she found were more bars. Still hot and thirsty, she stopped at one more of them, one that looked a little more kept up than the others, and had another beer. Only later did she learn that Dubuque, Iowa, across the river, was dry, so its residents came to East Dubuque for their alcohol consumption. East Dubuque was not a place any self-respecting young, unaccompanied woman would want to be after six o'clock in the evening!

By now Rita was more relaxed and no longer thirsty, but she was still worried about the apparent miscommunication concerning her arrival. Going back to the train station, she asked the stationmaster if there were any convents in the area. He replied that there were three or four and asked which one she wanted. When she told him that she was looking for Sinsinawa, he immediately understood and told her that Mr. Francis had been there a short while before looking for her. After making a phone call, the stationmaster assured Rita that Mr. Francis would return soon.

Suddenly Rita remembered the two beers she had consumed and the fact that she was on her way to a convent. Seeing a ladies' washroom nearby, she quickly went in and pulled her toothbrush and toothpaste out of her bag. After a vigorous brushing with a large amount of toothpaste, she was convinced that no one would be the wiser. But to be sure, she bought some chewing gum, which she chewed until Mr. Francis returned.

Rita arrived at Sinsinawa just as the sisters were heading into a music rehearsal. The first thing she heard was, "Where have you been? You are supposed to be at rehearsal. But, oh dear, first you must change your clothes. You look like you are on your way to a party!"

With that, Rita was given a black habit (a postulant garment) to put on. The pink suit disappeared into a closet, and she was ushered off to the rehearsal.

Rita's single room at Sinsinawa was very small, with just enough room for her bed, a night stand, and a small wardrobe closet, which held not only her few items of clothing, but also her books, music, and any other belongings which were not to be left sitting around. There were no radios or phones. Making phone calls, except in an emergency, was forbidden; however, family members could call in, in which case a postulant or novice could go to the office to receive the call. It had been made clear to Rita that the Church would not support any trips home to the Dominican Republic until she had been with the Order for eight years. In fact, it was 1971 before she next returned for a visit to her land of birth.

Sinsinawa Mound Center is just north over the Wisconsin state border from East Dubuque. Though not a town, as there is no commercial or municipal center and most area residences are farm homes, it does have its own post office, which serves the larger area. It is a large complex, which includes not only the convent, but also St. Clara Academy, a boarding school for high school students, and facilities for retreats.

Sinsinawa's outreach extends much farther. Founded in 1847, it is dedicated to "preaching and teaching." In fulfillment of that mission, it not only has its own resident boarding school but also has close ties to other area high schools and to two nearby colleges, Rosary College (now Dominican University) in River Forest, Illinois, and Edgewood College, in Madison, Wisconsin. Thousands of nuns have received their training at Sinsinawa, and they are found throughout the world serving not only as teachers but also in many other capacities, including law and medicine.

At Sinsinawa, Rita's schedule was highly regimented. She arose at 5:00 a.m. in order to be in church by 6:00 for prayer and meditation, followed by mass at 7:00. Breakfast was at 8:00. Academic classes began at

9:00 a.m. and lasted until 11:00, at which time Rita had hoped to have time to practice piano. However, early in her first year at Sinsinawa, Rita was given chores to do in preparation for lunch, chores which had to be done between 11:00 and the noon lunch hour. In frustration, Rita appealed to her superiors to be relieved from those duties so she could practice. Finally her request was granted, though one hour of practice was still a far cry from her former schedule of five or six hours of practice a day.

After lunch, Rita helped clean up the dining room and prepare for dinner. At 1:00 p.m., afternoon classes began and lasted until 3:00, followed by prayers, and, finally, at 4:00, a free hour for study. At 5:00 the novices once again assembled to help with dinner preparations, followed by prayers at 6:00 and dinner at 6:30. Dinner was followed by free time prior to a church service at 8:30. Then at 9:30, it was bedtime.

An early frustration for Rita was the convent's regulation that allowed for a shower of ten minutes every other day on a pre-assigned schedule. Rita had grown used to a daily shower, and so had another postulant. The two of them devised a plan whereby they would share their shower times, each developing the skill of dashing in and out on a precise schedule, in order to take a quick five-minute shower every day.

At Sinsinawa Mound, Rita especially enjoyed her classes in world history and geography. The teacher, Sister Eva, was a crusty and tough older nun, but she had a way of making the material very interesting. Rita was a puzzle to her, though. Sister Eva expected students to study an hour or more per day for her class, but when she asked Rita how much she studied, Rita responded, "About fifteen or twenty minutes."

"But you do so well on the tests. You must be copying from someone."

"No, I already know most of this material," Rita replied. "I studied it thoroughly in Santo Domingo and even tutored some of my classmates there."

"So, why are you taking the class?"

"Because I have been told it's the 'will of God' that I take the classes assigned to me."

"Well," replied the teacher, "the will of God is going to have to change."

From then on, Rita did not attend the class but instead met with Sister Eva most mornings for independent study lessons focusing only on American history and geography. As part of these sessions, Rita would also bring breakfast to the teacher, and the two would talk until it was time for Rita to go to her other classes. Rita very much enjoyed this friendship and even learned to respect the woman's contrariness. Often Sister Eva would pick lightly at her breakfast.

When Rita encouraged her to eat, saying that a hearty breakfast would be good for her, she would respond, "How do you know what's good for me?"

By Easter of her first year at Sinsinawa, it was clear that Rita had mastered the academics and other expectations of a first year postulant, and she was promoted to novice and began wearing a white habit in place of the black one. It was also at this time that the music teacher in the Sinsinawa boarding school, St. Clara Academy, became ill and died. Rita was asked to fill her position.

In many ways, Rita enjoyed her teaching at St. Clara. The school was small and the students were respectful and generally eager to learn. It was at St. Clara that she encountered one very special student on whom she would have a deep influence.

Mary Frances Lubahn had been orphaned as an infant when her parents were killed in an auto accident that occurred as they were taking her home from the hospital after her birth. She had been adopted by a kind, but non-musical, Wisconsin family. Her only remaining adult relative, an elderly grandfather, had been a professor of music, and his one request of the adoptive family was that his granddaughter be given music instruction if she showed a talent.

Mary Frances not only showed talent; she was highly musically gifted. It was in the spring of Mary Frances' freshman year at St. Clara that Rita began teaching music at the boarding school. During the next year, Rita had a profound influence on Frances' musical development, and the two of them became lifelong friends.

Rita had another dream in addition to her dream of starting a free music school. She wanted to see the three great rivers of the world, the Nile, the Amazon, and the Mississippi. This dream had begun when Rita's third grade teacher, Mercedes Cordero, had given an inspiring talk on the world's great rivers.

Living at Sinsinawa, Rita was only a few miles from the Mississippi River, but she had never seen it. In April 1965, the Mississippi experienced the worst flood in its recorded history, topped only by a later flood in 1993. Water lines rose to near bridge levels in many places.

Rita was obsessed with the thought of visiting this amazing phenomenon of nature. But how could she do it? Then an idea struck her. Dental emergencies experienced by the residents of Sinsinawa were treated by a dentist in Dubuque, Iowa, on the other side of the river. Soon Rita was complaining of a terrible tooth pain, which she claimed made it very difficult to eat. An appointment was set, and within a few days Rita was on her way to Dubuque.

The churning river lapping at the tops of the bridge support posts was truly a dramatic spectacle, and Rita was fascinated. With eyes glued to the many flooded buildings and submerged trees, she marveled at the power of nature.

When the dentist ushered her in and asked her where the pain was, she sheepishly confessed that she really didn't have any pain.

"So why are you here?" he asked her, puzzled.

"I came because I needed to see the Mississippi and the flood. Ever since third grade when I learned about the great rivers of the world, I have wanted to see the Mississippi. This was the only way I could do it."

"You played this trick, and you want to be a nun?" He looked at her in amazement.

"Yes, but sometimes when you have such strong dreams, you need to follow them."

"And what do you do at Sinsinawa?"

"I am a music teacher and a concert pianist," Rita replied defensively, sensing that the dentist was unsympathetic with what he had heard so far.

"Ah," he suddenly laughed, and his demeanor began to change, "you play music that tells stories, and now you are telling me a story. But there is a problem. How can I bill for my services if I do nothing for you?"

"Well, I do think I may have something caught in my teeth," Rita responded hopefully. "Tell them you needed to clean out some food that was caught in my teeth, but that we were happy to find the problem was no more serious than that."

The dentist sighed and shook his head, but he proceeded to pick away at Rita's teeth and give them a good cleaning. Soon she was on her way back to Sinsinawa and another close look at the powerful Mississippi. She would always hold those images clearly in her mind. Many years later, Rita would round out her dream of seeing the world's great rivers with trips to both the Nile and the Amazon.

CHAPTER 12

A Change of Plans

At about this same time, in the spring of 1965, there was troubling news out of the Dominican Republic. Rumors were circulating concerning political upheavals that were accompanied by much violence. Rita began to worry about her family and their safety. The inability to make phone calls to family members was especially disturbing to her, and she devised a plan to reach her brother Francisco, who was currently performing in Puerto Rico and who would know what was going on.

One duty Rita had at the convent, along with the other novices, was the periodic operation of the main telephone switchboard. Knowing that her brother was performing on a television program that extended from noon to 1:00 p.m., she made a person-to-person call to him at the station during that time. As a person-to-person call that didn't reach its recipient, the call did not appear on the convent telephone record, but it did prompt a return call from Francisco.

Rita's brother confirmed that after much fighting between Dominican factions, the United States Marines had moved in and taken control. While the presence of the marines was troubling, order had been re-established. Most important, Rita's family members were all fine. Francisco told his sister not to worry.

As she had done many times before, Rita regularly played either piano or organ for church services at Sinsinawa. In 1966, her last year on the Sinsinawa campus, a new chapel, the Queen of the Rosary Chapel was built, and she played for the inauguration. While her musical talents were appreciated at Sinsinawa, Rita nevertheless realized that she was slipping further and further from both her proficiency as a pianist and her dream of starting a free music school.

In May of 1965, a special visitor arrived at Sinsinawa. Katherine Bacon had been in steady letter communication with Rita. She wanted to know how her former student was faring and what plans the institution had for her future. When Rita told her that the nuns saw her primarily as a teacher for their boarding school and an occasional fundraiser for their projects, Katherine, who usually had a reserved, controlled temperament, became greatly disturbed. During a break in her teaching schedule, Katherine arranged a trip west which included a stop at Sinsinawa.

Katherine's agitation grew when she realized she would be given only minimal time with Rita and would not even be allowed to share a meal with her. She asked to have a conference with the mother general of the convent.

"Why can't Rita eat with me? Why can't we be discussing her future?" she inquired.

"Rita's place is here with us," was the reply. "She is providing us with valuable Christian service."

"Are you making it difficult for me to talk with her because you are afraid I will change her mind about being a nun?" Katherine asked.

Then she added, "No, I have already tried to do that, and I have learned to accept and respect her choice. But you must understand that God has given this girl a remarkable talent and it is important that she not waste it. If she is to be a teacher, she must at least be a teacher in a college or university, where she can work with advanced students and maximize her opportunities for serious performance. And for this, I strongly urge you to let her return to college in order to earn advanced degrees. Until then, it is important that she continue her piano studies with worthy teachers."

Katherine Bacon's words made an impression on the leadership of Sinsinawa, and after some deliberation, it was agreed that Rita should resume her piano studies with renowned pianist, Soulima Stravinsky, son of composer Igor Stravinsky, who was on the faculty of the University of Illinois. For many months, Rita made monthly trips from Sinsinawa through Chicago to Champaign-Urbana for lessons with Stravinsky.

In addition, it was decided that Rita would complete one more year as music teacher at St. Clara, during which time a replacement for her would be found, and then, in the fall of 1966, she would return to Juilliard as Sister Maria Ana Simó for further study.

CHAPTER 13

A Return to Juilliard

Back at Juilliard, Rita enrolled in the bachelor's degree program. Once again she studied piano with Katherine Bacon. Her past academic records left her one year short of the requirements for the bachelor's degree she would need before proceeding on to the graduate level. Since her music study had been extensive in her former years at Juilliard, the courses she needed to take were primarily in the liberal arts, and included 20th century world literature, astronomy, and an advanced level of mathematics, a subject in which she had always excelled. In the literature class, Rita developed a particular fascination with the German author Thomas Mann.

Though her living expenses were minimal, since she was living at the Corpus Christi Convent on 121st Street, Rita still needed a way to help pay for her schooling and music, as she had long ago stopped receiving money from the Dominican Republic. It was arranged that she would be given an assistantship in the piano for non-majors department. In that position, she became a keyboard teacher to a number of Juilliard students whose main course of study was voice or an instrument other than piano, since all Juilliard music students are required to have at least basic piano skills.

During the two years Rita taught in the piano for non-majors department, she had quite a few pupils who went on to illustrious musical careers. She continued to be grateful for everything she had learned in Frances Goldstein's keyboard harmony course during her first year at Juilliard. The wisdom she gained from those classes made up a large part of the material that Rita passed on to her students during the years of her assistantship in the piano for non-majors department.

Rita's experiences in New York during her final two years at Juilliard were very different from those in her first years in the city. As a nun at Corpus Christi, her life was much more regimented and confined. Along with her other duties at the convent, she often played for Corpus Christi church services. Between her studies, practicing, teaching schedule at Juilliard, and church responsibilities, she had little time for anything else.

Rita received her bachelor's degree from Juilliard in the spring of 1967, and the following fall she proceeded into the master's degree program. During the summer of 1967, she volunteered through Corpus Christi in a summer program at a local settlement house. Once again she met young people, many with talent, who were eager to study music and play instruments but unable to afford the lessons or pay for instruments. The experience deepened her dedication to the idea of creating a special music school for students like them.

As part of her continuing obligation to the Dominican Order at Sinsinawa, on December 2, 1967, Rita gave a benefit concert for Dominican High School in Milwaukee, Wisconsin, which is affiliated with Sinsinawa Mound. A reel-to-reel recording was made of the program by a member of the audience and given to Rita, who put it in a cardboard carton and forgot about it for almost thirty-five years.

During the early months of 1968, as Rita finished up work on her master's degree at Juilliard, there was another course of study that she was pursuing, one leading to United States citizenship. This goal was especially important to her, because on several occasions she had wanted to sign petitions relating to political issues but had learned she could not do so as a non-citizen.

One time she had signed a petition against the war in Vietnam and had received a letter from the Department of State warning her against signing her name as a non-citizen. This letter was a key motivator to Rita in her pursuit of citizenship.

It was in the late spring of 1968 that Rita Simó was sworn in as a United States citizen. When the presiding judge asked her why she wanted to become a citizen, the answer came quickly, "I want to be able to protest injustice in my new country." For a young woman who had grown up under repressive political conditions, this right was especially sacred.

The nuns of Corpus Christi planned a large party to celebrate Rita's new citizenship status. Rita was ecstatic. Everyone was talking about the 1968 national elections and their importance for the future of the country. Rita could now be part of the democratic voice of her adopted country, and she planned to exercise that right in many ways.

CHAPTER 14

Boston University

To qualify as a professor at the university level, it was now important for Rita to begin work on a doctoral degree, and for this step in her career she moved to Boston in the fall of 1968 to begin three years of studies toward a Doctor of Musical Arts in Piano Performance degree at Boston University. In addition to Boston University, Rita had also auditioned for entry to the Indiana University and University of Michigan doctoral programs and had been accepted as an applicant to both, but she chose Boston.

During her first year in Boston, Rita lived in a single room in a student residence hall on Ivy Street, which was operated by Catholic sisters, though those who roomed there were of all religious backgrounds. As she had done at Juilliard, Rita supported herself through an assistantship at Boston University teaching theory classes. Beginning in her second year, she also taught piano and theory classes at nearby Emmanuel College. After her graduation from Juilliard, Rita's friend Lily Siao, now Lily Siao Owyang, had accepted a teaching position at Emmanuel College. By the time Rita arrived in Boston, Lily was head of the music department at the college, and she arranged for a teaching position for her friend at Emmanuel.

At the beginning of her second year in Boston, Rita moved to an apartment in a three-flat building on Commonwealth Avenue, which she shared for two years with another doctoral student, Elizabeth Williams, whom everyone including Rita called "Bizza." A highlight of these two years for Rita was the December 16, 1970, 200th birthday of Ludwig von Beethoven. Rita and Bizza sent birthday party invitations to everyone they could think of, after which they spent several days decorating their apartment inside and out. The party began at eleven in the morning and lasted until eleven o'clock that night, with a continual buffet of German food and music, both live and recorded, by Beethoven. And a grand party it was, a worthy celebration in memory of the great composer!

The theory class Rita taught at Boston University provided her with a particular challenge, because it was scheduled for 8:00 a.m. Throughout her life, Rita has never been a "morning person," and she found it hard to be alert in the early daytime hours. At the end of her first year of teaching she was asked to evaluate her course. She used the opportunity to say that while the course had gone reasonably well, she was sure she would be a much more effective teacher if the hour were a little later. For the next two years, her theory course was scheduled for 9:00 a.m.

During the time Rita was taking courses at Boston University, a strong distraction existed less than a mile away, Fenway Park, home of the Boston Red Sox. Rita developed a strong loyalty to the team and attended games whenever possible. One spring she was enrolled in a course that ran from 1:00-3:00 p.m. Every now and then, she would go to the class and then leave in the middle in order to get to the park in time for the day's game. After this happened a few times, her professor called her to his office.

"Why are you leaving my class so early? Do you find it uninteresting?"

Rita figured it was best to tell the truth, and she confessed how much she loved attending the Sox games. Then she waited for the professor to continue scolding her.

"Well, all right, Rita, if you are up to date in your school work, you may occasionally leave class early to attend a game on one condition. The next day you come to class, you will have to give all of us the details of what happened." It turned out the professor was also a devoted Red Sox fan.

For the continuation of her piano studies, Rita's new teacher was Bela Nagy. Born in Hungary, Bela Nagy had been a student of Ernst von Donanyi, Zoltan Kodaly, and Leo Weiner, among others. In addition to his many years as a teacher, he was highly regarded as a pianist and had performed widely throughout the world. While he performed a considerable amount of contemporary music, he specialized in the late music of Beethoven and Liszt.

Professor Nagy was reserved and demanding, but Rita respected him as an excellent teacher. He was also quite a perfectionist. Often he would have Rita play a musical phrase over and over, sometimes without making much comment. When she would question this repetition, he would simply reply, "But you must understand that each time you play it, it is a little different. Each time, it becomes more and more your own. Each time, it is better."

For music history and analysis, Rita's professor was Joel Sheveloff, a highly regarded music scholar, author, and teacher. In addition to being a good teacher, Rita found him to be a kindly, supportive mentor, and she was pleased when she learned that Sheveloff was to be the supervisor of her doctoral dissertation.

From her earliest years at Juilliard, Rita had been troubled by the lack of access to and knowledge about Latin American music within North American universities and music conservatories. She was determined to have her doctoral thesis address this issue and perhaps bring about a change. While she planned to touch upon the entire historical spectrum of Latin American music in her dissertation, she felt strongly that many of the most important contributions to the repertoire had been made in the recent decades, and she decided to concentrate on the period beginning in 1930.

The title she selected for her dissertation was: "Stylistic Analyses of Piano Music of Latin America Since 1930." She created a general outline, working from information she already knew about Latin music, and began thinking about examples she might use to illustrate her points. Joel Sheveloff was impressed by Rita's motivation and subject matter, and in the spring of 1971, he approved Rita's dissertation subject and general plan.

Throughout her years in Boston, Rita continued to give recitals. One she particularly enjoyed occurred at the University in 1970 when she joined her friend Lily Siao Owyang, in a first performance of Linda Woodaman Ostrander's "Duet for Piano (4 hands)," a work in three movements, Prelude, Dance and Variations. Throughout their years together in Boston, the two pianists often performed together, and Lily continued to encourage Rita in the pursuit of her dream of a free music school.

Rita had also stayed in contact with her former St. Clara student Mary Frances Lubahn, and she was delighted when Frances, as she now called herself, enrolled in the Boston University masters' program in voice in the fall of 1970. During that academic year, Rita greatly enjoyed frequent visits with her former student.

Frances' teacher between 1970 and 1974 was Chloe Owen, who also had many students in New York City. After Frances received her master's degree from Boston, she moved to New York to continue her studies with Owen and to explore career opportunities. Her teacher, however, encouraged her to audition at various European opera houses. In the 1970s, it was widely understood that for an American to build an operatic career, it was important first to perform in European houses.

Following this advice, Frances set up a series of auditions in Europe. Her first contract, from 1975-77, was with the state theater in Oldenburg, Germany. In 1977, she was offered a contract with the Graz Opera in Austria, where she was invited to join their resident artist group as well as to become a professor at the Graz University for the Performing Arts. Though she performed in operas, oratorios and other concerts throughout the world, Graz would remain Frances' primary home throughout her musical career.

Rita continued to find much pleasure in tracking Frances' growing career. Later, when Rita had established herself in Chicago's Uptown neighborhood, Frances would spend a day or two with her former teacher during her annual visits back to the Midwest to visit family. On many of those visits, Frances would give recitals and conduct master classes at The People's Music School.

Though she performed primarily as a mezzo-soprano, Frances' vocal range was quite large. As Rita proudly proclaimed of her protégé, "She was one of the few sopranos I have ever heard who could sing a really good Queen of the Night in Mozart's *Magic Flute*."

While most of the concerts Rita performed during her years at Boston University were in the United States, a very important one occurred in the summer of 1971. Sinsinawa had provided funds for Rita to return to the Dominican Republic, her first visit home in eight years.

On July 17, she gave a benefit concert for the San Francisco de Marcorís Lions Club in the Palacio de Bellas Artes in Santo Domingo, where she had performed so many times in her younger years. The recital program consisted of works by Beethoven, Chopin, Stravinsky and Albeniz. It was a joyous homecoming, during which she reconnected with many relatives and friends after so many years away.

Also, by summer of 1971, Rita's required doctoral course work had been completed, and it was time for her to begin more concentrated research for her dissertation, as well as to begin her first college teaching job. Arrangements had been made through the Dominican Order at Sinsinawa for Rita to join the faculty at Rosary College in River Forest, Illinois. While Boston University required her doctoral dissertation to be completed and officially accepted by the spring of 1975, in the fall of 1971 when Rita stepped onto the Rosary College campus, that date seemed far away.

CHAPTER 15

Professor Simó at Rosary College

At Rosary College, Rita not only carried a full load of piano students, but she also once again taught courses in music theory. Many of the advanced piano students at Rosary requested Rita as their teacher and worked hard to meet her expectations. In addition, she developed musical connections throughout greater Chicago and performed in concerts with many of the area's finest musicians. On several occasions she performed piano quintets with the Chicago Symphony String Quartet, composed of Victor Aitay, Edgar Muenzer, Milton Preves, and Frank Miller.

Rita's teaching and performance activities kept her so busy that she had little time to think about her dissertation, which, for the most part, was put away and forgotten. It was in her second year of teaching at Rosary that a chance occurrence brought the whole project freshly to mind. She was at Roosevelt University in downtown Chicago on her way to attend a meeting of the Chicago Area Music Teachers Association (CAMTA), when, upon entering an elevator, she encountered three gentlemen, one of whom she knew from the Roosevelt faculty.

"Rita, you might be interested in meeting Juan Orrego Salas from Indiana University," her Roosevelt friend said, turning to one of the other gentlemen.

Rita was stunned. Salas was one of the Latin composers whose works she was analyzing in her dissertation. More significantly, his work had presented a particular problem on which she had spent a great deal of fruitless research time. The Salas composition that she was analyzing was a set of variations built on a central song or theme, called a pregón. These pregones were customarily folk melodies or segments of other well-known music. But after much searching, Rita had been unable to come up with the source of Salas' pregón. Now she had the opportunity to ask the composer himself. His answer was a simple one.

"I didn't take my pregón from any other source. I wrote it myself."

Rita's first reaction was one of angry frustration. "Do you know how much time I have spent searching for that pregón?" she asked.

But Señor Salas just smiled, totally disarming her. "I am so pleased you are so interested in my work," he said. And then he gave Rita's arm a friendly squeeze and wished her great success with her dissertation.

Rita enjoyed working with her students at Rosary, but by the end of her second year of teaching, a routine had developed establishing a pattern for the future, and it did not include any plan for a free music school. While many of her Catholic friends and fellow teachers admired her goal, it was becoming obvious that the Dominican Order was not interested in Rita's taking time from her teaching position at Rosary in order to start such a school. In order to realize her dream, Rita was becoming aware that she would have to do it on her own and not through the Catholic Church.

Rita was still weighing her options when she made a trip to Boston in the summer of 1973 to visit friends and check in with Joel Sheveloff. She decided to share her ideas of starting a free music school with Professor Sheveloff and confided in him that she was contemplating resigning from Rosary College in order to have time for the school. She further mentioned that since she would no longer be teaching in a college, she doubted that she would need a PhD degree, and she questioned whether it was necessary to return to Boston to write her thesis and complete her degree.

"So you want to start this free school, create it from nothing?" he asked.

When Rita agreed that was her plan, he continued, "And you expect people to believe you are capable of doing this? How can you expect people to trust you? If this is your plan, you are going to have even more need for your doctoral degree. You will need to convince people that you have the proper credentials for such an ambitious task."

Back at Rosary College in the fall of 1973, Rita began making plans for her return to Boston University for the 1974-75 academic year in order to complete work on her doctoral dissertation and prepare for its written and oral presentation. By Christmas, after much self-reflection, she had reached the conclusion that if she were to fulfill her dream of starting a free music school, she would have to do it on her own, and it would take all her time and energy. She would need to resign from Rosary College and also leave her Dominican Order.

By then, Rita had told the administrators at Rosary College that during the 1974-75 academic year she would need to take a leave of absence to return to Boston to complete her doctoral dissertation. What they did not know was that she would never return to Rosary as a professor.

In May of 1974, Rita gave an all Beethoven concert at Rosary. The program was especially well received, and it was followed by long and enthusiastic applause. As an encore, Rita played "Für Elise," a composition played by virtually anyone who has ever been a serious piano student. But instead of playing the piece at a light, quickly flowing tempo, as it is most often heard, Rita played it as Beethoven is said to have intended it, at a very slow, contemplative tempo. Once again, the audience responded with appreciative applause.

Within a few days after the concert, Rita told Rosary's president that she had just mailed a letter to Sinsinawa requesting release from her vows as a Dominican nun. She also was tendering her resignation from Rosary College in order to follow her dream of creating a free music school.

CHAPTER 16

"Doctor" Simó

Rita returned to Boston University in the fall of 1974 and moved in with Ann Kelley, a friend whom she had met through the Harvard Catholic Center during her first years in Boston. Ann had also been a Sinsinawa nun, but she had left the Order several years earlier. At the time of Rita's return to Boston, Ann was completing her ThD dissertation in Church History from Boston University and was teaching and working at the Harvard Catholic Center. She would remain one of Rita's closest friends throughout many years ahead. Ann's apartment was on the Cambridge side of the Charles River, and to support herself, Rita joined the faculty of Lesley College near the apartment.

The year began with Rita busily occupied with the usual adjustments that always come with starting a new teaching position. Then, early in November Rita received an urgent phone message from Joel Sheveloff. He insisted Rita get in touch with him right away. He wanted to know if she was close to completing the written part of her dissertation. Rita responded that she had done very little writing on her thesis, since she had been busy with her teaching obligations. She had assumed she had many months before the end of the school year to complete the work.

"It doesn't matter that your teaching has kept you so busy," Professor Sheveloff responded. "Both the written and the performance parts of your dissertation must be completed and accepted by the end of this academic year, and in order for everything to fit into the required schedule, I must have your finished written draft by the second week in February. I think you had better put this on the top of your desk right away."

Rita had not focused on the fact that the submission of her written thesis would need to be followed by several weeks of analysis by the acceptance committee, after which would come her oral presentation and accompanying concert performance. The concert schedule was already filling up, and Rita's doctoral concert would need to be scheduled soon. There was much to be accomplished both in writing and in preparing for the concert.

Even then, Rita continued to procrastinate. Ann Kelley tried to help prod her friend into action. Every morning Ann was up early, preparing for her classes. Before she left, she would be sure a sleepy and grumpy Rita was up and beginning work on her thesis. In her frustration, Rita's response was usually a defensive one, "What is one more dissertation? Who cares, anyway?" But she would soon be at her desk, working.

In early February, Ann Kelley asked to see what Rita had written up to that point. While Ann was impressed with the general content, she was astonished to realize how little Rita understood about the traditional form and language expected of a doctoral dissertation. The fact that English was Rita's second language was clearly an impediment.

"I'm afraid that there is much that needs fixing, " she told Rita. "We need to talk with Richard Griffin."

Richard Griffin worked with Ann at the Harvard Catholic Center, and he was already a published writer. He also knew Rita well. The three agreed to a plan. They would meet every morning at nine o'clock and work together for an hour or two, going over Rita's text line by line, with Richard and Ann paying attention to the language usage and sentence structure. Rita remained solely responsible for the substance and for all musical notations.

This schedule continued for several weeks, with Rita being asked endless questions by her friends: "What do you mean by this?" "Why does this have to be this way?" "Why did you choose this example?"

Little by little the manuscript was revised. By Sunday morning, a day before the written dissertation was due in Professor Sheveloff's office, all revisions had been completed, and all that remained was the retyping of the document with its footnotes. the addition of the musical examples, and the copying of extra sets for the three professors who would judge the dissertation: Joel Sheveloff; María Clodes, a Brazilian pianist on the faculty; and John E. Hasson, Associate Professor of Musicology.

The spring of 1975 pre-dated the era of personal computers, and the retyping of the dissertation, which was 121 pages long, along with the final adjustments to the detailed musical examples, which had to be hand-written, took most of the rest of the day and night. Nevertheless, the finished thesis was ready for submission to Professor Sheveloff on schedule the following day. Rita was exhausted and also worried about what unknown errors there might be in her manuscript. So when on Wednesday Professor Sheveloff phoned her and said he needed to see her immediately, her heart sank.

"Rita, did someone write this for you?" he inquired. "It is better English than I get from most students who have always lived in the United States."

Rita told him the whole story, stressing that all of the ideas and examples were hers, but that she had received help in stating her ideas in clearer and more correct English. Professor Sheveloff had only one further comment. At one point Rita had expressed an idea she had heard Sheveloff state that she assumed was general knowledge.

"No," he replied, "This is my original thought, and you need to give me credit in one of your footnotes. That is all. After you make that correction, I am ready to give the copies to the other two judges. Good job."

By the middle of March, the written part of Rita's dissertation had been approved by the committee, and her oral presentation and concert had been set for April 18, 1975.

In her doctoral thesis, Rita focused on the fact that though there are a few contemporary Latin American composers who are well known around the world, such as Alberto Ginastera, Heitor Villa-Lobos, and Carlos Chávez, there are many others worthy of serious attention who are largely overlooked. Her analysis went on to show that while most Latin composers have been influenced by various styles of Western European and North American music and also by music from a wide spectrum of music history, from early classical through 12-tone, they also have developed creative individual musical voices and styles of their own. Their compositions often incorporate the unique rhythms and folk elements of their Latin culture. In fact, the use of rhythm is central to much Latin music, and the presence of conga, cinquillo, pasillo, and samba beats can often be found woven in interesting ways into the fabric of Latin American compositions, resulting in works of great complexity and interesting musicality.

Yet works of individual Latin composers vary greatly in style and content. To prove this point, Rita proceeded to reference a long list of Latin composers, in many cases giving detailed analyses of their work and in other cases giving shortened analyses or simply making reference to them.

Composers Rita referenced, in addition to Ginastera and Villa-Lobos included:

Juan Orrego Salas (analysis)
Manuel Simó (analysis)
Andres Sas (semi-analysis)
Ernesto Lecuona (analysis)
Francisco Mignone (analysis)
Manuel Ponce (reference only)

Hilario Gonzales (analysis)
Juan Francisco García (analysis)
Lorenzo Fernández (analysis)
Camargo Guarnieri (analysis)
Alejandro García Caturla (analysis)
René Amengual (analysis)
Julian Orbón (analysis)
Héctor Campos Parsi (analysis)
Alfonso Letelier (reference to an analysis by another)
Juan Carlos Paz (analysis)
Roque Cordero (analysis)
Roberto García Morillo (analysis)
Eduardo Mata (analysis)
Juan Lemann (reference only)
Alcides Lanza (short analysis)

In all her examples, Rita stressed that these Latin composers were creating a new and vibrant fusion of styles and rhythms, resulting in "a mature and cosmopolitan form of expression," in respect and advancement of "the universal values of music."

Rita had also been hard at work on her doctoral performance presentation, which she gave at 1:30 p.m. on the afternoon of Friday, April 18, 1975, in the Marshall Room of the College of Fine Arts at Boston University. Starting with an oral historical overview of Latin music, she proceeded to illustrate the many influences and inspirations present in the music. She then performed works by seven Latin composers grouped according to various influences in their music:

Romantic Influences (various short musical excerpts given as examples)

Nationalistic Influences
      Capricho Criollo (1941).....................Juan Framcoscp Garcia
      Preludio, No. 3 (1955).....................Hilario Gonzales
      Danza Negra (1946).........................Camargo Guarnieri

Non-nationalistic Influences
      Sonatina, Allegro (1938)...................René Amengual
      Tercera sonatina (1933).....................Juan Carlos Paz
      Tercera iluminación.........................Manuel Simó

The program concluded with three dances written in 1937 by Alberto Ginastera:

La danza del viejo boyero
La danza de la moza donosa
La danza del gaucho matrero

Rita's performance presentation was a huge success, and in June 1975 she was awarded the degree of Doctor of Musical Arts in Piano Performance. She did not attend the graduation ceremony. She had more important things on her mind. It was time to begin paving the way for her new free music school.

CHAPTER 17

Planting the Seed

Returning to Chicago in the early summer of 1975, Rita moved into an apartment with Fran Holtzman, a retired grade school teacher with whom she had become friends during her years at Rosary College. Rita and Fran had become acquainted through their mutual efforts in protest of the Vietnam War. Through these protests, the two of them also had become friends with a young Jesuit scholastic named Joseph Mulligan, who would figure into Rita's future life in several important ways. In 1973, Rita and Fran had driven to Detroit for Joseph Mulligan's ordination.

Fran's apartment was on North Hermitage Avenue near Lawrence in the Uptown area of the city. At the end of July, Rita moved again, this time into an apartment at 1446 West Berteau, which she shared with three other nuns. Her request to be released from her vows still had not been officially accepted, so she was still Sister Maria Ana Simó. Rita continued living at the West Berteau address until the summer of 1976, when she moved to her own apartment, a large studio apartment at 4240 N. Clarendon, where she remained for the next two and a half years.

As Rita had grown familiar with the city of Chicago during her teaching years at Rosary College, she had found herself drawn to the Uptown area. It was an area of great ethnic diversity, with a constant stream of immigrants and refugees from Latin America, Africa, Southeast Asia, and, as the Soviet Empire began collapsing a decade later, Eastern Europeans. Most of these newcomers were eager, like Rita, to become productive citizens in their new country. Uptown also included both middle and working class families, and it was an area that had cultivated a unique sense of community. Rita saw Uptown as a good location for her new free music school.

Though Rita was no longer on the faculty of Rosary College, three senior class piano students who had studied with her previously made a special request to have her serve as their teacher for their final year, and Rosary arranged for her to use a studio on Monday afternoons to give them lessons. While Rosary paid her for these lessons, Rita chose to donate most of the earnings back to the college, feeling that was only fair given the circumstances of her departure. But that left her needing to find a way to finance her new life.

One day in July, Rita read about a two-year-old government program called CETA that had been created to put those needing jobs in touch with employment opportunities. There was an office nearby for matching clients with CETA jobs, and Rita decided to make an appointment. After she handed the CETA representative her application form, she was asked more questions about her background.

"You have a PhD? Then I'm afraid you are overqualified for anything we can offer," said the representative.

"But people with a PhD need jobs, too, and some do not have them," responded Rita, somewhat irritated, "I need a job, and I am willing to take almost anything."

"There is a social services organization on Devon with a program for children with challenges. They need a person to wash the windows in their building."

"I'll take it," said Rita.

Later that day, the CETA office called Rita and said that her job assignment had been changed. Instead of the job on Devon, she was to report to Father James Dunkerley at St. Peter's Episcopal Church on Belmont near Broadway in the Lakeview neighborhood.

On the following Monday, Rita arrived at Father Dunkerley's office to learn that her assigned job was to recruit participants and help with a free lunch program that the city of Chicago was funding for senior citizens at the church. Rita also learned that Father Dunkerley's plan was to expand the hours of the lunch program to include various enjoyable activities. He told Rita that it was especially important to create a "feeling of family" for the participants in the program, so that it didn't feel like just a "handout."

He then introduced Rita to the church secretary, and told her to assist Rita as needed. With the secretary's help, Rita created flyers to pass out to potential clients for the program. In addition to telling a little about the program, the flyers invited people to attend an informational meeting to be held at the church the following week.

Knowing that low-income senior citizens often looked for an inexpensive place to have lunch, Rita took her flyers to a nearby McDonald's restaurant, where she sat down at a table near the door. Within a few days she had passed out hundreds of flyers.

The day of the information meeting arrived. Though it was not scheduled to begin until 3:00 p.m., Rita arrived early to get things ready. By 1:30, people had already begun to arrive, and by 2:45, seventy people were gathered ready to hear about the program.

Father Dunkerley warmly welcomed them, "We want you to treat our church as a home, not just a restaurant," he said.

Rita then told the assembled group about some of the activities she had planned, and announced that she would be at the church between 9:30 a.m. and 2:00 p.m. every Tuesday through Friday. Among the activities Rita planned were movies, sing-alongs, Bingo, and "complaining days," where people could air their gripes and worries. On an average, around fifty people came each day for lunch and most of them stayed for the activities.

Rita continued her job at St. Peter's for more than two years. After she ceased having piano students at Rosary, she expanded her time at St. Peter's to include Mondays. When the CETA grant expired, Father Dunkerley found other money to continue Rita's employment with the program. In time, he also took an interest in her plans for a free music school and asked the church secretary to help with any printed materials or letters Rita might need.

Soon after arriving in Uptown, Rita had started attending church services at St. Thomas of Canterbury Catholic Church on Kenmore Avenue just north of Lawrence, the church attended by her friend Fran Holtzman. She enjoyed many things about the church, but found the music to be weak. One day she approached the priest, Father Michael Rochford, and volunteered to help improve the music for the services. He was dubious at first, but before long was delighted with the changes she brought. When she told him of her dream for a free music school, he listened with great interest and told her he would try to help her in any way he could.

Rita continued as music director at St. Thomas for many years on a totally volunteer basis, but to her the rewards far outweighed her service to the church. Many members and regular visitors of St. Thomas became devoted financial supporters and hands-on workers in her efforts to start The People's Music School. Looking back, she is convinced that she couldn't have done what she did without their support, especially in the early days.

CHAPTER 18

The Tiny Seed Begins to Grow

In September of 1975, a flyer arrived at Rita's apartment on West Berteau from the Saint Francis House of Hospitality, a Catholic Workers House on North Kenmore Avenue a few blocks south of St. Thomas of Canterbury Church. It was an invitation to attend a series of presentations and discussions on the theme of "The Theology of Hope," led by her friend, Father Joseph Mulligan. Rita was intrigued by the idea and decided to attend. Several weeks into his presentation, Father Mulligan asked the participants to tell their dreams of things they would like to accomplish. Rita told the group of her dream of starting a free music school.

"But," she added, "I haven't figured out how I can make it happen."

To her amazement, several in the group spoke up and expressed their willingness to help. Rita asked for their suggestions on how to get started. One talked about the papers she would need to file. Others offered to help if she found a location that needed fixing up. Several gave Rita their names and phone numbers and told her to call them when she needed help.

One person who responded with special encouragement and enthusiasm to her plan was Jim Duignan, the executive director of Chicago's Friendship House. Rita was greatly encouraged. With people like these in her new community, she just might have enough support to get started on her dream.

Rita next began asking fellow musicians she knew if they would be willing to become volunteer teachers at her free music school. Mary Therese O'Neil, a voice teacher at Roosevelt University and a former nun, and Sister Rosemarie, a music teacher at Academy of the Sacred Heart on North Sheridan Road both accepted the challenge. Mary Therese volunteered to teach voice and start a choir, and Sister Rosemarie agreed to provide instruction in flute and clarinet in addition to teaching theory classes.

To get things started, Rita was told that The People's Music School, the name she had selected for her school, must become incorporated as a not-for-profit organization with the State of Illinois. Next, the school would need to file for tax-exempt status with the Internal Revenue Service so that donations could be tax deductible. In order to be incorporated, the school needed to have a board of directors, so Rita approached several of her friends, asking them to join her in forming a board. Fran Holtzman and Jim Duignan agreed to serve.

The incorporation process with the State of Illinois was accomplished without difficulty. On November 13, 1975, Rita, accompanied by Fran and Jim Duignan, went downtown to the State of Illinois building and received the official incorporation papers establishing The People's Music School as a not-for-profit organization in the state.

The IRS filing proved much more difficult. When Rita first looked at the papers explaining the process, she was totally confused by the legal language. There was a phone number to call for more information, so Rita called. The IRS representative on the other end of the line was initially wary about Rita's explanations of her plans and asked her to supply more information about the people who would teach at the school and their credentials. When Rita gave her the information, the woman's attitude changed. She was astonished that people with such impressive backgrounds would be willing to teach for no pay. But from that point on, she became very helpful to Rita in moving the request forward.

Rita next focused on two important tasks. First she traversed the Uptown neighborhoods looking for an affordable space that could serve as a location for the school. Second, she wrote personal letters to everyone she could think of who had expressed interest in her plan for a school asking for their financial support on whatever level they could afford to help her get started. Sent from her apartment address on West Berteau, the letters read:

November 1975

Dear_____
For a long time now I have been thinking together with others about the possibility of starting a music school for individuals unable to pay for lessons. Having completed my doctoral program at Boston University last spring, I have been supporting myself by working part time with senior citizens and teaching in the Music Department at Rosary College. Because music has been so much a part of my life, I want to be able to share my talent and enthusiasm with others, especially the poor.

*Traditionally, professional music appreciation and education
has been another luxury enjoyable by an economic elite.*

*At long last, things are beginning to come together to make this
music school a reality. The school will be established in the
Uptown community of Chicago, which is home to many low
income families. In addition to teaching people with limited
means to become professional musicians, a secondary goal is to
develop an appreciation of classical music for future generations.*

*In the process of opening such a school, I have had to deal with
the reality of money. Therefore, I have spent some time doing
related research in order to submit proposals to various
foundations for their support. If you have ever done anything
like this, you know how difficult it is to get. I am going to start
the school now without any assurance of serious funding. This,
after all, is the way the poor must live. Also, if something is in
operation, it can enhance the possibility of funding.*

*In order to move ahead, I need your help. The school has
recently been incorporated as a not-for-profit corporation with
friends and professional associates coming together to form a
Board. It has been suggested that I contact a number of friends
to ask a monthly commitment of five, ten, or more dollars during
the next twelve months. If you are able to make such a
commitment, I will be most grateful. A monthly reminder will be
sent. Each month, with the reminder, I hope to include a brief
newsletter about progress at the school. Such donations are tax
deductible. Thank you for your interest and friendship.*

Sincerely,
Rita Simó

Soon, donations began to arrive along with cheerful words of
encouragement from friends across the country. Many responses came
from Rita's wonderful group of friends in Boston, friends who would
continue to support the school generously for many years. (Appendix I)

On December 16, Beethoven's birthday, the first meeting of the new
Board of Directors of The People's Music School was held in the apartment
on West Berteau. Those present included the three Board members along
with several prospective teachers, including Mary Therese O'Neil and
Sister Rosemarie.

At the meeting, Rita announced that she already had $650 in donations in hand and that she had found a street-level former beauty salon with approximately 600 square feet that had been vacant for two years at 4417 N. Sheridan Road that could be rented. "It's a mess, but it's cheap," she told them. The group gave Rita their support and told her to reserve the space with a $200 security deposit plus $200 for the first month's rent. At first the landlord would not sign the lease, concerned that the school had only $650 in the bank. But the plan moved forward when Father Rochford stepped in and signed an agreement saying he would be responsible for the rent payments if the school could not make them.

Since so much work was needed in order for the space to be habitable and pass city inspection, it was agreed that the lease period would begin in early February. Before then, volunteers from the school would be allowed access to the space in order to make the needed cleanup and decorating.

The layout of the space was discussed. It was decided that the area in the front, near the door and the only external window, would be used for a piano and chairs where parents of students or an audience could sit. It was here that the general music or theory classes would also be held. The office area was relegated to the back of the space, with the single bathroom off to the side. Paying for a telephone would be a big expense, so it was agreed that Rita would use her home phone as the contact number for the school for the time being.

The next few weeks produced a flurry of activity at 4417 N. Sheridan. The walls were thick with the by-products of the old beauty salon, including massive amounts of hairspray, which needed to be peeled or sanded off. All surfaces had to be scrubbed and then painted, including the small bathroom at the side in the back.

Rita made the rounds of local stores and any place else she could think of looking for donations of the supplies needed in the cleanup and painting efforts. Several cans of paint were donated from a surplus supply at the local office of the Chicago Housing Authority. Additional paint and other supplies were donated by the Ace Hardware store north of the school on Broadway. Other local establishments also chipped in. After making her rounds of the neighborhood, Rita would reappear with the paint, brushes, and other donations she had received.

With many volunteers offering a hand, some scrubbing, some painting, and some attending to the electrical and plumbing needs, the space gradually began to show its potential. It helped that Rita arranged to provide a steady supply of food and beer for her volunteer workers.

CHAPTER 19

"Welcome to the People's Music School in the Music Center of the People"

In early February 1976, the lease period began on the storefront at 4417 N. Sheridan. The City of Chicago inspectors arrived and gave approval, except for one thing. City regulations required that any building operating as a school had to have a minimum of two bathrooms, and the space at 4417 N. Sheridan had one bathroom. The building could not be called a school, but through a strange loophole it was acceptable for The People's Music School to operate in a section of the building called the Music Center of the People. The papers were filed under that name.

Before the school could open, there were several critical needs. Office furniture, including desks, chairs, and file cabinets, would be needed. But most important, there was the need for a piano. Rita had had her eye on a piano at St. Thomas of Canterbury Church for quite some time. The church had two upright pianos of similar quality, but had little use for the second one. Father Rochford told Rita he would love to give the second piano to her for the school, but that it was not his decision to make. Both of the pianos were owned by the Archdiocese of Chicago. Rita persisted.

Finally, Father Rochford sighed, "All right, Rita. I will write a letter to the Archdiocese explaining, and if they do not object, you may go ahead and take the piano."

Several weeks later, a group of husky male volunteers from Prologue Alternative High School were wheeling the piano down the middle of the streets between St. Thomas of Canterbury Church and 4417 N. Sheridan to the astonishment of those passing by. As Rita encountered the amused smiles and questions of those they passed, she used the opportunity to talk about her new school and to invite everyone she met to the upcoming opening celebration, which was planned for the end of the month.

As they neared their destination, a police car stopped, and one of the officers asked Rita what she was doing with a piano in the middle of the street. Her answer was simple," Can't you see what I am doing? I'm moving a piano."

After a chuckle and a warning to be cautious, the officers allowed the parade to proceed, though they continued to keep an eye on the ragtag group. Once the piano was in place, Rita followed up on an offer made by a retired piano tuner, a participant in her CETA program at St. Peter's, who had kindly agreed to tune any pianos in the school for free.

The closing of the St. Vincent DePaul parochial school, with which Jim Duignan had special connections, presented an opportunity for The People's Music School to acquire desks, chairs and other office furniture in exchange for removing them from the premises. Once again, Rita's volunteer "army" rose to the occasion with an assortment of pick-up trucks and vans, and the furnishing of 4417 N. Sheridan was completed.

With the piano and office furniture in place, the focus turned to planning for the event which would acquaint the community with the school and its teachers. During the first week of February, Rita sent out a letter to everyone on her growing list of people who had shown interest in the school. Those letters and a large number of flyers for general distribution were printed through the continuing generosity of Rita's friends at St. Peter's Church:

> *Dear Friends,*
> *The People's Music School is a reality. We are at 4417 N. Sheridan Rd., Chicago 60640. The place is called the Music Center of the People........We have been cleaning and painting. So far we have no instruments, but have learned of several possibilities that might (hope) come true next week.*
>
> *As the enclosed flyer indicates, we are planning for a grand opening on Sunday, Feb. 22nd at 3:00 p.m. Some people will play, and I hope all present might participate in some musical experience. If you are nearby, please come and share with us in this important moment. Looking forward to seeing as many of you as possible. I thank you for your support.*
>
> *Sincerely,*
> *Rita Simó*

Rita and her friends discussed the plans for the day. In addition to giving information about the school to those in attendance, there would be a concert featuring Rita at the piano, an instrumental ensemble made up of Sister Rosemarie's students from Sacred Heart, and a community sing-along. Several of Rita's friends offered to bring refreshments. A large sign was placed in the front window with colorful music symbols and details about the grand opening, and the flyers about the event that had been printed at St. Peter's were distributed throughout the neighborhood.

There was some concern that a day in late February might bring inclement weather, so everyone was grateful when the day dawned cold but clear. By three o'clock, over a hundred people had gathered at the space at 4417 N. Sheridan. Before the afternoon was over, 122 people had signed the guest book, and forty-five had registered as students.

While the lessons would be free, Rita had two requests of her new students. First they needed to exhibit that they were serious about their study of music through their attendance and practicing. Second, the student or a family member was obligated to donate a minimum of two hours a month in volunteer time to keep the school running.

As Rita repeated on numerous occasions, "Some people have more money than others, but all people have the same amount of time, twenty-four hours in a day."

Rita's March letter to her friends and supporters reflected her pleasure with the February 22 open house:

> *Dear Friends,*
>
> *Our open house was an overwhelming success with over a hundred people enjoying an afternoon of piano music, small band ensemble and community singing. We are now into a regular schedule with students coming each day and a total enrollment of fifty-six students ranging from 5 years old to senior citizens. Because of the large enrollment we have three general music classes: two beginning classes, one for 5 to 10 year olds and another for eleven and older, and a third for a few that already have had some music training.*
>
> *Besides myself we have a voice teacher, a guitar teacher, and a band teacher each coming one afternoon a week, and one person to do the adult general music. None of this would have been possible without your fantastic generosity and continued support.*
>
> *Thank you,*
> *Rita*

CHAPTER 20

Carter Hoyt III, Judith Johnson and Alta Jacko

The March newsletter referred to a new teacher who would continue to teach at the People's Music School for many decades. Carter Hoyt III had attended high school in the north suburbs of Chicago, but he was very much aware of the privileges that he had enjoyed there. In March, he joined The Peoples Music School faculty as a teacher of guitar and theory. A recent music graduate of Roosevelt University, Carter taught without pay until April 1, 1977, when he was able to qualify for an eighteen month CETA grant.

"Music is ultimately an intricate part of everyone's soul. It's a part of humanity and what sets us apart from other species," he later reflected in a Chicago Sun Times interview.

Beginning in early February, Rita had made inquiries with moving companies and storage facilities throughout the Chicago area to see if any of them had pianos that had been left behind. During March she was informed of a spinet piano that had been abandoned in a storage center in Rogers Park. Enlisting the help of a friend with a truck, she picked it up and brought it to the school. The People's Music School now had two pianos.

Moving ahead into the spring and summer, Rita's monthly letters continued to speak of growing success and enthusiasm for The People's Music School:

April 1976
Dear Friends,
We have been in operation for five weeks and the people's interest continues to increase. We have expanded to 6:30 p.m. on Tuesdays and Wednesdays in order to adjust to people's schedules.

On March 20th, there was a small article in the Action Line column of the Chicago Tribune together with a picture. As a

*result of it, we got $350.00 of unexpected donations. We can
now begin work on partitions for a sound-proof practice room,
so that some of the students can practice here, since they don't
have their own instruments at home.*

*Happy Easter to all,
Rita Simó*

Rita insisted on handwriting each monthly newsletter, which was then
duplicated. These letters were a reflection of the personal approach she
always took toward her students, volunteers, teachers, and other supporters.
When the task of preparing the mailings by herself became too large, she
asked parents of students to address the envelopes, always by hand, but she
continued to write each letter herself. These handwritten monthly letters
were continued until Rita's retirement. With few exceptions, her only
typewritten newsletters were the lengthy December letters that summarized
the accomplishments of the school throughout the preceding year.

The Action Line column to which Rita had referred in her April
newsletter was in answer to an inquiry by a North Side resident looking for a
low cost way to pursue music study. It described the school, Rita and her
background, as well as the fact that The People's Music School operated
totally through volunteer teachers and donations. With the funds generated
in response to the article, Rita was able to buy materials to create two
soundproof practice rooms. Karl Meyer, a carpenter and member of the St.
Francis Catholic Worker organization, volunteered to help. Working on
weekends, he and several other helpers he recruited constructed the two
rooms within a few weeks.

There were other exciting developments, as well:

*May 1976
Dear Friends,
As I mentioned to you in last month's letter, we started building
two practice rooms with the donations we got as a result of the
Action Line article. They are up now. Our next step is to tack the
acoustical tiles on the inside walls and place the carpet to deaden
the sound; then we will plaster and paint the outside walls.*

*We received a donation of a set of rhythm instruments and several
singing books, which will be used in the general music classes. In the
first week of June we are starting a new general music class, since so
many new people have shown the desire to join.*

Thank you for your continual support. If you are near by please feel free to come and visit. If not, write.

Thanks,
Rita Simó

June 1976
Dear Friends,
Many things are happening! The practice rooms are finished, the inside walls are covered with sound-proof material, and there is a rug on the floor so the sound is well controlled.

A family from Des Plaines donated a French horn, some music, and a music stand. A woman from River Forest sent a big package of beginner piano books, a woman from Oak Park gave us a big new rug, and a friend from Boston sent a package with many good records. To them all, as well as to all of you, we say thank you.

As the enclosed flyer shows, we are having a flute and piano recital on Sunday, June 13. If you are near by, please come.

Sincerely,
Rita Simó

The flute player joining Rita in the June 13 recital was new flute teacher, Judith Johnson. Like Carter Hoyt, Judith would continue to teach for over twenty-five years at The People's Music School, instructing students in theory as well as flute. She also often collaborated with Rita in concerts and educational residencies in local schools.

Up to this point, all letters had been sent from Rita's West Berteau address. Beginning with the July letter, the return address given was that of the school, 4417 N. Sheridan Road. Rita was now no longer a nun, and she had moved into her own apartment on N. Clarendon.

July 1976
Dear Friends,
Summer classes at the music school are going well. Although some of the teachers and students are gone for the summer, I was able to find two teachers to cover for the months of July and August from the CETA program through the Catholic School Board.

On June 7th we had a good article in the Chicago Daily News, which brought us some donations. On Sunday, June 13th, we had a flute and piano recital as part of our program to bring good music to the community. About seventy people attended despite the terrible, hot weather. A friend from Boston donated to us a Renaissance and a Baroque recorder; another one gave us some records and another gave us several textbooks. To them all, and to you, too, we say thanks.

Have a good summer,
Rita Simó

One of the female teachers hired for the summer months through the Catholic School Board's CETA grant was Alta Jacko, a music teacher at Academy of the Sacred Heart. After the summer, Alta continued teaching piano and music theory at The People's Music School and also conducted the adult choir. Years later, she started the school's first piano laboratory, a program in which a group of students could begin their keyboard studies in one classroom together on donated electronic keyboards.

Rita's August newsletter spoke of more donations of instruments, as well as a $2,000 donation from the Sisters of Saint Joseph of the Third Order of Saint Francis, which Rita happily announced would be enough to pay the rent for the entire next year. The fall term brought further interest in the new school. In October, Rita wrote on newly created letterhead stationery:

Dear Friends,
As you can see, we finally got a letterhead. The fall semester has started and we have fifty-five students: twenty-four adults and thirty-one children.

On November 7th at 3:00 p.m., Mr. Omer Reese, our new voice teacher, will give a recital here. He will sing music by Brahms, Purcell, Vaughan Williams, and Charles Ives. I hope that those of you who are near by will come to hear him.

During the months of August and September, we received a gift of a saxophone from a young woman in Chicago. We are still in great need of an additional piano; if anyone knows where we can buy one in good condition, let us know.

Sincerely,
Rita Simó

CHAPTER 21

An Agreement with Jake

It did not take long after the opening of the storefront school for the homeless to begin stopping in, sometimes to get out of inclement weather or find a few peaceful minutes to rest, but often because they were curious about the musical sounds they heard coming from the building. A few even asked to take lessons and were accepted as long as they followed the protocol set for all students, including the requirement to volunteer at least two hours per month toward the maintenance of the school.

Some of the homeless who entered the school ended up asking Rita for money in order to get something to eat. Rita was street-smart enough to know that money given through such requests often went for alcohol or drugs. Still, barely scraping by on her minimum salary at St. Peter's Church, she appreciated the hunger that these individuals might be suffering.

Rita's solution to this dilemma came through a conversation with Jake Siegal, who owned a fast food restaurant on a corner south of the school. Jake specialized in chicken, burgers, hot dogs and shakes, prepared in various unique ways, and he did not have a liquor license. Rita's proposition was simple:

"If I sign my name on the back of my business card, give the person who brings it to you something wholesome to eat. At the end of the week, I will square up my bill with you."

At first Jake was dubious, but he agreed to give it a try. When Rita paid her bill promptly at the end of the first week, he realized he could trust her. The arrangement continued for the next ten years, up until the time the school moved to new third floor quarters in the Ecumenical Institute building in 1986, where it became much more difficult for the street people to walk in.

CHAPTER 22

A Special Friendship Begins

As soon as Rita moved to Uptown, she began giving piano recitals and participating in other programs throughout the wider Chicago area. Sometimes these programs were organized to raise funds for projects Rita felt were worthy of her support. But often they involved fees for service, money she quietly put toward support of The People's Music School.

In September 1976, Rita was asked to play for an anniversary event in remembrance of Salvador Allende, the deposed President of Chile, who had committed suicide rather than be taken by the forces of his foe, the dictator Augusto Pinochet. The organizer and primary speaker for the event was Martín Gárate, a Chilean priest who had fled persecution following the 1973 coup and was residing in South Bend, Indiana, where he was involved with the Center for Justice and Peace of the Congregation of the Holy Cross.

Martín Gárate's roommate in South Bend was a priest named Tomás Bissonnette. Originally from Detroit, Tomás had recently joined the Spanish Speaking Catholic Commission located in South Bend, which promoted and supported Hispanic apostolates in the five state Midwest region.

In 1967, Pope Paul VI had issued a "moto proprio" restoring the ancient practice of ordaining to the diaconate men other than those who were candidates for priesthood. This opened up that area of service to a much larger segment of the male Catholic population, men who would need extensive training.

Tomás Bissonnette had been the first priest to train Hispanic men to serve as Catholic deacons, preparing them to assist parish priests in their pastoral duties. As he had previously developed these training programs in the Detroit and Kalamazoo dioceses, Tomás was asked to join the team working with Hispanics within the larger Midwest region, which was based in South Bend.

In addition to this responsibility, Tomás, who had always been an avid reader and scholar, had developed a book distribution service, acquiring and distributing Spanish language books to various Catholic institutions as he received requests. First begun as a voluntary service to local institutions, as word spread, so did the territory that Tomás served through this project.

As an outgrowth of his duties at the Spanish Speaking Catholic Commission, in 1975 Tomás was asked to assume the position of Director of the Hispanic Institute at Mundelein College in Chicago. One of the Institute's goals involved the turning of a fledgling project in support of Hispanic interests in the wider Chicago area into a fulltime program at the college. In this role, Tomás was involved in structuring programs which furthered bilingual and bicultural education and outreach for people who were working with the growing Latin populations in various neighborhoods of Chicago and the Midwest area.

In early December of 1976, a friend, Father Bob Stark, invited Tomás to accompany him to the Uptown home of Renny Golden and Michael McConnell for an Advent Day of Reflection. One of the other guests invited to the event was Rita Simó. Tomás and Rita conversed for a time, and Tomás remembers thinking at the time that she seemed to have a rather aggressive personality.

During the conversation, Tomás asked Rita about her childhood home. When she told him that she had grown up in the Dominican Republic, he casually mentioned that he was planning a trip to the Dominican Republic that December after visiting his parents, who had retired and were living near St. Petersburg, Florida.

Rita immediately brightened. "I will be there then, also. I will meet you when you arrive."

Tomás was flustered at the firmness and forthrightness of this declaration, but he could think of no graceful way of refusing. So the two agreed to meet at the Santo Domingo airport upon his arrival.

When he returned to South Bend that evening, Tomás mentioned "a forward-speaking Dominican woman" whom he had met that day to his roommate Mártin. When Mártin, remembering conversations with Rita during her participation in the Allende anniversary event, began to sing her praises, Tomás became more interested.

After spending Christmas with his parents, Tomás went to the Tampa airport for the flight to the Dominican Republic. As he approached the Quisqueyana airline counter, he saw a flurry of active between staff and irritated patrons. The problem soon became clear. The airline had gone bankrupt and, with no advance notice, service was being discontinued immediately. Tomás pictured Rita standing at the gate at the other end and wondered how she would react.

When both had returned to Chicago, Tomás called Rita to explain what had happened. Rita already knew about the cancelled flight, as she had heard about the bankruptcy while waiting at the airport in Santo Domingo, but she now had something else on her mind.

At St. Thomas of Canterbury Church, Father Rochford had been responding to the Catholic Church's new policy, arising from Vatican Council II, allowing for mass to be conducted in vernacular languages. With the growing diversity of his congregation, Father Rochford was eager to offer mass in more languages, especially Vietnamese, Laotian, and Spanish. He had already found priests who could celebrate mass in Vietnamese and Laotian, but while Father Rochford was able to read the words of the mass passably well in Spanish, he was not comfortably conversant in the language. He was looking for a way to better serve this growing segment of his congregation. Rita was convinced that Tomás, with his interest in outreach to the Hispanic community, would be just the person to conduct mass in Spanish at St. Thomas.

Tomás agreed, and he quickly came to enjoy his work at St. Thomas of Canterbury Church and the friendship of Father Rochford. In addition to welcoming Tomás to the church, Father Rochford offered him a room in the rectory in exchange for Tomás' help in seeing to the special needs of the Hispanics in the parish. Tomás happily accepted this expansion of his responsibilities. He was glad to be living in the rectory, as it brought a more active and varied social life than he had been able to have in his dorm room at Mundelein. Father Rochford also found space for Tomás' growing Spanish books distribution service in an attic room.

From that point on, Rita and Tomás regularly crossed paths in their work at St. Thomas. While Rita greatly respected Tomás' talents and dedication to service, at first she found him rather formal and reserved.

The new practice of celebrating mass at St. Thomas in Vietnamese and Laotian presented a challenge for Rita. Since she knew neither language, she had problems knowing when the priests were ending their chants or prayers and her music was to begin. She had special trouble with the Preface prayer of the mass, which was always followed by the music, "Holy, Holy, Holy." Finally, she solved the problem by asking the priests, whose hands were usually raised, to lower them for a few brief moments before raising them again, as a signal that they were finishing their prayers, and she should get ready to play.

CHAPTER 23

A First Anniversary and a Disaster

As the 1976-77 school year progressed, more instruments were donated to The People's Music School, including several wind instruments, a cello, miscellaneous percussion instruments, and a second spinet piano, which Rita excitedly noted was "in quite good condition." Also, as a result of the circulating word among musicians, several new teachers offered their services, expanding the offering of instruments on which students could receive instruction.

Curiosity about the school spread across the Uptown neighborhood, and local people would stick their heads in the front door to see what was going on, intrigued by the sounds of a piano, a flute, a guitar, or a set of snare drums. All visitors were warmly welcomed by Rita and her teachers. There was only one strictly enforced rule. Visitors must at all times behave respectfully to the staff and students and to their music making.

By December 1976, the progress of the students at The People's Music School had reached a point where Rita felt comfortable scheduling the first student recital, which took place on December 19. An enthusiastic audience of parents, teachers and friends proclaimed it a great success.

On February 20, 1977, The People's Music School celebrated its first anniversary with a recital by students, teachers, and several guest artists. Compositions by Mozart, Schubert, Scriabin, and Debussy were performed, featuring piano, voice, clarinet, trumpet, and guitar. The afternoon ended with a sing-along, something Rita would often incorporate into the school's programs over the years, so that all attending could be participants as well as audience in the experience of making music.

Because so many people were involved in the first anniversary program, the recital was held in St. Thomas of Canterbury Church. Afterwards, there was a big party with much food and celebration.

Then one week later, disaster struck. Someone broke into the school and stole all the instruments that were portable, leaving only the one upright and two spinet pianos. Instruments stolen included a flute, two clarinets, a trumpet, a French horn, and two guitars, as well as miscellaneous percussion instruments.

Everyone was devastated, but once again Rita used the publicity to her advantage. A picture of Rita playing a cello, one of two instruments that had been donated to the school after the robbery, appeared in the Chicago Sun Times along with the story of the school and what it was trying to accomplish.

Letters of sympathy poured in, along with donations of money and instruments, and the school soon ended up with more instruments than before the robbery. In fact, with the donation of quite a few string instruments, Rita now put forth an appeal in her March 1977 newsletter for a volunteer string teacher.

CHAPTER 24

The Friendship Blossoms

At the beginning of 1977, Tomás Bissonnette planned a weeklong intensive live-in program for the Hispanic Institute at Mundelein. As part of the program, he wanted to include a half-day workshop on Hispanic music. He discussed his ideas for the program with Martín Gárate, and both agreed Rita would be a good musician to include in the plans.

Rita was very impressed with the outreach mission of the program, and readily agreed to take part. She found the event very satisfying and enjoyable, so she was amazed when a check for $250 arrived in the mail in payment for her services. Tomás had neglected to tell her that she would be paid. Delighted with this new prospect for raising funds for her school, Rita quickly contacted Tomás' secretary at Mundelein, Sonya Rendón, and told her that she would gladly participate in any further programming the institute might offer.

A few months later, Tomás informed Rita about another program he was planning at the Hispanic Institute for the summer of 1977, a program in which he hoped she could participate. Unfortunately, the date conflicted with a trip she had previously planned to visit and perform with friends in Boston; however, wanting to be sure Tomás wouldn't be discouraged from asking her in the future, she told him, "Be sure to check in with me in September after I return, and let me know what you are planning. I will be back at 4417 Sheridan beginning Labor Day weekend, cleaning up for the opening of school."

In the meantime, positive developments were occurring at The People's Music School. In April, the school was awarded its first CETA grants, which provided funds over an eighteen-month period for two teachers, Carter Hoyt and Dianne Mayners, as well as a secretarial assistant, Bonny Rhoads.

Bonny had played a little guitar as a young teen and had always hoped to improve her playing. After seeing one of the posted notices, she attended the February 1976 opening of the school, and became one of Carter Hoyt's first guitar and theory students. She also sang in the adult choir.

When her eighteen-month CETA grant expired, Bonny enrolled at Northeastern Illinois University in Chicago, but many years later she recalled: "It took several years and jobs later before I realized what a privilege I'd been given to be able to work at the music school among accomplished people who had a sense of creating something larger than themselves and being part of a community. The experience seeded many later experiences in my life and provided me with direction and purpose. I did stick with the guitar and eventually learned to express myself on it. Over the years playing and singing have been a real gift and source of strength through all of life's ups and downs."

In late April, the school realized $700 from a benefit concert that Rita gave at the People's Church on Lawrence Avenue. A few weeks later, a $3,500 gift arrived from the Sisters of St. Joseph of the Third Order of St. Francis, along with expressions of sympathy over the loss of the stolen instruments. Further attention was drawn to the loss when NBC, WMAQ-TV, news aired a widely-viewed segment about the school and the robbery, which resulted in a number of new friends and supporters, and, of course, more students.

On Labor Day weekend, Rita and various of her volunteer helpers were cleaning up at the school when Tomás Bissonnette suddenly appeared at the door and, seeing the scurry of activity within, rolled up his sleeves and announced that he was ready to be put to work. Rita was pleasantly surprised to discover this more relaxed and informal side of her new friend.

Once the cleanup was completed, Tomás told Rita that he had come to tell her about more events he was planning at the Hispanic Institute, in which he was hoping she could provide a musical component. Rita suggested that they continue the conversation over coffee at her apartment.

Several tentative fall dates were discussed for the next program at the institute. Rita rejected one of the dates, saying she was scheduled to attend a Lyric Opera performance that afternoon. She mentioned that she had two tickets and would be glad to share one of them with Tomás. Tomás was pleased with the invitation. He had frequently attended concerts during his years in Detroit, but that city had no major opera company. He agreed to meet Rita at the Civic Opera House at a mutually agreed time before the opera.

As was her custom, Rita took the bus downtown on the day of the opera. About half way there, the bus drove by a car stopped at the side of the street with a flat tire. It was Tomás' car. Rita waited near the box office of the Civic Opera house until the final seating bells began to ring. Leaving Tomás' ticket with the box office, she sighed and went in to her seat. Once again, despite his best intentions, Tomás had failed to arrive at the designated meeting time and place. Later, when he joined Rita after the first intermission, Tomás could only offer his apology and share his frustration at the slow arrival of the AAA roadside service.

CHAPTER 25

New Contacts with the Arts Community

In November 1977, Rita learned about a meeting dealing with funding opportunities for arts organizations, and she decided to attend. One of the people making a presentation was the director of the Illinois Arts Council. When Rita approached him afterwards with questions, he suggested she visit his office for further discussion. Rita immediately set up an appointment, and within a few days she was sitting in the director's office, explaining her accomplishments so far and what she hoped for the future.

The director listened sympathetically and then asked her how many paid employees she had. She told him that other than three CETA-funded employees, there were none. He explained that this was a problem, as the Arts Council was prohibited by law from giving financial support to volunteer organizations with no internally paid staff. He suggested that Rita give herself a salary as executive director, which then might be covered by a grant.

"But if the grant money goes for my salary, no money would go to the school," she replied.

"There's nothing that prevents you from donating the money back to the school," he told her. "We won't be awarding our next major grants until September, but you could submit a proposal now asking for a one-time seed money grant of no more than $1,500, if you specify that the money would be used to pay your salary. The Council will be meeting in a few months, and we could review your seed-money request at that time."

He then gave Rita the form to fill out to apply for the seed money grant as well as the papers for applying for a larger grant for the following year.

As 1978 began, the bustle of activity increased as The People's Music School made plans for their second anniversary celebration on Sunday, February 26. The main event scheduled for the day was a production of the operetta *Peter Rabbit*, put on by the school's children, who were eagerly showing up every afternoon to practice their parts. Rita found to her amusement that they were taking their roles so seriously and working so hard that her newsletter sent in early February announced:

> They all seem to be secure in their parts already. We
> are experiencing a rare occasion in the world of show
> business, being ahead of our schedule deadline.

It was also in February that a woman from the Chicago Council for the Fine Arts came to visit the school. She informed Rita of a federal grant program which would provide financial support for selected not-for-profit community arts organizations over a two-year period. The Chicago Council for the Fine Arts was to be the local partner in determining and distributing the grants. The visitor asked many questions, and said that while she had many other organizations to visit, she would consider recommending The People's Music School for one of the grants. She also said it would probably be a number of months before the decisions on the grants would be known.

In her March 1978 newsletter, Rita announced plans for a new fundraising event, a benefit dinner dance on April 1. One of the school's Board members managed a ballroom in the area and had arranged for the donation of the space for the evening. Music for dancing would be provided free of charge by Carter Hoyt and his band. Thus began a tradition repeated over many years, as Carter and his band continued to provide free music at many of the school's benefit events, a generosity Rita deeply appreciated.

The March newsletter also contained the exciting news that a grant of $1,500 in seed money had been approved by the Illinois Arts Council. It would provide Rita with a $250 per month salary until September. Rita now began preparing the application to the Arts Council for a grant for the 1978-79 year beginning in September. In her proposal, she asked for $7,000, $6,000 for a $500 monthly salary for herself and $1,000 for a theory teacher.

Unfortunately, March ended with a new challenge. A major water pipe broke and flooded the school, requiring massive cleanup and repainting. Hard earned new money was needed for repairs.

CHAPTER 26

From Friendship to Marriage

Rita performed at one more of Tomás Bissonnette's lecture programs at
the Hispanic Institute during November of 1977. As he became more
acquainted with her, Tomás' admiration grew for this talented and
tenacious woman, who clearly shared many of his interests and his passion
for service. Though he was uncertain about Rita's feelings toward him at
this point, by spring of 1978 Tomás had reached the important decision
that this was the woman he wanted to marry, a decision that would require
his departure from the priesthood. He confided his decision to his parents
in Florida and his sister, who still lived in Detroit.

By June, unknown to Rita, Tomás had written the prerequisite letter to
the Pope asking to be relieved of his priestly obligations and duties.
Coincidently, at the same time, Martín Gárate also was petitioning to leave
the priesthood in order to marry, though he and Tomás did not share their
plans with each other until the process was well underway.

Toward the end of the spring term at the school, Rita received a phone
call from an older couple she knew who were moving from their home into
an apartment. They were offering to give the school their baby grand piano.

In her excitement, Rita danced around the school exclaiming, "A baby!
A baby! We're going to have a baby!"

Word of this exuberant scene reached Lloyd Green, a reporter for the
Chicago Sun Times, who happened to be walking through the neighborhood
at the time, and he wrote an article about Rita's announcement of a "baby"
arriving at the school. Along with a lengthy description of the school, the
article included a picture of Rita at the new piano, surrounded by students.
Green was also part of a national news syndicate, and papers throughout
the country picked up on this humorous, heart-lifting story.

One of the papers that ran the story was The Detroit Free Press. After Tomás had discussed his plan to ask Rita to marry him with his family, they had excitedly told several close friends. One of those friends, Bertha Rom, showed a copy of the article to Tomás' sister.

"I think this is the girl Tomás wants to marry," she told her.

With his petition to leave the priesthood under review, Tomás decided the time had arrived to ask Rita to be his wife. He proposed to her at her North Clarendon Avenue apartment on a warm June afternoon and asked her to accompany him to Detroit over the Fourth of July weekend to meet his family. His parents would be traveling up from Florida to spend their usual month with his sister in Detroit.

Rita was thrilled and honored by the proposal, but she couldn't resist responding playfully, "But I have a baby, and it's called The People's Music School."

"Yes," responded Tomás, indulgently, "I know. I can live with that baby."

Rita knew that it was important at this point to honor Dominican tradition by phoning her widowed mother in San Francisco de Marcorís for official permission to marry.

Ana Isidra Rodríguez had only one question for her daughter, "Does he speak Spanish?"

Rita told her that Tomás spoke very good Spanish, and then she handed the phone to Tomás who quickly proved his proficiency in the language.

Back on the phone with her daughter, Ana Isidra laughingly responded, "I approve, I approve."

Though Rita was very nervous about the trip to Detroit to meet her future in-laws, she and Tomás arrived to a warm welcome from Tomás' family. They referred to the article about the new "baby" at The People's Music School, and they asked Rita many questions about the path she had taken leading to the founding of the school. From the beginning they could see that Tomás had made a good choice.

Wedding plans began, and Rita Simó and Tomás G. Bissonnette were married in the LaBagh Woods, just east of the Eden's Expressway at Foster Avenue, at 2:00 p.m. on Saturday, October 21, 1978, in a clearing near a gazebo-style shelter building. Father Joseph Mulligan and Father Jay Samonie officiated at the ceremony. Since the Chicago Park District did not give permits for private ceremonies such as weddings, the permit for the gathering was entered as: "Autumn Festival for St. Thomas of Canterbury."

The day was sunny and unseasonable warm, with a high of 85 degrees. Rita and Tomás had brought wood for a fire to counteract any chill, but it proved unnecessary. Rita wore a long white dress that had been made by her mother for concert performances during her time as a nun. In her hair, she placed several bright leaves from the surrounding fall foliage, and around her waist she tied a long sash made out of autumn-colored ribbons, which reached to the ground. Tomás wore a light tan suit.

Those in attendance included Rita's mother; her brother, Alfredo, and his daughter, Oresty; Judith Polanco, one of Rita's closest childhood friends; Tomás' parents; his sister, Carol, her husband, Bob, and their daughter Amy; family friends from Detroit; Rita's old friend, Ann Kelley; Father James Dunkerley of St. Peter's Episcopal Church; Father Mike Rochford; Jim Duignan; and many teachers from the People's Music School and parishioners of St. Thomas of Canterbury, as well as a number of Catholic priest and deacon friends.

The music for the day was led by voice teacher Mary Therese O'Neil, accompanied by The People's Music School's two guitar teachers, Miguel Muñoz and Carter Hoyt. At the end of the ceremony as the newlyweds recessed through the crowd, Father Rochford playfully introduced the new couple as, "Tomás Simó and Rita Bissonnette."

The feast, which followed the ceremony, was truly a grand one, with both hearty fare and delicacies representing cultures from around the world. Rita and Tomás had asked that their guests not bring wedding presents, but instead provide food dishes and beverages for all to enjoy. When pressed, they had agreed that they also would gratefully accept contributions to The People's Music School.

There was only one tense moment in an otherwise perfect day. Rita had stressed that she wanted everyone to dress casually and comfortably, and she specifically had instructed the clerics, including Father Mulligan and Father Samonie, not to wear their priestly collars. All complied with her wishes. Shortly before the wedding began, however, Father Dunkerley had sent Rita an emergency call saying that he had been detained by an engine problem with his car and would not have time to change out of his priestly garments. Would she be upset if he arrived without changing? Of course, Rita told him to come as he was.

As the ceremony was ready to begin, Tomás parents began looking anxiously around the group. Finally they confided to their son that they were distressed that they did not see any priests in clerical clothing in attendance. How could it be a legitimate Catholic wedding with no priestly vestments? Just then, James Dunkerley arrived in his clerical collar. Tomás' parents took one look at him and smiled and nodded. They were now satisfied that the wedding would be a proper Catholic wedding. No one told them that Father Dunkerley was Episcopalian.

CHAPTER 27

Beginning A New Life Together

Rita's November 1978 letter started out with a warm thank you to everyone for their kind thoughts and wishes for her wedding, and for the many generous donations made to the music school as wedding gifts. She also announced plans for a bake sale at the school, the first of many bake sales that would take place over the years ahead to raise money for the school's programs. Her December letter gave a summary of the year's progress:

Dear Friends,
Greetings for the holiday season. We want to thank you again for the support you have given to the People's Music School this year... we would like to update you a bit about the school.

For our second anniversary in February, children of the general music classes presented the operetta "Peter Rabbit." The Exceptional Children's Convention invited us to perform it again in May at the Museum of Science and Industry. We also had student recitals at the end of the spring and summer semesters. In April we had a workshop of African and jazz rhythms by a guest musician, and last month we had a voice recital by an excellent soprano. All of these programs have been well attended by our students as well as by people from the community, which shows how much they enjoy these opportunities.

The student population of the school has increased to 97. We now have three classes for children seven to twelve years of age and one class for little people five and six years old. There are three classes for adults. During the year, we were also able to add violin and drums to our private lessons in piano, voice, flute, clarinet, and guitar.

As our student population increases, so do our financial needs......Since September of this year, the Ilinois Arts Council has given us a grant of $7,000, which is used to pay me a salary of $500 a month. Our CETA grant for the salaries of two teachers has been renewed through September 1979. Since the teachers have been with us for two years, they will not qualify for any further extensions. So we have been writing proposals to private foundations for their salaries after May. In early spring, we had a benefit dance at a ballroom owned by one of our Board members. The band in which Carter Hoyt, one of our teachers, plays donated its services to the dance. The students organized a quite successful bake sale last month. As you can see, we have been hard at work........

Thank you for your interest and friendship,
Rita Simó, Director

With the December letter distributed and school closed for the holidays, Tomás and Rita departed for a delayed honeymoon trip to Mexico City.

CHAPTER 28

Continuing the Spread of Music

In January 1979, Tomás and Rita returned from their honeymoon to a Chicago deeply covered in snow. Just before the wedding, Rita had moved to a two-bedroom apartment that she and Tomás had rented on West Lakeside Place, a one block long street between Sheridan Road and Clarendon, just south of Lawrence. They would remain there for approximately a year and a half before moving into a large brick house at 4645 N. Beacon Street.

West Lakeside had not been plowed when the newlyweds returned from their trip, and the snow was piled up so high that the taxi had to leave them off at the end of the block. Having just arrived from warm Mexico and still dressed in warm weather clothing, Rita and Tomás found the sudden return to the severe Chicago winter to be a great shock.

Soon, however, Rita was enthusiastically welcoming students back to the new school term. As she reported in her January newsletter:

> Saturday we woke up to find ourselves covered with more than 20 inches of snow; nevertheless, 14 new students showed up for their first class, showing that this is really important to them. Unfortunately, our rent has increased by $30 a month at the same time that our student body has increased considerably, and we need more teachers and materials.

The third anniversary of the school was celebrated on February 25. Soon afterwards, on Tuesday, March 6, Rita was interviewed on Spanish radio station WEDC. As a result, her March newsletter reported that the school had acquired many new students. By April the student body of The People's Music School had increased to more than 120 students.

In March 1979, Rita traveled to the Dominican Republic to perform the Beethoven 3rd Piano Concerto with the National Symphony and also to visit her family. While she very much enjoyed reconnecting with family and with her former musical colleagues in Santo Domingo, Rita was also pleased that the money she received from playing helped greatly with expenses at the school.

After returning to Chicago, she also told her teachers, woefully, "I played on a fantastic Steinway. I wish we had a piano half as good here."

With the growing body of students at the school, it became clear that more space would be needed for lessons. The building contained two unused rooms at the rear of the space the school occupied, and Rita negotiated with the building's landlord and arranged to rent them. That meant not only an increase in rent, but also the hiring of a carpenter to build a doorway into the new area. For once, Rita was not able to use volunteer help, since city code required that a licensed carpenter had to be used. Good news was announced in the May newsletter:

> *The Chicago Council on Fine Arts came through with $3,500*
> *for us. We also got the word that Prudential Insurance*
> *Foundation has allocated us $500. And last Saturday we*
> *had a bake sale....We made $161.90.*

The July newsletter spoke of the new People's Music School t-shirts, which students were proudly wearing to concerts of the Chicago Symphony Orchestra at The Ravinia Festival in Highland Park. For a second year in a row, the school had been given free pavilion seats as part of the outreach program operated by the Ravinia Festival Women's Board. Rita saw these visits as an opportunity to educate her students on good concert behavior, in addition to providing them with a fine musical experience. Before each visit, she would discuss proper concert behavior with the participants, as well as prepare them for the music they would be hearing.

Rita was concerned, however, that festival patrons might be wary of a group of young, ethnically mixed students in their midst. She had no need to worry. A follow-up letter from the program's chairman, Margaret Harris, informed her that several patrons had commented on the fact that The People's Music School group was better behaved and more attentive than many adults in the audience. The partnership between Ravinia's outreach program and The People's Music School continued for many years, presenting many of the school's students with their first opportunity to hear live classical music by world-class artists.

In August, the long-delayed project to open a door to the two new rooms at the back of the school was finally underway. Classes had closed down for the summer, and teachers Carter Hoyt and Alta Jacko, alternated being at the school during the construction. In the meantime, Rita and Tomás were planning a special trip to Ecuador.

While Tomás' was working at Mundelein, his secretary was a master's degree student named Sonya Rendón. An Ecuadorian native, Sonya had developed a friendship with Pat McTeague, a former nun working in Quito who was associated with the Sisters of Charity of the Blessed Virgin Mary (BVM). The two began to share a dream of building a special school in Ecuador that would include children from the poorest neighborhoods.

Once at Mundelein, as part of her work towards her Master's Degree in religious studies, Sonya designed plans for the experimental project. A new school, to be called Nuevo Mundo, would be created. Tuition funds from a morning educational program, attended by students from middle and upper class families, supplemented by other charitable gifts, would provide financial resources for a free afternoon school for students from poor families. Parents of the afternoon school students would provide in-kind services or, in some cases, be employed by the school or by the parents of the morning students.

Seeing many parallels with her own efforts to create a free school, Rita had agreed to travel to Ecuador to give two recitals. The first, in Guayaquil on August 17, 1979, was for the purpose of raising funds for Nuevo Mundo. The second, at the National Conservatory in Quito on August 20, was to fulfill a government regulation that any concert for which admission was charged had to be balanced by a free public concert. The trip to Ecuador included a few days of much appreciated rest for Rita and Tomás, along with the pleasures of exploring the country where Tomás had once studied.

Upon her return to Chicago, Rita was greeted with good news. For a second year, the school had received an Illinois Arts Council grant of $7,000 for the 1979-80 year beginning in September. This was very much welcomed, as the CETA grants supporting Carter Hoyt and Dianne Mayners could not by law be extended beyond the end of September.

With Dianne's departure, violin teacher Barbara Ferrel volunteered to take the general music theory class for five to seven-year-old students, while Rita found it necessary to increase her own teaching load to make up the difference. At the same time, Rita was busy preparing for an October 7 recital at nearby Immaculata High School on Irving Park Road. The concert earned $800 for the school, an amount, as Rita pointed out in her October newsletter, which was enough to pay for almost three months of rent.

In the same October newsletter, Rita spoke of a great need for 1/8 and 1/4 size violins, reflecting a growing interest among very young students in the instrument. That appeal was soon echoed in a television broadcast that reached across the Chicago area. Harry Porterfield, a CBS, WBBM-TV news anchor as well as an amateur violinist, had been one of the earliest supporters of The People's Music School and its mission. In October, he presented a special feature on the school during one of his evening broadcasts in which he stressed the need for donated instruments and especially student-sized string instruments. Soon after the broadcast, donations of instruments of all descriptions began arriving.

Rita expressed her gratitude for these new gifts in her year-end letter. She also excitedly pointed out that this year's December Christmas Concert would fall on a special day:

What better date for a concert than on Beethoven's birthday!

CHAPTER 29

The House on Beacon Street

The fourth anniversary of The People's Music School was celebrated on February 24, 1980, and included a performance by young students of part of the musical *The Electric Sunshine Man*, about the life of Thomas Edison, a concert they would repeat during the year for several community groups. The month of February also included several visits by student groups from The People's Music School to Orchestra Hall to hear the Chicago Symphony Orchestra as part of the symphony's outreach program.

As the school grew, faculty changes became a challenge. In May, it was announced that two key teachers Gayle Kremers, woodwinds, and Fred Teuke, percussion, were moving, and in her May newsletter Rita pleaded:

> *If anyone knows of a woodwinds or drum teacher willing to teach for little pay, please send them our way.*

After three years, Rita had found that to retain good teachers, she had to pay a modest stipend. Beginning about this time, and for a number of years into the future, most of the teachers were paid $8.50 a lesson, an amount still much below what they were able to command in their other teaching positions.

Since their wedding, Rita and Tomás had looked forward to the day when they could have a house of their own, a house that they envisioned filled with friends, festivities, and food. In early 1980, Rita received funds from the sale of family property she had inherited in the Dominican Republic, and the couple began searching nearby neighborhoods for the right house. By late spring, they had set their sights on a lovely, large vintage brick house at 4645 N. Beacon Street, not far from Truman College.

The Beacon Street house consisted of fourteen rooms, including six bedrooms and three bathrooms. A large open porch stretched across the front of the house. At the back of the lot, there was a three-car garage. Across the alley from the garage, there was an open public area with a play lot, where children and families would gather on warm afternoons.

Rita and Tomás moved into their new home in July of 1980. With so many rooms, they found they were comfortable occupying only the first floor, which included large living and dining rooms, a kitchen, a bedroom and a bath.

For several months, Rita's brother Alfred joined them and used his skills to convert space on the third floor into two rooms, which, along with rooms on the second floor, including a small kitchen, were rented out to a succession of friends. A large finished basement provided additional sleeping quarters and a spacious room for entertaining guests.

Homes across the street were more heavily shaded by tall trees, and Tomás and Rita soon started adding trees to their front yard, first an elm and then an evergreen tree, a Christmas present from Tomás to Rita. A previous owner had painted the home's molding, and Tomás spent several years stripping the paint from baseboards, door and window trim, and the main staircase.

On the first floor, Rita's piano occupied a strategic position at one end of the large dining room. The adjoining living and dining room areas of the home were separated by a partial half wall, resulting in a combined open area so spacious that a large audience could be accommodated for the many chamber concerts, some planned and others occurring spontaneously, that took place at 4645 N. Beacon Street.

Many wonderful traditions were created at the house on Beacon Street. In addition to regular concerts and holiday picnics, Rita and Tomás each year hosted a New Year's Eve party, which, as the invitations stated, welcomed guests to join the party anytime between 8 p.m. on New Year's Eve and 8 a.m. on New Year's Day. Many friends would arrive during the evening, converse, eat and toast the New Year, and then rest a few hours on one of the many guest beds before rejoining their friends for an early morning breakfast.

For over twenty years, the Beacon Street home was filled with activity, laughter and music. Local friends and out of town guests came and went, and many of them have special memories of their visits.

CHAPTER 30

The Classical Music Taxi Driver

From the first days of their residence on Beacon Street, Rita and Tomás developed friendships with families living nearby, friendships which would continue for many years. One of these new friendships was with the Valdés family, consisting of Goyo, Aurora, and their nine-year-old daughter, Maria. The Valdés family lived on the second floor in the building next door.

Goyo Valdés was well known throughout the area as "the classical music taxi driver." Customers with a taste for other forms of music were politely told, "the radio in this cab only tunes into classical stations." Others who preferred classical music would often ask for Goyo by name when requesting a taxi. Some claimed that Goyo seemed to know as much about classical music as the announcers of the programs.

A strict parent, Goyo expected his daughter Maria to excel in school and to avail herself of every opportunity for development. It was not long before Maria was enrolled as a piano student at The Peoples Music School. Though she first studied with another teacher at the school, within a few years Rita had become her teacher, and a special bond developed between them that went far beyond the study of music.

Goyo was an especially helpful parent at the school, often putting in service time well beyond what was required. He proved to have many skills that were useful to the maintenance of the school.

While Goyo took advantage of many of the free classical music programs and other music-related events in Chicago and was a regular attendee at Rita's frequent musicales next door, his favorite event was the annual Do-It-Yourself *Messiah* held every December at Orchestra Hall. Though not a singer himself, he found few experiences in his life to be more inspiring and exhilarating than sitting up front in this historic hall while it filled with thousands of voices, both trained and amateur, and the accompanying orchestra, in Handel's great musical depiction of the life of Christ.

Even after he retired to Miami in later years, Goyo continued to fly to Chicago every December for the Do-It-Yourself *Messiah*. By then there was another reason why this annual event gave him so much pleasure. His daughter, now Maria Valdés-Vargas, had become the program coordinator for the International Music Foundation (IMF), the event's sponsoring organization.

CHAPTER 31

Continuing Challenges, And a Visit from a Clown

From the earliest days of The People's Music School, Rita had ended each school term with a concert featuring the students and often also members of the faculty and other guest performers. The programs were free and open to all who wished to attend. At first these concerts were modest events, held either at the school or in a community space at St Thomas of Canterbury Church. But gradually the audiences increased in size, and larger venues were needed.

By 1980, the concerts at the end of the summer term of The People's Music School were becoming large community events, involving not only the school's students and their families, but also people from the entire Uptown community. Held on a late summer Sunday in Lincoln Park near Montrose and Lake Shore Drive, the day usually began with a picnic and ended with everyone participating in a sing-along. Rita happily referred to these summer concerts as "Ravinia of Uptown." Unpredictable weather could present a challenge, but in general the afternoons were sunny and pleasant.

Rita's biggest problem was keeping the space secured for the day. Even though the school obtained the necessary permits from the city, Rita found she had to stake out the territory beginning early in the morning, to "shoo off" other groups hoping to set up an impromptu picnic or sports event. The summer concert on August 3, 1980, was especially exciting, as a crew from the Chicago Council on Fine Arts made a videotape as part of their documentation of arts programs in the city.

The concerts at the end of the school terms were not the only times the school reached out to the entire neighborhood. From the beginning, The People's Music School, as part of their mission, had arranged for students and teachers to give performances throughout the Uptown community, sometimes for a small fee, but often for free. By 1980, the school was broadening that circle and participating in events across the city.

To aid in this outreach mission, the school fashioned a continually changing group of faculty ensembles, building upon the musicians available at the moment. In October, one of these ensembles presented an especially well-received concert of Baroque chamber music, which included the first public performance of a secular cantata by Alessandro Scarlatti. Soon after the concert, Rita announced the formation of The People's Music School Chamber Players, a more permanently defined group of teachers from the school that continued to perform at various festivals and other events, usually for a fee that went to the school.

Nevertheless, fundraising for the school remained an ongoing challenge. The bake sales and dinner dances continued to be popular and successful community-building events, but they rarely brought in more than a few hundred dollars. After several major grant proposals had resulted in disappointment, Rita was finally able to announce at the beginning of the 1980 fall term that the school had received a grant of $8,000 from the Illinois Arts Council, an increase of $1,000 from the year before.

But the financial challenges continued. In the fall of 1980, a proposal had been sent to the National Endowment for the Arts (NEA) following an encouraging visit from one of their representatives, who had written a strong recommendation for the school and encouraged them to ask for $19,000. By early 1981, word had circulated of a proposed 50% cut in the NEA budget, which did not bode well for a first time applicant. In her March newsletter, Rita announced that the school had joined a coalition of Chicago arts organizations in collecting signatures and letters to send President Reagan, and she urged everyone to write their U.S. Congressman.

By 1981, the school was looking for a new, larger venue for its anniversary concerts, and the fifth anniversary concert on February 22 was held at the Hull House Gallery on Beacon Street, with over 100 in attendance. The benefit dinner dance, held six days later at St. Thomas Church, proved to be the most successful one to date, netting $850.

As spring progressed, students and faculty from the People's Music School continued to perform both within their Uptown neighborhood and throughout the city. On May 2, the children's choir joined other musicians in a "Peoples, Yes" concert celebrating the contributions of everyday working people, put on by the Center for Continuing Studies at the University of Chicago. The following day, the school's Chamber Players performed for the Hispanic Festival of the Arts at the Museum of Science and Industry, a program they would repeat in July at Truman College for the chamber music organization Mostly Music. In the meantime, the adult choir prepared for a late May performance in Evanston.

The People's Music School continued to provide an atmosphere of fun along with serious music study. In her June 1981 letter, Rita announced:

> *On Tuesday, June 16, we have a surprise for our youngest*
> *students. A clown is coming to visit and help me teach their*
> *general music class.*

Mixed news arrived in July of 1981. The NEA informed the school that they were providing a first time grant of $2,500. It was far from the school's $19,000 request, but it was an important first "foot in the door." At the same time, because of cuts in the Illinois Arts Council budget, the school's IAC grant had been reduced from the prior year's $8,000 to $6,500, making the NEA award even more welcome. As Rita quipped in her July letter:

> *Does anyone have an idea on how to make a music school*
> *part of the defense budget? They are the only ones getting*
> *what they ask for.*

The summer concert in Lincoln Park, on August 2, drew a record 200 people, and most of them stayed even as threatening clouds approached. As Rita's August letter reported:

> *Just as the chorus finished singing "If We Only Have Love,"*
> *the rain started to come down. It poured. We all got*
> *drenched; still we all had a marvelous time.*

In the meantime, the number of new students registering each term was growing beyond the school's capacity to serve them, and for the first time Rita found it necessary to cap the fall 1981 student body at 150. A waiting list of twenty-one prospective students was formed, and new, more strict rules were put in place, putting additional pressure on all enrolled students to continue to maintain high attendance and music practice standards, in addition to their volunteer duties at the school.

In support of this tightening of the rules, teachers began filling out weekly evaluation sheets, and students were expected to reach established levels of proficiency in a reasonable amount of time, both in performance and in their general music class. As the students advanced in proficiency, more levels were added to the general music classes, which all students were required to take. Rita announced the general music faculty for fall of 1981: the beginning classes for children would be taught by piano teacher

Elizabeth Knapp; Judith Johnson, the flute teacher, would teach intermediate classes of 5-7 year-olds; Carter Hoyt would teach the first two levels of the adults; and Rita would teach the intermediate and advanced levels for both children and adults.

A problem that had occurred in January 1981 also needed to be addressed. Some of the 168 students who had registered at that time for the spring term had never returned. To help assure the commitment of those applying for admission to the school, beginning in the fall of 1981, a $5 refundable registration deposit was required each semester from each student. If the student had one unexcused absence, he or she would lose half that deposit. With a second unexcused absence, the other half was lost, and unless the student agreed to avoid future unexcused absences and paid a new
$5 registration fee, lessons were terminated and a member of the waiting list was invited to begin lessons.

Some people questioned Rita's practice of taking students on a first-come, first-served basis, resulting in growing lines on the school's registration days. Rita always answered by saying, "No one is more important than anyone else, so the only fair way to enroll students is on a first-come basis. If people are serious enough about studying music, they will come early."

Rita was especially pleased when, by the fall of 1981, one of Judith Johnson's flute students made the All-City Orchestra, and a ten-year old piano student was preparing to take part in the highly selective Society of American Musicians competition the following February. Still, Rita recognized that not all of her students would excel as performers.

As she more than once stated, "Let's say that only one in a hundred becomes a professional performer or a music teacher. That still leaves 99% to develop into a good, intelligent audience and to continue to understand and love good music. I want to make sure that music learning is not isolated from life."

A bright spot in the fund raising area for the school was created by the growing popularity and support for the dinner dances at St. Thomas. Originally held once a year, by 1981 several yearly dances were held, bringing in much needed funds. Everyone celebrated when the November 7 dinner dance netted a record $1,200, an amount that would be duplicated the following February 20 at a Mardi Gras theme dinner dance. In what had become their generous tradition, Carter Hoyt and his band provided the music free of charge, and many students and parents donated food for the event.

CHAPTER 32

A Casket Filled with Broken Instruments

The week before classes began in January 1982, the boiler in the building at 4417 N. Sheridan broke down. Quite a few water pipes broke, resulting in a number of leaks in the ceiling and part of the south wall of the school's space. Within a few days, plaster was falling from the ceiling and the walls. All classes had to be moved to the rear of the building. Feeling this additional limitation in a space that had felt cramped even before the disaster, Rita began seriously considering a move to a new location. But with the financial uncertainties that the school was facing, such a move seemed unlikely in the near future.

However, enthusiasm among the school's students, now 163 in number, remained at high pitch. As Rita wrote in February:

> The weather and damage to the building have been against us
> for the last four weeks, but amazingly most of the students have
> shown up for their classes and lessons.

Amid the chaos, plans progressed for the sixth anniversary concert on February 28, again held at the Hull House Gallery. The concert was an all-Haydn program in celebration of the 250th year of the composer's birth.

By March, the repairs to the building had been completed, and a new fund-raising project, made possible by the generosity of one of the school's Board member, was causing much excitement. At the May 16 spring concert, a prize of a Caribbean cruise and airfare voucher for two would be raffled off. Students and friends of the school all joined the effort to sell books of raffle tickets. With a limit on the number of tickets to be sold, hopes for selling all of the tickets ran high. The winner of the lottery drawing, which followed the spring concert, was Eleanor Wheeling, a senior citizen who was a member of the school's adult choir. The $2,600 profit produced by the raffle was greatly needed, as both the state and national arts funding organizations continued to have reduced budgets for grants.

Rita and The People's Music School staff had always recognized and appreciated the existence of another outstanding non-profit music school in the city of Chicago, the Merit Music Program. While some students at Merit did pay tuition, many from lower income families were on scholarship. Students at Merit were chosen through audition.

By summer of 1982, two students who had begun their music study at The People's Music School were participating in the Merit program. Rita welcomed this opportunity for her more accomplished students to expand their music study opportunities and to perform with other advanced music students in larger ensembles at Merit.

In September, Rita happily announced that two more students from The People's Music School, twin brothers Jonathan and Benjamin Crocker, a clarinetist and a violinist, would be auditioning for scholarships at the Merit Music Program. The Crocker brothers were children of Reverend Joseph Crocker and his wife, Marilyn, both of whom were deeply involved in the work of the Institute for Cultural Affairs at 4750 Sheridan Road.

The two boys were in the 7th and were good students as well as quite accomplished on their instruments. But they also had a playful streak. Since they were identical twins, Rita had trouble keeping them apart, but she quickly learned to do so by the instrument case they were carrying. To tease Rita, the boys would occasionally arrive at the school carrying each other's instrument, sending things into utter confusion and amusing everyone greatly.

The Crocker twins continued to excel in many ways beyond music, and both later became internists at Boston's Massachusetts General Hospital and members of the faculty of the Harvard Medical School. They also both continued to perform in community music groups.

In the years ahead, Rita often promoted opportunities for advancement and new challenges for her students. Many students from The People's Music School would become members of the Chicago Youth Symphony Orchestra, the Chicago Children's Choir, and other area youth performing groups. Many would win prizes in Chicago-area youth competitions.

Before the end of 1982, Rita had also worked two trips into her busy schedule. In August, she and Tomás returned to the Dominican Republic for a three-week visit with family, and at the end of November, she went to Boston to play a fund-raising recital for The People's Music School at the Cronkhite Graduate Center in Cambridge. Her close group of Boston friends, who had provided key support for the first months of the school, had continued their active dedication and generosity to the school. As she reported in December, upon her return:

> The recital was very successful and provided me with an
> opportunity to talk about the developments of the school to
> our generous supporters there. Most of them have been
> contributors to the school since our beginnings. I am still
> overwhelmed by their generosity.

On February 27, 1983, the seventh anniversary of the school was celebrated at a new venue, the Uptown Baptist Church. The children performed an operetta titled *The Runaway Snowman*, which was so well received that they were invited to repeat it on March 20 at St. Augustine College. Also in February, Rita announced that administrative demands at the school had become so large that a part-time administrative assistant, Miriam Lugo, had been hired.

Unfortunately, this expansion of the staff preceded more bad news in the funding area. In early March, Governor James Thompson's office announced a proposal to eliminate the Illinois Arts Council totally from the budget. Rita's first response was to ask all of her students and supporters to write letters of protest. In April she mailed a package of 140 letters to the governor's office.

Already, however, another plan was taking shape in Rita's mind. On May 7, she gathered a large group of students and faculty for a trip by bus to the governor's Fullerton Avenue home to stage an impromptu "serenade." The date of May 7 was chosen because it was the 150th birthday of Johannes Brahms. All the music the group performed that day was by Brahms.

Wanting to maximize the effect of the event, Rita's also notified her various friends in the media of the upcoming "serenade." As she reported in her May newsletter:

> About 200 students, parents, faculty and friends were there.
> We brought along a casket with broken instruments,
> paintbrushes, books of poetry, dancing slippers, etc., to make
> our point more visually clear. The president of our Board,
> Thomas McLaughlin, was dressed up like Brahms and
> presented a letter to the Governor. We sang some Brahms
> songs to him, accompanied by violins, flutes, recorders,
> trumpet, sax and guitar. The whole affair came off very well.
> The Governor spoke to us and listened to our concerns. We

> *got good publicity from the papers, radio and TV. Now we*
> *wait to see what the results are.*

No one can say with certainty what role the "serenade" played in the outcome, but by early August news had circulated that Governor Thompson had just signed a budget allocating a larger sum for the Illinois Arts Council than in previous years. Equally important, The People's Music School was awarded a larger grant than they had received the year before.

CHAPTER 33

Maria and Nalini Kotamraju

The adult choir at the People's Music School was an eclectic group. In addition to individuals studying voice or an instrument at the school, others who had schedules too busy for music study or were studying privately elsewhere found pleasure in joining the adult choir. One of those individuals was Maria Kotamraju-Fraai.

Born in Curacao, Netherlands Antilles, Maria developed a love of music at a young age and performed in choirs both as a child in Curacao and as an adult in the Netherlands. After marrying Dr. Baburao Kotamraju, she and her husband moved to Uptown with their young daughter, Nalini. By 1982, Maria had discovered The People's Music School and its choir.

Daughter Nalini took music classes at her school, the nearby Academy of the Sacred Heart. She began piano study with a teacher there, but her mother also enrolled her in the children's choir at The People's Music School.

Tragedy struck the family in 1984 with the unexpected death of Baburao Katmraju. In 1986, Nalini's closest friend also died unexpectedly. Shortly before her friend's death, Nalini had begun piano lessons with Rita Simó.

"The People's Music School became an important place for me at that point," Nalini recalls. "It was often the place I would come after school or following a school activity. Rita would put me to work organizing things, filing or sorting. She valued my competence, but I later realized that she was also providing me an opportunity to feel needed and was keeping me busy as I navigated through these losses."

Both Maria and Nalini continued their involvement with The People's Music School for many years. Maria served on the Board of the school for over a decade. For several years, she rented rooms in Rita and Tomás' Beacon Street house while teaching at nearby Truman College.

It was widely understood that Maria Kotamraju was the person connected with the school who was most successful in dealing with Rita. She was the one other Board and staff members would turn to when difficult school matters needed to be discussed with Rita. Maria's soft, diplomatic manner would usually lead to mutual understanding and support among all parties.

Nalini continued volunteering at the school even after she had graduated from high school and become a student at Harvard University. In 2001, while pursuing a PhD at the University of California, she made a special trip back to Chicago in order to attend the school's 25th anniversary.

"Other than my parents, Rita Simó is the adult that has had the most influence on my life," she says.

CHAPTER 34

Growing Pains

Late in the summer of 1983, Rita and Tomás returned from a vacation in Greece to learn upsetting news. Though the school had received significant grant support from the National Endowment for the Arts for several years, there would be no grant for the coming year. This was especially puzzling because the NEA representative who had visited the school the prior March had made a very positive evaluation of the school and had encouraged Rita to request $15,000 in her application.

Further inquiry brought an explanation. The school's application had been rejected because of its open admissions policy. New NEA guidelines stated that support would be given only to programs requiring an audition for entrance. Rita found this new policy very upsetting. As she wrote in her October 1983 newsletter:

> This policy is discriminatory to the poor. How does a child
> from a home with no exposure to classical music ever know
> whether he or she has any talent?

It seemed to her that if the goal of the NEA was to increase interest and participation in the arts across a broad spectrum of the nation's population, the new policy was counterproductive to that end. Rita wrote to the chairman of the NEA explaining her frustration with the new policy and asking that it be reconsidered.

Another initiative taken by The People's Music School in the fall of 1983 turned out more positively. On October 24, Rita and the president of the school's Board met with representatives of the Midwest Chapter of the National Guild of Community Schools for the Arts (NGCSA) who had come to determine whether the school would be a good candidate for membership.

While membership in the NGCSA would not produce funds, it would provide interaction with a strong network of arts organizations. With its widely respected professional standards, it would also add considerably to the status and credibility of the school. The visit with the representatives went well, and by mid-December word had been received that The People's Music School had been accepted as a member of the guild.

In December, the school received an invitation from the office of Mayor Harold Washington for the children's choir to perform at the Christmas tree lighting ceremony in Daley Center Plaza. A student group from The People's Music School had performed for the Mayor's inauguration the prior April on Navy Pier, so Washington was already familiar with the school.

For the ceremony, the children sang the gospel hymn by Andre Crouch, "Soon and Very Soon, We Are Going to See the King," in three different languages, English, Spanish and Vietnamese the native languages of the children in the group. Afterwards, the mayor came up to Rita and expressed his amazement that the children could alternate so effectively from one language to the next. Rita pointed out to him that while the children were able to sing all the words in the three languages, it didn't mean that they were conversant in all three languages.

The school's fund raising efforts were given an important boost in early 1984. The Chicago Council on Fine Arts in conjunction with the Chicago Community Trust presented The People's Music School with a two-for-one challenge grant. If the school raised $4,000 in new donations within a two month period, it would receive an $8,000 matching gift.

Rita was excited at the news, but it came at a busy time for her. In addition to her full teaching schedule, plans for both the school's upcoming eighth anniversary celebration on February 19 and the Mardi Gras dinner dance on March 3 were in full swing. At the same time, Rita needed to find a new office administrator. Miriam Lugo had resigned to take a new job, and a replacement Rita had hired had lasted only a few weeks. Now, on top of everything, she would need to increase fund raising efforts.

Yet, as she announced plans for the February 19 anniversary concert, which was to include an all-French music program presented by the school's faculty, she remained steadfastly thankful and optimistic:

> *As we prepare to celebrate our eighth anniversary, we look back*
> *with our hearts filled with gratitude....The common thread which*
> *runs through all of you is your conviction that music is*
> *fundamental; music is a joy; music is a right for everyone....With*
> *friends such as all of you, can we feel anything other than grateful.*

In her March 1984 letter, Rita joyfully announced that the challenge grant goal had been met and that the Mardi Gras dinner dance had brought in a record $1,600 profit. Classes were going well, and the school now included thirteen part-time dedicated teachers in addition to Rita. In most respects things were looking positive, but one big challenge remained: the uncertain future of the school's current space and the growing awareness that more space was needed.

In the meantime, The People's Music School's ambassadorship within the greater Chicago metropolitan area continued to grow. Faculty ensembles regularly performed on the Mostly Music concert series and in a Classical Music series on Monday nights at Hobson's Choice Restaurant on N. Clark. In May 1984, several ensembles from the school participated in a Mexican Fine Arts program at the Field Museum. Rita, herself, performed often in numerous venues around the city, including regular recitals in the Chicago Cultural Center, sometimes solo and sometimes with other faculty members. For Rita, each of these performances was another opportunity to tell people about the People's Music School and to make new friends for the school.

In May, the school finally was able to hire a new office administrator, Alban Fisher. Alban's hiring proved a fortuitous choice, and he continued to serve the school faithfully and competently for a number of years.

But the difficulties with the school's location continued to grow. Rita's July 1984 newsletter outlined some of the problems:

> *Our building has been sold. We were able to negotiate certain concessions with the new manager. Previously the heat in the summer was our greatest problem due to the water heater for the building being located below us. They have now moved it to another part of the building, and the temperature inside is now ten degrees cooler than in previous years. They raised the rent to $500 a month, but agreed on a lease until August 1985.*

Summer of 1984 was a memorable one for Rita and Tomás. In August they traveled to Germany, where Rita presented a lecture/recital at the American School in the Bavarian town of Kitzingen. The two of them then traveled throughout West Germany and Austria, giving special attention to the areas where the great classical composers had lived and worked. Rita especially enjoyed exploring the places where Beethoven had lived or often visited, including the woodland paths near Vienna that served as inspiration for many of his compositions.

Though the August trip focused on male composers, upon her return, Rita began preparing with her faculty for an October Illinois Arts Festival week featuring women composers. Their program included works by Florence Price, Katherine Hoover, Emma Lou Diemer, and Beth Anderson. It was repeated in March 1985 in the Louis Lerner Auditorium at the Sulzer Regional Library as part of the Chicago Public Library's celebration of Women's History Month.

As Rita wrote to a friend, "The wealth of music composed by women is amazing. It is a pity that most of it is rarely played."

On November 12, 1984, The People's Music School received important national recognition when Rita gave a presentation about the school at the Conference of the National Guild of Community Schools for the Arts in Detroit. To open her presentation, Rita recited Robert Frost's poem "The Road Not Taken," an appropriate reflection upon her own career path. After returning to Chicago, she reported that everyone was very receptive to her story and impressed with the accomplishments of the school.

Within a few weeks of Rita's return from Detroit, news broke of an imminent strike by Chicago public school teachers. The strike, which occurred in December, lasted for ten days before an agreement was finally reached. During that time there were no classes in Chicago public schools.

Rita always saw her school as not only a music school but also as an extended family for her students, and the response of The People's Music School to the public school crisis reflected this philosophy of community support: "We have decided to open two hours early in order that our students can come and have two hours of supervised study time before our regular classes begin."

The year of 1985 began smoothly with the school's well-received ninth anniversary concert featuring music by Handel and Scarlatti, in celebration of the 300th anniversaries of their births. News also had been received that the City Arts Council in cooperation with the Chicago Community Trust had again presented the school with a matching grant challenge of $11,744, to be given if $3,910 in new funds could be raised.

The school decided to meet the challenge partly through a new initiative. On March 30, Johann Sebastian Bach's tri-centennial birthday was celebrated one day early at the school's first "performathon." All students and faculty members were encouraged to perform works by Bach. Students and faculty alike worked hard to line up sponsors, and everyone was delighted when $2,000 in new contributions was earned to put toward the challenge grant.

On the same day as the performathon, an evaluator from the National Endowment for the Arts made a visit to the school. Rita never knew if her letter of protest a few years before had made a difference, but by now the NEA policy against programs with open admission had been rescinded. Rita was pleased that the evaluator had chosen this busy day for her visit and that she seemed to be impressed with the enthusiasm and accomplishments of the students and teachers and sympathetic about their need for larger space.

Several food and bake sales were also planned during the early months of 1985, helping the school meet its new challenge grant. To Rita, these sales were very important for reasons beyond their fund raising results. Perhaps equally significant, they created a wonderful spirit in which school families from a wide range of backgrounds and traditions came together, sampled each other's food, shared recipes, and developed friendships. Rita smiles as she recalls one of her favorite stories:

"At one of our food sales, a woman brought a dish that was just like one I used to be served at home when I was growing up. I told the lady who brought it, that she must be from the Dominican Republic. She said, no, she was from Africa and this had been a dish she had been served as a child. I excitedly turned to another mother nearby who had come from the Dominican Republic and told her she must meet the lady from Africa and share more information about the similar cooking traditions each had experienced. The beautiful thing is that these two ladies from very different backgrounds became the best of friends." There are many similar stories of friendships created through the sharing of food at The People's Music School.

Though music proficiency and knowledge were the primary concerns of the school, Rita often dealt with more serious problems faced by her students and their families, including housing, immigration, and, in a few cases, domestic violence. As Rita understood it, The People's Music School family was her family. Whenever she found a need to be addressed, she tried to meet it. In an article that appeared several years later in Chicago Magazine, she was quoted as saying, "A good teacher goes beyond just book knowledge and helps students establish the basis for a meaningful and productive life."

As the spring term ended, Rita proudly listed the many invitations her children's choir had received to perform throughout the community, including a concert for Joseph Cardinal Bernardin during a visit he made to Uptown. She knew that children are often the most convincing ambassadors, and she saw how meaningful this way of giving back to the community was for everyone involved. As she wrote at the end of her May newsletter:

One of the songs the children are singing says "spread some sunshine everywhere," and we feel this is our way to do just that.

CHAPTER 35

Celebrating Ten Years

Rita's June 1985 newsletter addressed her biggest concern as the end of the school's current rental lease approached:

> *We started summer classes last week. As usual we turned away over thirty people for lack of space. We have started looking around for a bigger place but the rents are outrageous around here. We have even considered buying a place, but that would be quite a task.*

On July 28, the school celebrated the 235th anniversary of Johann Sebastian Bach's death with a special lecture and recital featuring all fifteen of the composer's two-part inventions performed by students and faculty.

As Rita later reminisced with friends upon remembering that day, "I see this as one of the greatest accomplishments of our early years. Here was a small music school with students who hadn't studied all that long, and all of them were involved in performing the Bach inventions. I keep thinking about my own early transformation in growing to appreciate Bach. It has always been important to me to try to bring a passion for the music of Bach to my students."

The September newsletter announced a wonderful opportunity for the school. The children's choir was invited to sing with the Niles College choir in a program featuring a piece by Carl Nilsen for mixed chorus, soloist, children's choir, and orchestra. It was the first time the children's choir had performed with another group is such a professional setting.

The children's choir had also impressed Cardinal Bernardin during his visit to Uptown a few months earlier, and in late October the group received an invitation to perform at the Cardinal's Christmas reception in the

Archbishop's Residence on North State Parkway, an invitation that was repeated for several Decembers thereafter.

The 1985 fall newsletters talked about the beginning of preparations for the school's tenth anniversary year. In recognition of this special milestone, Rita and the Board had commissioned an operetta by local composer and educator Hugo Teruel to be produced the following May. Also, since the actual anniversary date of the opening of the school, February 22, fell on a Saturday, that day would be celebrated with a concert featuring faculty, current and former students, and both the adult and the children's choirs, followed by a "lavish banquet." The February celebration took place at St. Augustine College on West Argyle.

In her March 1986 letter, Rita happily announced:

> *Our tenth anniversary celebration was a great success. Over 300 people came to be with us that night. Mr. Fred Fine, the Commissioner of Fine Arts for the city, was there for the whole program and said a few words afterwards. We were all very honored with what he said. Also, our alderman, Jerome Orbach, came and brought us a proclamation from the city.*

The printed program for the concert carried many tributes from area businesses and friends, as well as Rita's thanks to the financial sponsors of the event. But one page had special meaning for Rita. Under the title "Best Wishes" there were three segments: the first one brought greetings from Harvey and Ethel Bissonnette; the second accompanied by the message "Felicidades en los primeros diez años y prosperidad en el future" was signed by Ana Isidra, brother Alfredo, his wife Myrna, his daughter Rimir, and the family's longtime maid and nanny, Gracia; the final one was from Tomás.

Toward the end of the printed program, Rita thanked her Board, led by Thomas McLaughlin, and also her faculty: Mariano Arcenas, George Blanchet, Anne Costello, Steve Edwards, Carter Hoyt, Carlos Jimenez, Judith Johnson, Betty Lewis, Becky Pavlatos, Annie Randall, and Robert Richman. It was a day all would remember.

Rita with favorite toy, age 2

The young pianist, age 6,
at the family's "new" piano

A young equestrian, Rita at her father's farm, 1942

109

Teodoro Simó Knipping

Pretending to be Carmen Miranda

Eighth grade graduation, 1947

Rita with father Teodoro

Graduation concert, Conservatorio Nacional de Música, 1954

Rita with religious mentor Father Dermot Brennan, 1961

Rita with Juilliard piano teacher Katherine Bacon, 1968

Ecuadorean dress worn by Rita in many recitals

First meeting between Tomás and Ana Isidra, 1978

Wedding day for Rita and Tomás, October 21, 1978

The children's choir at the Christmas tree lighting ceremony,
with Mayor Harold Washington, 1983

Members of the children's choir with Cardinal Bernardin,
Christmas reception in the Archbishop's Residence, 1985

(Many of the school photos in this book were taken by photographer Charles Lewis.)

CHAPTER 36

The Search for a New Home

A little over a month after the tenth anniversary celebration, The People's Music School suddenly found itself in crisis. Rita's April 1986 letter began:

> So many things are happening. I never expected that the second decade was going to begin at such hectic pace. On April 2 we were given notice that we must vacate our place by May 31st due to complete renovation of the building.......We are very nervous about finding a place in such short notice. At the same time, we hope that now we can find a larger place to be able to expand.

By the end of April, the owners of the building had told Rita that the school could stay on until renovations began in the middle of August; however, Rita was never able to get them to put it in writing, which made the arrangement precarious.

The May newsletter was the first one Rita had ever typed, other than the year-end reports. She wrote that there was so much information to cover that it would never fit on one handwritten page. On May 6, the city had turned off the water to the building, because the owners were too far behind on their water bills. In typical fashion, Rita marshaled her students and faculty into a demonstration in front of the building, which resulted in enough publicity that water was restored on May 8, though the building's owners were greatly irritated.

Then, on May 10, Alban Fisher opened the school to find that a flood, which had originated on the 7th floor, had damaged rugs, furniture, and light fixtures in the school. There could now be no delaying. The school would have to move.

First, however, Rita realized that money earmarked for other purposes would have to be spent in cleaning, repairing, and replacing damaged items. Carter Hoyt's thoughtfulness once again eased some of Rita's distress. He was now working for Illinois Bell Telephone Company and was earning a comfortable salary.

"When I didn't have a job, you helped me get one through CETA," he told Rita. "I now have a job and would like to give lessons for the next year at the school without pay."

When Rita protested, Carter insisted that he would hear of no other option. For once, Rita did not get the final word.

As the building crisis had grown, Rita had been busily scouring the neighborhood for an alternative location. She explored many rental possibilities throughout the area. Most of them charged rents far above the school's ability to pay. She even investigated several abandoned buildings that might be purchased for reasonable sums.

One possibility held out hope. Parents of several of the school's students were participants in the Ecumenical Institute, an organization that had originated several decades before within the Church Federation of Greater Chicago, along with its companion organization, the Institute of Cultural Affairs. Both groups worked as advocates for social change, both locally and internationally, through various programs and through the sponsorship of seminars and conferences, many of which were held in the building the institute owned and occupied at 4750 N. Sheridan. Since the institute was in the process of program reorganization, some of the parents thought space might be opening up and available.

With several parents from The People's Music School by her side, Rita visited the Ecumenical Institute and explained her situation to the lady at the front desk. While the woman was sympathetic, she was doubtful that the institute could be of help. At the present time, with the scheduled programs and seminars, there was little available space, and rents for whatever rooms might be spared would probably be unaffordable for the school. However, she promised to bring the matter up with the program's director. Neither of them knew that the director was standing nearby and overheard part of the exchange. After Rita left, he asked for more details.

"I think this is the kind of program we want to help," he said. "I think we can find space for this school."

At first the Ecumenical Institute promised to provide space only for the summer months, as there had been some talk that the building might be sold. Beyond that they could only promise a month-by-month extension while plans for the future were clarified. Since there was no guarantee that the space would be available beyond the summer, Rita continued exploring other alternatives. Already she was beginning to understand the virtue of the school's having its own building, so it would not be at the mercy of the vicissitudes of the rental market. As she wrote to students, friends, and supporters:

> *We are looking at a vacant firehouse that is being used for storage*
> *by the city. I went to see it with an architect, who said it is only*
> *four walls, but that it has great possibilities. He estimated that*
> *$60,000 to $80,000 would have to be invested into it to make it*
> *into top shape. We are going to write a proposal to the city for a*
> *50-year lease at $1.00 per year. We started a building fund last*
> *October, which to date has grown to $10,000.*

As a final farewell to The People's Music School's first home, the spring concert took place as scheduled, on Sunday, May 18, 1986, at 4417 N. Sheridan. It featured the newly commissioned operetta, *Friends Without Words*, by Hugo Teruel, which was thoroughly enjoyed by all who attended. Rita shared her delight with the program in her May newsletter:

> *The children sang perfectly and followed all the directions that*
> *Marlene Zuccaro, the stage director had given them. We made a*
> *video of it and perhaps can use it for publicity purposes.*

CHAPTER 37

Settling into New Space at 4750 N. Sheridan Road

Moving day, May 26, arrived with much fanfare. Rita had rented a truck and was delighted when her flute teacher, Judith Johnson, offered the services of her husband as driver and general moving helper.

"He has always dreamed of being a truck driver," Judith laughed.

More than fifty other students and parents volunteered to help as well, and with so many people participating, the move progressed efficiently and was accompanied by much joviality. When it had been completed, everyone was invited to Rita's house for one of her famous picnics.

Soon, the school was setting up for the summer opening of classes on Monday, June 2. Through all the upheaval, Rita's Boston friends had continued sending both much needed funding and also heartfelt moral support. One contribution received that June from Boston came with a button enclosed, which was inscribed, "Winners Never Quit."

The space the Ecumenical Institute had made available to The People's Music School at 4750 N. Sheridan consisted of three large rooms in the front of the third floor. The rent was $500 a month, the same that the school had been paying at their former location. While the school's new home had the same number of rooms as before, the rooms at 4750 N. Sheridan were larger, airier and more pleasant.

The only negative was that being on the third floor, the school was less accessible to both students and to the parade of local residents who had regularly walked by and stopped in to listen and exchange greetings with students and staff. While the students quickly made the transition, visits from other local residents and from the street people largely ceased.

The summer of 1986 brought another important move, as well. For a number of years, Tomás' Spanish language book distribution service had been growing steadily, and it had become clear that more space was required. When Father Rochford moved from St. Thomas of Canterbury Church to St. Jerome's Catholic Church in 1984, Tomás moved his book service to a room of the school at St. Jerome's.

By 1986, however, he had outgrown that space. In the summer of 1986, he rented a storefront at 5127 North Clark Street, expanded his inventory to include books of general interest to the Hispanic community, incorporated as "Spanish Speaking Bookstore," and set up shop. Within a few years, Tomás again felt a need for expansion, and he and Rita bought a building at 4441 North Broadway, the bookstore's final location. While no longer operating on a strictly volunteer, break-even basis, Tomás continued to structure his bookstore business as a low-profit operation, in service to the Hispanic community.

In August, following trips to the Dominican Republic and Boston, Rita gleefully announced:

> We just got a donation of a Kimball baby grand piano in very good condition. We are continually amazed at people's generosity.

She also announced that she had not given up on the prospect of turning the abandoned fire station into the school's next home. However, the city was still showing no signs of responding to the request.

Fortunately, talk of selling the Ecumenical Institute building had subsided, and it appeared that The People's Music School could remain at its new location for the near future. In fact, planned program changes at the Institute could mean that more space would be available at some point.

Following the fall registration, enrollment at The People's Music School stood at 160. Half were five to twelve years old and the other half were thirteen and older, including four senior citizens. The requirements made of students remained the same as they had been in the school's former location, except the refundable entry fee was now $10. Absences, except for last minute emergencies, had to be approved ahead by Rita or one of the other teachers. For every unexcused absence, $5 was deducted from the fee. If a student had a third unexcused absence, he or she was asked to leave to make room for someone on the waiting list.

As had been the case from the beginning, all students, or their parents or guardians, were required to donate a minimum of two hours of volunteer service per month to the care and other needs of the school. This service could take many forms. Some students and parents did maintenance chores. Some offered help in areas of their expertise, everything from plumbing to secretarial chores. Others planned and administered the various fund raising activities or greeted and ushered at the various recitals and other programs. Still others supplied food for special events and for the fund-raising food and bake sales. Some parents were allowed to hand address the envelopes for the monthly newsletters, a "plum" volunteer service job, but only if their penmanship passed Rita's strict test.

The required pattern of study for new students also remained the same as it had been from the beginning. All students were expected to begin with four sessions of "general music," or theory, before they could start lessons on their chosen instrument. In these sessions, students were introduced to music fundamentals, including common terms, symbols, and definitions.

Following the four sessions, which they were required to attend, students could begin lessons on their instrument. However, they were also required to continue attending and participating in general music or theory classes, which on more advanced levels included exploration of general musical literature. Rita wanted to make sure that her students were serious about their commitment, and she firmly believed that general musical knowledge must accompany the development of technical skill for her students.

Except for unusual circumstances, the students were also expected to perform several times a year in concerts given by the school, including the annual performathon. At these performances, students were not allowed to wear athletic shoes or jeans. On occasions where this was a financial hardship, money would surreptitiously appear for the purchase of dress shoes, often from the nearby secondhand store.

Rita's September 1986 letter expressed gratitude for the continuing support of the Illinois Arts Council, and announced that the school would celebrate Illinois Arts Week with two events: a faculty recital featuring music of Liszt and Weber and a concert by a guest, Guatemalan classical guitarist Alejandro Herrera.

In January 1987, it was decided that the budget would allow an increase in the number of students at the school, and enrollment was raised to 170. Even then, more than fifty applicants had to be turned away. By now, students were coming from all over the city of Chicago, many arriving at the school by public transportation.

Rita continued to perform in a full schedule of concerts. On January 23, she exhibited that her keyboard skills extended beyond piano and organ when she performed an evening of harpsichord music titled "Go for Baroque."

As she was preparing for this program, however, Rita had a more serious concern on her mind. Tomás had agreed to travel with a delegation from Witness for Peace to the U. S. Embassy in Nicaragua to protest United States funding of the Contra War there. He was leaving near the end of January. While the group was planning a peaceful demonstration, their safety was far from certain in that war-torn country where many innocent people had been killed.

Amid her worries that Tomás might be putting himself in a position of danger, Rita made a silent promise to herself and to God. If he returned safely, she would do something Tomás had long urged her to do, give up her cigarette smoking habit. By the end of the first week in February, Tomás had returned home safely, along with many new books for his Spanish Speaking Bookstore. From the day of his arrival, Rita never smoked another cigarette.

The People's Music School celebrated its eleventh anniversary on February 22 at its new home with a concert of music by living composers, followed as always by a dinner. Rita's February newsletter referred to the upcoming hotly-contested aldermanic race and expressed her hope that the winner would be supportive of local arts efforts and expansion. The April election brought new leadership to the district in the person of reformer Helen Shiller, who through her long tenure as the District 46 alderman would lend much helpful support to Rita and the school.

Rita's February 1987 letter also mentioned a special event at the school in celebration of Black History Month:

> *Last week we had Geraldine de Haas from the Illinois Arts Council talk to our students about Marian Anderson and sing some spirituals. For many of our children it was the first time they heard a real contralto. They were really impressed.*

The school's ongoing search for a more permanent home was aided in March by the news that the Illinois Arts Council had awarded them a grant from its "Build by Design" program, which would allow the school to hire someone to look for a building to either buy or lease long term and to help with feasibility studies relating to renovation needs and code requirements. The grant could also be used to hire consultants to help the school begin planning for a capital campaign, a critical part of any ambitious move.

In the meantime, The People's Music School once again moved in April, this time to an area in the back of the third floor of the Ecumenical Institute. Rita welcomed the move. In addition to containing more space, including three practice rooms and a separate large combination administrative area and concert room, the location was an improvement, as Rita mentioned in her March letter, because everything would be together in one area and would be separated from all other activity on the floor.

The school year ended with dwindling hope for converting the abandoned fire station into suitable space. The city remained noncommittal, and consultants hired through the "Build by Design" grant questioned the desirability of the building for the school's purposes. Rita valiantly repeated her commitment to continuing the search, and she asked her students and parents to bring her any ideas they might have of possible sites from around the community. A church building that was being sold on Lawrence Avenue near Beacon Street proved upon inspection to require too much renovation as well as costly asbestos removal.

For a while Rita was excited about the former Sulzer Library building at 4544 N. Lincoln that the city was selling. But it also proved to require too much expensive renovation before it would be suitable for school needs. In addition, it was much too large. That building subsequently became the new home of the Old Town School of Folk Music. A former car repair shop on Foster Avenue east of Broadway caused excitement for a while but also proved unsatisfactory upon closer scrutiny.

In June, a special feature on The People's Music School was broadcast on the NBC, WMAQ-TV, primetime news at 6 p.m. It resulted in a large number of responses from new people interested in learning more about the school and, in some cases, in making contributions, either of money or of instruments and other musically related items.

June also brought an invitation for the school's children's choir to perform their operetta *Friends Without Words* at Greeley School in Winnetka, as part of the TWIG program, a summer camp which brought together children from the inner city and the northern suburbs in an intercultural day camp experience. The invitation came about through a friend and generous supporter of The People's Music School, Anita "Onnie" Darrow.

Several years earlier, Rita had been invited to join the Wieboldt Foundation Board as a result of her friendship with a staff member at the foundation. It was while serving on that board that she met Onnie Darrow.

A granddaughter of William Wieboldt, a German immigrant who rose from poverty to establish the Wieboldt's department store chain, Onnie had grown up in a family devoted to charitable service, much of it through their Wieboldt Foundation. Like other members of her family, Onnie had always been a strong advocate for equality and justice. In 1967, she had welcomed the first African-American family to her Winnetka neighborhood and had personally escorted the children to their first day of elementary school. The prior year, she had joined other Winnetka residents in creating the TWIG program.

Onnie was also an amateur viola player, and many years later, when she had moved to a retirement community and was no longer able to play her viola, she donated the cherished instrument to The People's Music School. Rita often referred to Onnie Darrow as "my guardian angel."

Rita served on the Wieboldt Foundation Board for over a decade. While her membership on the board prevented her from receiving any funds from the foundation for her school, Rita received a priceless education in the workings of foundation boards, and her involvement with the Wieboldt Board put her in touch with many people in the wider Chicago philanthropy community.

CHAPTER 38

Twelve Years: Manuel Simó and 12-Tones

The 1987 fall term at the People's Music School started with a record student enrollment of almost 200. An October article about the school in the Claretian magazine *Salt* gave the breakdown of ethnicity as: 45% Hispanic, 20% African-American, 18% white, 12% Oriental, and 2% American Indian.

A new office manager, Precedia Massey, had also been hired. Precedia's job was to administer the day to day activities, while Alban Fisher, who had now gone back to school to work on a degree in clinical psychology, continued to take care of the proposal writing, general reports, and the financial books on a part-time basis and without pay. During the summer, The People's Music School had received a grant from the Community Arts Assistance Program to publish a brochure and an annual report, and these projects were responsibilities Alban also accepted.

Rita was especially pleased when a grant was received in October from the Albert Pick, Jr. Fund that allowed several students to accompany her to perform at the 50th anniversary convention of the National Guild of Community Schools for the Arts in New York in early November. A competition was held to determine which students would make the trip, and the winners were Maria Valdés, piano; Anissa Balverde, violin; and Bryan Apolinar, snare drum. Upon their return, Rita reported that all had performed well and had also served as excellent ambassadors for the school.

The year ended with a special Christmas Concert, again featuring the operetta *Friends Without Words* by Hugo Teruel, held at the spacious O'Rourke Performing Arts Center, home of the Pegasus Players. In expressing her gratitude to the theater group, Rita commented on how much her students had enjoyed the large stage and the availability of plenty of seating for over two hundred people who attended.

Rita's January 1988 newsletter spoke with excited anticipation about the 12th anniversary celebration scheduled for February 21. With the money from the Community Arts Assistance Program grant, she planned to publish a special brochure about the school that could be ready for distribution at the anniversary celebration:

> *Since we never had an Annual Report, we are making this brochure our "Twelve Year Report." For the cover we are using a twelve-tone row from a piece by Manuel Simó. It will represent the twelve years of the school, and it almost matches our ups and downs over that time.*

By February, the People's Music School had its first professionally printed brochure, a multi-paged booklet that outlined the school's programs and other activities, as well as the story of the school's history. The opening pages contained letters from both Rita and the president of the school's Board, Robert G. Clarke. Rita's comments in the booklet were particularly poignant:

> *I can hardly believe that 12 years have passed since we began our music program at the People's Music School. Many of you still remember when the idea of opening a music school that would be free of charge to community residents was just a dream in my head. Many told me the school would never last, that there would not be the interest and commitment, let alone the finances, for such an operation. Well, here we are, and still going strong.*
>
> *I would be lying if I said that everything has gone smoothly through the years. There have been many joys along with disappointments. Yet, we have survived and flourished through the help of many. Faculty members, students, their families, local residents, board members, and our many supporters throughout the Chicago area and across the country have all worked together to make the People's Music School a possibility. We are a community music school. Our strength is the people whom we serve and give a chance to put music into their lives.*
>
> *As a professional musician, I know what the arts have meant in my life. I know many of you understand the importance of the arts in a child's education, in giving adults an opportunity to*

expand their horizons and use their time more creatively.
Through these 12 years, we have reached over 1,500 students,
the majority of whom probably would never have developed
their musical talents if our program had not been available.
We have identified many gifted students and given them the
opportunity to develop their skills. Now they compete with
others who were able to pay for their own music education.

The School is the product of more than one person. As I look
back over the last 12 years, the people who have stayed with
our program over this time never cease to amaze me. Carter
Hoyt has taught the beginning adult theory classes and guitar
classes since the first year the School opened. Mary O'Neill
Siebel has served on our board and directed the adult choir for
many years while still serving as a faculty member at Roosevelt
University. Judith Johnson has taught flute and theory to
younger children since the first year we were opened. Thomas
McLaughlin, our long-time board member, who stepped down
as president this year, also deserves special recognition for his
time and commitment to the growth of our School. The list goes
on and on, including those who never fail to send a monthly or
yearly check. I want to express my heartfelt gratitude to
all..........

I look to the future with great hope. I see our School
expanding to reach over 250 students in our very own
facility. Another dream! But we know of what we are
capable and believe in the work we are doing. This dream is
also attainable.....

Very truly yours,
Rita Simó

CHAPTER 39

The People's Music School Is a Teenager

The year of 1988 continued with a full calendar of activities and performances at The People's Music School. On April 15, the percussion ensemble, consisting of five boys and one girl, performed at the Daley Center in celebration of Mayor Harold Washington's birthday, and the following day the school's fourth performathon took place, with 135 students and faculty members playing from 2:00 to 7:15 p.m. It netted almost $2,200. At the same time, plans were underway for the largest spring concert yet, to be held at Truman College on May 21.

Rita's talent for perfect musical pitch never ceased to amaze her students and staff. Often she would pass a classroom where a student was practicing and react with an admonishment, such as, "Not f-natural; that's an f-sharp."

One staff member recalls with amusement the day a shrill-sounding vacuum cleaner was circulating the floor of the building. Rita came around the corner shaking her head and muttering, with a nod in the direction of the sound, "Such an irritating e-flat!"

Students and staff enjoyed the informal, friendly atmosphere of the school. At one point, Rita got the idea of earning a little extra money from soda pop purchased by the case from the local Aldi store, which the school would sell can by can for a small profit. Rita would only sell grape, orange and citrus, feeling these were the only healthy flavors.

As soon as the little refrigerator in the reception room started to look bare, the familiar routine would begin. Rita would arrive in front of the school with the cases of pop and turn on her car's flashers. Staff would be ready with a large wobbly rolling office chair, which they would load with the drinks and somehow maneuver to the elevator for transportation to the third floor, and a careening journey down the hallway to the refrigerator.

Another school fund-raising tradition was the periodic bazaar sale. Out would come the bins and boxes of donated items collected over the previous months, including various records, CDs and sheet music, as well as clothing and other items left too long in the lost and found. Students staffed the sales with their volunteer hours, and most shoppers found treasures either for themselves or to use as presents. While these sales usually took place during the time between Thanksgiving and Christmas, they could also occur spontaneously whenever the boxes and bins got too full.

These happy activities, however, were periodically interspersed with sad news. In May, Rita reported the car accident death of saxophone and clarinet teacher, Carlos Jiménez, a Cuban refugee, who had taught at the school for five years.

Summer of 1988 proved especially challenging as temperatures soared, bringing a record number of over 90-degree days to Chicago. While classes continued uninterrupted, Rita observed that the children seemed much quieter than usual. It was clear everyone was feeling the oppressive heat.

Registration week in the fall once again brought a deluge of applicants. Rita reported in her September newsletter that the school now had 185 students, which was the maximum number the space would allow, and that the school had now extended teaching hours to 8:00 p.m.

In the same letter, Rita announced both good and bad news in the area of funding. While both the Albert Pick, Jr. Fund and the Chicago Tribune Foundation had come up with grants for the school, there would be no money from the Illinois Arts Council. When Rita asked for an explanation, she was told no money was being given that year to youth programs unconnected with or unsupported by local public schools or their boards of education. She sadly commented that the way most Chicago public schools operated in the area of the arts, it was not likely they could be of much "support" to a program like the People's Music School.

October brought much better news. The Prince Charitable Trust had given the school a $15,000 grant, which would serve as a much-needed offset to other funding cuts. The good news arrived as Rita and her staff were making plans for participation in the late November convention of the National Guild of Community Schools for the Arts, which that year was scheduled to take place in Chicago. The main concert at the convention, to be held at the Chicago Cultural Center, featured students from various schools throughout the Midwest. Three of the more advanced students from the People's Music School were preparing to perform a string trio. Rita was especially pleased at this opportunity for some of her more advanced students to share the stage with other accomplished young musicians. As she wrote:

> *Slowly our more talented students are realizing that*
> *professional aspirations in music are a true possibility*
> *for them.*

In January 1989, Rita's newsletter announced a new plan for the 13th anniversary celebration:

> *Since the school is becoming a teenager, the teenage students are*
> *planning the celebration. It will be on Sunday, February 26. The*
> *concert will be performed by all our young people, who will be*
> *playing music written by composers when they were teenagers*
> *or else music specifically written for young people. The concert*
> *will be followed by dinner consisting of pizza and pop. I am very*
> *happy to see our students getting excited about the music and so*
> *ready to work on this event. The concert will include music by*
> *Mozart, Mendelssohn, and Prokofiev, and the children's choir*
> *singing, among other things, the song from Chorus Line, "Hello*
> *Twelve, Hello Thirteen.*

CHAPTER 40

City-wide Recognition for Rita and the School

In May 1989, Rita announced that The People's Music School had been selected by the Prince Charitable Trust as one of two organizations to receive 250 reserved seating tickets to *Golden Bird* a special "jazz fairy tale opera" to be presented July 19 at the Petrillo Music Shell in Grant Park. Composed by William Russo, a much admired local jazz artist and composer, who also co-wrote the lyrics with Albert Williams, the story was drawn from the Brothers Grimm and told of a young boy who ignored the advice of a wise old fox in his pursuit of the "golden bird." The performance by the Grant Park Orchestra under Michael Morgan included Roy Leonard as narrator, baritone and soprano soloists, and the Lynda Martha Dance Company.

Since the program was popular, it was decided to sell the tickets for $5 each, both as a fund raising opportunity and also to assure that the tickets would go only to those serious about attending. In her July newsletter, Rita reported:

> *All of us attending had a marvelous time. At the end of the*
> *performance, the conductor, Michael Morgan came out and*
> *talked to all of us. For our students, it was a thrill of a*
> *lifetime.*

By summer, The People's Music School was once again looking for an office manager. In the meantime, former students Nalini Kotamraju, by now a Harvard University sophomore, and Maria Valdés, who was entering Roosevelt University's Chicago Musical College as a freshman, took turns managing the front desk through the summer months. They both proved so competent that Rita was sad when it was time for them to return to their studies.

Nalini's summer employment at The People's Music School was funded by a Harvard Public Service Fellowship, a grant which was renewed by Harvard in several future summers. In applying for her fellowship, Nalini had written a case statement outlining the school's need of a new facility and giving her ideas on how a capital campaign could be structured. She had also mentioned the important role the school had played in her life: "The school is so much a part of me and my life. It means more to me than just a summer job."

Rita announced the hiring of Diana Altstadt as the new office manager in her September 1989 newsletter, adding that she now hoped to be able to focus more on her teaching. Unfortunately, Diana's employment lasted only a few months. In January 1990, Charlotte Moxley Vinson was hired as the latest office manager in what would continue to be a "revolving door" of employees in that position, much to Rita's frustration.

In her September letter, Rita also gave an update on the search for a new permanent location for the school. After examining many buildings for sale, Rita and The People's Music School Board were becoming convinced that instead of trying to convert an existing structure, it might be better to look for a lot on which to construct their own building. The costs might not be much greater, and the building would be new and constructed exactly to their needs. A lot on the corner of the convergence of W. Peterson, N. Ridge and N. Clark was considered, but Rita was concerned about both the high traffic and the distance from the current neighborhood, where many of the students resided. The search continued.

As their participation in Illinois Arts Week, the school's faculty gave a program on November 12 featuring all French music, in recognition of the 200th anniversary year of the onset of the French Revolution. Soon thereafter, plans began for the celebration of the 14th anniversary of the school, to be celebrated on February 22 with a faculty recital and dinner. The recital, titled "Music of the Americas," included works by composers from Canada through South America.

In early 1990, Rita received a very special honor. The Chicago Tribune had selected twelve Chicago women whom they called "Chicago's Most Beautiful Women: Their Good Deeds Bring a Glow from Within." Rita was featured as one of the twelve and her photo and an article about The People's Music School appeared prominently in the Tempo Woman section of the January 28 issue of the newspaper. The article discussed how through their service and leadership, the women selected had brought enduring value to the city. Again, new interest was generated throughout the Chicago metropolitan area in the school and its mission.

Another award was presented to Rita on March 31 by the Boulevard Arts Center during a program titled, "A Tribute to Children Artists," at the New Regal Theater. The children's choir from The People's Music School performed on the program, along with student violinist Michele Quach. Rita later commented on what a special experience it was for all of them to perform on such a large stage and in such beautiful surroundings.

An exciting new educational collaboration was announced in Rita's May newsletter. Through a grant from the International Music Foundation (IMF), Rita had designed and administered a six-week music education residency program which had taken place during the spring at Stewart School, 4525 N. Kenmore. While the IMF had funded Rita and her teachers for single concert/demonstration programs in area schools for several years, this was the first extended, in-depth, educational project with a local school.

Over the six-week period of the residency, Rita met with two different classes once a week, presenting the elements of music, familiarizing students with the different musical instruments, and bringing guest musicians from her faculty into the classrooms to demonstrate. Rita repeated this six-week residency program at Stewart School in 1991 and in 1992, both times under IMF sponsorship. In May 1990 she wrote:

> *I hope that by the end of the six weeks the students will be able to do some simple rhythm patterns, read in the F and G clef, and learn some simple songs. Hopefully, the classroom teachers will be able to continue what we are starting. We are giving them lots of material that they will be able to follow.*

Officers of the International Music Foundation were pleased with the results of Rita's music residency series in Stewart School and in subsequent years, they funded a number of similar extended residencies conducted by Rita and her faculty in other area schools, including Manierre, Brennemann, Dodge, Hibbard, and Swift, as well as the Duncan YMCA.

Several years later, Rita and her teachers designed and administered extended music education residencies in still other area schools, this time funded through Marshall Field's newly formed "Arts Partners" project. These included a partnership with Howland School of the Arts that was repeated over several years.

However, most of the school residencies run by Rita and her faculty continued to be funded by the IMF. Though Rita's primary focus continued to be on The People's Music School, her artistic and educational talents were gradually touching more and more young lives in the city of Chicago.

Beginning in 1990, Rita's faculty piano trio included two new young African-American musicians from the Chicago Sinfonietta, Edward Kelsey Moore, cello, and Terrance Malone Gray, violin. In addition to participating in many of the public school residency series, the trio gave a number of lecture performances at the Chicago Cultural Center to which students from a combination of schools were bussed.

From his early years, Terrance Gray was passionate about encouraging young musicians. Having studied violin with former Chicago Symphony concertmaster Victor Aitay as well as the current co-concertmaster of the orchestra, Ruben Gonzalez, Terrance very much appreciated both the excellent training and strong encouragement he received as a young musician. In time he expanded his musical interests to conducting, and in addition to conducting engagements with the Chicago Sinfonietta, the Grant Park Orchestra, and other local orchestras, he was named Associate Conductor of the Chicago Youth Symphony Orchestra.

Throughout his developing musical career, as well as after he had established himself as a symphonic conductor in Chicago, Terrance continued to teach at The People's Music School and to lead the school's chamber ensembles. While Ed Moore enjoyed life as a professional cellist and teacher, he also loved to write. Soon after turning forty, he began to write short stories. In 2013, he published an award winning novel, *The Supremes at Earl's All-You-Can-Eat.*

On June 17, the National Association of Music Merchants held their annual convention in Chicago, and at a banquet dinner, Rita received a Special Recognition Award. As important to Rita as the award itself, the program for the banquet included the showing of a videotape about The People's Music School, which greatly impressed many of the representatives at the convention. Little by little the school was establishing its reputation as a major contributor to Chicago's arts culture. Now, more than ever, it needed a home of its own.

CHAPTER 41

A Vacant Lot and a New Dream

Rita's August 1990 newsletter, while still handwritten, was unusually long. It announced an exciting new development:

> Since February we have been trying to get an empty lot from the city with the hope that we can one day build a school. We have gone through two of the eight steps in the process. On Tuesday, August 21, at 2:00 p.m., we met with The Department of Urban Renewal Board for the city of Chicago, which in the third step agreed to sell us the lot. We were hoping to get it for $1.00, but as it stands, the price is $43,424.50. We have until November 1 to decide whether we want the lot or not. The sooner we make the decision, the sooner the process will move to the fourth step. We wish we had some connections to make the price lower.....I am petrified but excited, because we have never been this far before. Even though we were hoping not to have to pay for it, the price is certainly a lot less than other lots we have seen. We'll see what happens. I will keep you informed.

The "city lot" to which Rita was referring was located at 931 West Eastwood Avenue and had previously served as a community garden. Its location was ideal, on a quiet street very near the school's current home at the Ecumenical Institute.

In September, Rita announced that the Board of Directors had met and voted to make a bid to buy the lot from the city, though they were still hoping to negotiate a lower price. By early October, the Chicago Department of Housing had made the school's bid public and stated that if no other bidder came forward by October 22, the request would move to the Chicago City Council.

Negotiation over the details of the purchase proceeded, with Helen Shiller as the school's primary advocate in dealing with the city. However, the timing could not have been worse, as Chicago's City Hall was undergoing revisions to some of its long-standing policies on public lands. For many years, Chicago aldermen had been able to target certain vacant properties in their communities to be gifted to non-profit organizations free of charge. By 1990, however, the city was looking for new revenue. Also, there were many who felt that the privilege of the gifting of public lands had too often been abused, and a new policy was adopted requiring all public properties to be sold at fair market value.

Two major grants received late in 1990 helped the school move ahead with plans. The Illinois Arts Council gave the school a $27,400 grant in their Building by Design Program to hire an architect to begin preliminary designs for a new building, and the J.D. and C.T. MacArthur Foundation awarded them a grant for the hiring of a capital campaign consultant. By early 1991, J. J. Quinn & Associates had been hired to oversee the design of a capital campaign as well as to set up a management plan for executing it.

As the school prepared to celebrate its 15th anniversary on February 27, 1991, at the Dance Center of Columbia College with an all-Mozart concert by the faculty, Rita felt confident enough with the developments to date to make an announcement in the printed program that was distributed at the event: "Plans are underway to purchase or build a permanent home that will provide space to accommodate at least 250 students."

The 15th anniversary celebration began a new tradition with the awarding of the school's first "Fred Fine Democracy in the Arts Award" to Al Booth, founder of the International Music Foundation and originator of the annual Do-It-Yourself *Messiah* concerts in Orchestra Hall. The award, given "for dedication to making the Arts accessible to all," was established to honor Chicago's first Commissioner of the Department of Cultural Affairs, Fred Fine, who had been appointed to the position in 1984 at the time Mayor Washington created the department. Subsequently, Fred Fine awards were given at five-year intervals to mark significant anniversary years of the school. Through this award, the school continued to honor some of Chicago's major cultural leaders.

The year of 1991 also brought new recognition for Rita. In March, she was presented with an Illinois Alliance for Arts Education Award, and on October 6 she received the Nordstrom Service Award. On December 7, she received the Illinois Arts Alliance Foundation's Sidney B. Yates Arts Advocacy Award. Rita always saw these awards as less about her, and more as opportunities to make new friends for The People's Music School.

CHAPTER 42

Creating an Architectural Plan

In May of 1991, an important, stabilizing addition was made to The People's Music School staff. Hazel Leukaufe was hired as office manager, taking charge of the front office activities and supervising the student and parent volunteers. Hazel would end up as one of the school's longest employed and most valued office administrators. Over the next nine years, she became much beloved by the school's students, parents, and teachers, as well as earning Rita's gratitude for her thoughtful, competent service. Hazel began working at the school just as activity was picking up relating to architectural plans for the school's new building.

In 1984, when Rita started to think ahead to the time when the school could move into its own building, she had concluded that it was important to have someone with architectural knowledge on her Board. Looking for the right individual, she approached several people with whom she had become acquainted at the Chicago Architectural Assistance Center. She found that all of them were unable to devote the time, but they suggested she talk with a young intern named Paul Gates, a recent graduate of the University of Notre Dame with a bachelor's degree in architecture.

Paul Gates immediately saw Rita's school as the type of volunteer commitment that interested him, and he agreed to join The People's Music School Board of Directors. But his Board tenure was interrupted in the fall of 1985, when he enrolled in the Columbia University masters program in architecture and moved to New York.

Following his year at Columbia, Paul returned to Chicago, where he worked for the architectural firm of Tigerman McCurry. He rejoined the Board of The People's Music School, and during 1989 and 1990 served as its president. In late September of 1990, he again resigned from the Board, to travel to Nicaragua to work on a three-month volunteer architectural project.

In the meantime, he had become engaged to Marie Franchett, a young graduate student working on an MBA at DePaul University. When Paul left for Nicaragua, he suggested to Marie that she join in the efforts of The People's Music School to raise funds for their new building, and she agreed to chair the "friends and individuals" committee of the campaign.

After receiving the Building by Design Award from the Illinois Arts Council in late 1990, Rita and her Board began the process of hiring an architect. Their first thoughts were of Paul, and Rita contacted him in Nicaragua and asked him to submit a proposal.

At their January 1991 meeting, Board members decided they wanted Paul to be their architect for the project, and they sent him a letter offering him the position. Soon after, however, several Board members became concerned that the school might face legal or governmental issues by not having opened the interview process to other prospective candidates. With Paul's support and understanding, the position of architect was advertised and other applicants were solicited. Over the next few months, four additional architects submitted proposals. By early May, the Board had carefully reviewed all proposals, had held interviews with three applicants, and had concluded that Paul's proposal best fit their needs.

Even before Paul was hired, Rita and the Board had begun to discuss what a new building might look like. Should it be one story or two? Should there be a basement? How many teaching and practice rooms would be needed? What about parking and security issues? How could the new facility maintain the welcoming feeling and family-friendly ambience that had been achieved in the school's first two locations? It didn't take long for Rita and the Board to realize that given the size of the lot on West Eastwood, the new school would need to have two stories to accommodate its needs.

In early April 1991, Paul Gates and Marie Franchett were married. On their wedding gift list, they suggested that donations be made to The People's Music School's building fund. The couple's original plan had been to move to Minneapolis, Marie's hometown, after the wedding. Once Paul received the commission to design the new building, however, the couple remained in Chicago through the rest of the year. When Marie finally moved to Minneapolis in January 1992 to begin her new job with the St. Paul Planning and Economic Development Department, Paul remained in Chicago for the first half of the year to complete the design work for the new building, commuting to Minneapolis on weekends.

Meanwhile, concrete plans began to take shape regarding how the school should structure the capital campaign for the new building. At first a target of $600,000 was established for the land and the new building, which was originally estimated to encompass about 6500 square feet. A Capital Campaign Steering Committee was appointed, headed by former Board president, Tom McLaughlin, and a tentative budget was set.

By early spring, a detailed plan had been created for what needed to be done to set up the fund raising campaign, and a projected time frame had been established for accomplishing it. Potential donors who might help with leading gifts were identified and a plan established for visiting them. J. J. Quinn & Associates met with Board members, steering committee members, and others involved in campaign solicitations to instruct them in effective techniques for approaching potential donors.

Paul Gates' first project as design architect for the new building was to create two questionnaires, one for students and parents and the other for faculty, to get their ideas on how the new building could best serve their needs and desires. The teachers wanted to be sure the soundproofing was adequate, and they stressed that practice rooms of varying sizes were needed, some for solo instruction, others for ensembles or group instruction.

The students had ideas, too. Several of their suggestions were details Paul hadn't thought of, such as drinking fountains and lavatory basins on two heights, to accommodate all ages. Some students also suggested vending machines with pop and treats, but Rita vetoed that idea.

"We are a school, not a commissary," she said.

Paul also began serious conversations with Rita and the Board about the overall building plan. Should they allow for a potential third floor addition at some point? If so, that decision would have to be made from the beginning. Both Rita and the Board felt it was important to leave that option open. Also, all agreed about the desirability of having an outdoor performance space, where music could be shared with the neighborhood. For security reasons as well as for optimum effect, it was decided to integrate this small performance area into the second floor of the building.

As ideas were exchanged and preliminary drawings modified, the desired building size grew from 6500 to 7365 square feet. Of course, all of these changes also raised the cost projections. By October of 1991, the estimated cost of the project had grown to over $900,000.

Paul had one further idea. A small-scale model of the new building should be constructed to aid in fund raising. "There's nothing that raises interest in a project more than a physical model of what it will look like," he told Rita, and within a few months he had constructed a simple model of the proposed new facility.

Paul Gates continued to play a central role in the coordination of the building project. By fall, he had been contracted to oversee all aspects of the project up to its completion, including everything from dealing with the city on building permits to hiring the supporting consultants, including acoustical, mechanical and structural engineers. Most important, he was put in charge of the process of hiring the construction company that would oversee the actual building of the facility.

Even when Paul joined Marie in Minneapolis in mid-1992, he made countless trips back to Chicago at his own expense to oversee numerous details of the project. His dedication and continuing attention to detail were deeply appreciated by Rita and her Board.

Not everyone was comfortable with the grand plans for the new building. In mid-October of 1991, Rita received a letter from the campaign consulting firm stating that they felt compelled to terminate their contract with the school by the end of the year, as they could no longer support the "current goals and direction" of the campaign.

As stated in their letter: "A campaign goal in excess of $800,000 is unrealistic. To date, a firm leadership commitment has yet to be identified. Our view is that campaign goals should be upheld with research and facts. The current goal is clearly beyond our ability to support."

The firm's analysis had concluded that in the economic recession being experienced in 1991, with its significant government and corporate funding cutbacks, the school would never be able to raise the amount of money it would need for the project as designed.

The partners of the consulting firm were not the only ones dubious of the ambitious new building plans. Several members of the school's Board were also nervous about overcommitting to the project and argued for a more conservative approach.

There was one major flaw in all of their analyses. They were not reckoning with the determination of Rita Simó. Rita's students knew better. One day a group of them presented her with a tee shirt with the inscription, "Never say 'no' to Rita Simó."

CHAPTER 43

Cops and Angels

In early 1992, Brooke Tippett was hired as the new coordinator for the capital campaign for the new building. Within a few weeks, she had organized committees focusing on different funding sources, and they were meeting regularly and reporting back on their various contacts.

Under Brooke's inspiration and guidance, the designing of a capital campaign brochure also began to take shape. It was decided to limit the ink colors used on the brochure, thus saving quite a bit of money. Instead, children from the theory classes volunteered to color in certain parts of the design, adding a personal touch as well as a reminder that children would be the primary beneficiaries of a new school building. Amid the activity, the one thing missing was one or more donors to make a large leadership gift.

Paul Gates was still convinced that one of the greatest tools for generating donations was an actual model of the building. He had created an earlier version, but now many more of the details of the plan were established. In early February, he set to work on a new highly detailed to-scale model, complete with interior and exterior refinements and landscaping. It would be a highly labor intensive project which would take him until July to complete, but Paul was determined to do it, assuring Rita and the Board that he would personally absorb any costs. After the school used the model for fund raising, he could use it as part of a personal portfolio of architectural projects.

On Monday, March 9, 1992, an article about The People's Music School, with a photo of Rita and some of her students, appeared in the Chicago Sun-Times. It spoke of the school's mission and its challenges, including the problems of renting space on the upper floors of an old building, where a few weeks earlier a pipe had burst, flooding several rehearsal rooms. It also spoke of the comforting and positive atmosphere created in this "place of the spirit," where a local cop often walked in "to get away from the problems of the streets for a moment and feel good again." It spoke of Rita Simó's efforts to raise funds for the new building and how she only had been able to raise about $150,000 toward her goal of $950,000. It quoted her saying, "I need an angel."

Sitting in a waiting room at O'Hare airport near Chicago, one of the city's premier musicians was waiting for a flight to Europe and the beginning of a concert tour. The plane was late, and Richard Young, violist with Chicago's internationally renowned Vermeer Quartet, was distractedly thumbing through the morning paper when his eyes lighted upon the article about Rita and the school. Young was instantly and deeply moved. Rising from his seat, he hurried to a phone and called the school. Rita answered the phone and immediately assumed that Young was interested in making a monetary gift to the school, but he had a very different thought in mind.

"Rather than money, I want to give you something more valuable," he told her. "As soon as I return from my tour, I will call you to plan a visit."

Several weeks later, Richard Young's visit only served to increase his determination to help Rita and The Peoples Music School. Through his many contacts, he immediately began to arrange for musician friends to become involved at the school, starting with his fellow Vermeer Quartet members, Shmuel Ashkenasi, Marc Johnson, and Mathias Tacke. Over the years ahead, he also recruited many musicians from the Chicago Symphony Orchestra, the Lyric Opera Orchestra, the Chicago Chamber Musicians, as well as visiting touring professionals, and professors from area universities, many of whom gave "mini-master classes" at the school. Some participated in public recitals, with proceeds going to the school's building fund.

At one point some years later, it was determined that Richard had personally persuaded over 100 prominent musicians to give master classes at The People's Music School. These classes were of immeasurable educational and inspirational value to the school's students and faculty alike.

Over the following years, Richard Young continued his strong involvement at the school in other valuable ways. Working closely with Terrance Gray, he helped bring continuity and direction to the string curriculum, and he regularly participated in the bi-annual student "string juries." Often he would recruit fellow musicians to help with the juries, which, in addition to evaluating student progress, gave valuable pedagogical suggestions to the school's teachers and students. But perhaps Richard Young's most poignant contribution occurred with two inspiring speeches he gave, one at the groundbreaking and the other at the opening ceremony for the new building on W. Eastwood Avenue on November 1, 1995. (Appendices II and IV)

Another well-known Chicago celebrity who had begun to take a special interest in the school during the spring of 1992 was author and legendary radio personality Studs Terkel. On June 3, Terkel came to The People's Music School to interview Rita and two students for his show on local public radio station WBEZ.

Rita's spirits had been greatly lifted a few weeks before Studs Terkel's visit with word that the capital campaign had received its first leadership grant from the Chicago Community Trust. It consisted of $100,000 for the campaign, as well as an additional $15,000 "management grant" to prepare a strong management plan for the operation of the new facility. These two grants were in addition to a $15,000 general grant from the trust for the current year's operating budget, which was especially appreciated, as Rita and her Board were hoping that gifts for the capital campaign would not replace grants to support the ongoing expenses of the school.

On September 10, 1992, The People's Music School received more good news. A letter arrived from The John D. and Catherine T. MacArthur Foundation announcing that they were committing $125,000 to the capital campaign, in addition to the foundation's gift of $25,000 to the operating fund. Of the new $125,000 capital grant, $50,000 would be in the form of an outright gift, but the remaining $75,000 would be given in segments as certain matching targets were reached. Under the arrangements for the match, the McArthur Foundation would contribute a dollar for every two dollars raised by the school over a two-year period, between the dates of January 1, 1993, and December 31, 1994.

Though some were concerned about meeting this new challenge, Rita never doubted that $150,000 in new dollars could be raised during the two years of the agreement. Several other proposals that had been submitted to various companies and foundations were currently receiving thoughtful consideration as a result of the continuing diligent work of Brooke Tippett, so as 1992 progressed, Rita and her Board were full of optimism.

Another major step forward occurred in September with the hiring of a management-consulting firm with the funds earmarked for that purpose by the Chicago Community Trust grant received in May. After reviewing proposals from several firms, the Board hired Management Cornerstones, Inc., a consulting firm for non-profits. Several years later, when Brooke Tippett returned to school to complete certification for teaching, Management Cornerstones, through partners Pam Moore and Pat Wyzsbinski, also began providing guidance in the school's capital campaign, in addition to their help in designing a strong management plan.

As everyone celebrated these important developments in the capital campaign, one dark cloud appeared, dampening the jubilant mood. Ana Isidra's health had been deteriorating over the year. During the August break between classes, Rita and Tomás traveled to the Dominican Republic. Alfredo was anxious to have his sister back with the family, as it was clear Ana's life was near an end.

After several weeks of comforting communication between mother and daughter, Rita gave her mother a final hug, knowing it would be her last, and returned to Chicago. Ana Isidra died on September 12, 1992, the first day of the fall term at The People's Music School. By agreement with Alfredo, Rita did not make the return trip. But she knew exactly how the service would proceed. Ana Isidra, in consultation with Rita, had outlined very detailed plans for the funeral.

CHAPTER 44

A Capital Campaign Kick-off

While the architectural planning for the new building continued to move ahead, final arrangements for the acquisition of the land were still in limbo. In February of 1992, the city had sent a contract to the school, listing the $43,424.50 purchase price. The school was given six months in which to respond, but the Board of the school felt this was not enough time to work out a plan. Further talks with the city resulted in an agreement to extend the time to eighteen months. Still hoping to work out a long-term leasing arrangement for the land, similar to one the city had recently made with the Museum of Contemporary Art, Rita and her Board put the signing of the contract on hold.

The school's delay in confirming the contract, however, brought a new problem. By late 1992, the city informed The People's Music School that the price of the land at 931 West Eastwood Avenue had been raised to $60,000. Rita was dismayed, but not discouraged. Helen Shiller pointed out to her that if she could negotiate to have payments of the $60,000 spread over twelve years, interest free, it would result in annual payments of $5,000 and would not be such an onerous obligation. Both Rita and the city were convinced a reasonable accommodation could be reached, and negotiations continued.

With two leadership gifts secured, on November 19, a "Capital Campaign Kick-Off" event took place in the Preston Bradley Hall of the Chicago Cultural Center. Studs Terkel served as master of ceremonies. His participation was all the more meaningful because he was an Uptown resident, and he spoke of the importance of the school in the community. Representatives from the Chicago Community Trust and The J. D. and C. T. MacArthur Foundation also were honored and thanked for their leadership role.

Since many of the school's families were unable to travel to the Chicago Loop for this ceremony, a second more informal campaign kick-off party for families and others who were unable to attend the Cultural Center event was held on November 21 at the school, complete with a potluck supper.

Publicity sent out from the school about the kick-off celebrations brought significant media coverage. Mary Schmich wrote a heart-warming story in the Chicago Tribune about Rita, the school, and the plans for the new building. In early November, Harry Porterfield interviewed Rita for his CBS, WBBM-TV series "Someone You Should Know." Local stations WGN-TV, Channel 9, and WSNS, Channel 44, also aired special reports on the school and their dream for a new building.

Rita laughingly announced at the December 16 Board meeting, "After the program on Channel 44 last Thursday, by Saturday we had received seventy-eight phone calls. Unfortunately, nobody offered us money; everyone wanted to become a student."

At the December meeting, Rita also announced that "fantastic" master classes had recently been given by Marc Johnson of the Vermeer Quartet and Ruben Gonzalez, co-concertmaster of the Chicago Symphony Orchestra. She further informed the Board that Richard Young had started coming to the school every Friday at 4:30 p.m. and would continue through the following May, to listen to the string students and to help them with the pieces they were studying. Perhaps the most exciting news, however was that the Vermeer Quartet was planning a concert on Sunday, February 7, 1993, in the Charlie Chaplin Auditorium of St. Augustine College, with all proceeds going to The People's Music School building fund.

CHAPTER 45

A Welcome for Nelson Mandela

Rita's schedule for the spring of 1993 was as busy as ever and her list of accolades continued to grow. In late April, she traveled to Boston to receive the Dean's Arts and Humanitarian Services Award from Boston University. Another honoree at BU that day was *Seinfeld* star Jason Alexander. When Rita returned, the staff and students were greatly amused to learn that Rita was seated next to Jason during the ceremony, but had no idea who he was.

As part of her award, Rita was given a chair with "Boston University" inscribed on the back, which she took to the school. Staff and faculty remember with amusement that she never sat in it, and only rarely did anyone else. Instead, it was always stacked high with music books.

Most of all, Rita was pleased that the Boston University honor included several interviews with the Boston media, both radio and newspapers. As she wrote to Francine Cabonargi of the MacArthur Foundation before her trip: "I hope to win some new support for the school while there. I've got my fingers crossed, as always."

In May, Rita returned to Rosary College to receive the honorary degree Doctor of Humane Letters. While many of her former colleagues had retired or had moved on to other universities and colleges, she still was able to reconnect with old friends and memories.

It was also in May that Rita was selected by Sculpture Chicago as one of a hundred Chicago women, past and current, honored for their outstanding achievements. Each woman had her name and accomplishments written on a plaque, which was secured to a three-foot high, half-ton rock. The rocks were placed in public locations around the city, where they remained through the summer. Rita's rock was in front of Rose Records on Wabash Avenue. Many illustrious women were included in this project, including Jane Addams, Ida B. Well, Ardis Krainik, and Gwendolyn Brooks.

On June 5, The People's Music School children's choir sang for the grand opening of the new Uptown Chicago Public Library branch at the corner of Buena and Sheridan, a project that had received strong support from Helen Shiller. Marie Haley, a former music student of Rita's, was head of the children's section in the new library. Her assistant, Karen Griebel, was so moved by the children's performance that she told Rita she was hoping to enroll as a student at the school on the next registration day.

The summer of 1993 brought a special visitor to Chicago. Nelson Mandela was in the United States raising support for the African National Congress (ANC). On July 6, the first day of Mandela's two-day visit in the city, Mayor Richard M. Daley honored the South African leader at a reception in the Harold Washington Library. Through the Chicago Department of Cultural Affairs, The People's Music School piano trio, consisting of Rita, Terrance Gray and Ed Moore, was invited to provide the evening's music.

The trio members were excited about performing at the Mandela reception, but they found their schedules allowed them very little time to practice as a group. Terrance provided Rita and Ed with copies of a large book that contained an extensive collection of string trio music, and the three agreed to work on their individual parts on their own.

When the day of the reception arrived, the musicians took their places in a recessed area next to the ninth floor domed Winter Garden room, where the reception was to be held. As the guests arrived, they began to play, starting with the first trio in the book, with Terrance signaling the tempo they would use at the start of each movement.

Many guests had been invited to the event, and as the reception continued for over two hours, the musicians, who had taken only one small break, found they were getting near the end of their trio books. Quietly they agreed to start over at the beginning if needed, but that became unnecessary. The reception ended just as the musicians were performing the final work in the book.

All three were pleased with their performance, which had gone off quite well in spite of the lack of practice time. The music had also attracted the attention of Nelson Mandela, who made a special point of going over to the group and, after a short conversation, giving each member a warm hug.

CHAPTER 46

An Invitation to Maestro Barenboim

In March 1993, Rita pointed out with great excitement that campaign donations had passed the halfway point, and it was time to start thinking about plans for a groundbreaking ceremony for the new building. Certain guests would be important to include in this event. Most lived in Chicago and could generally be available. But Rita's heart was set on having Chicago's premier maestro, Daniel Barenboim, the conductor and music director of the Chicago Symphony Orchestra, at the ceremony to help wield the first shovel of dirt.

"For this special occasion, the school should have the biggest and best," she vowed.

Rita realized the event would have to be planned around the maestro's busy international schedule. Barenboim had often spoken of the importance of reaching out to Chicago's wider community, especially its ethnic minorities, so she was optimistic. Barenboim would be in Chicago in late September for the Chicago Symphony Orchestra opening concerts. Rita began planning her groundbreaking for late September.

When she spoke with the administrative assistant to Chicago Symphony President, Henry Fogel, in the late spring, however, Rita was told that Barenboim's participation was unlikely given his busy schedule. At any rate, nothing could be decided before his return in the fall. She would need to call back in September.

In the meantime, Rita and the school participated in the planning of another musical event. Early in 1993, the German Consulate in Chicago had contacted Rita about co-sponsoring a well-known student orchestra from Tübingen during their concert tour of the United States. The group's travel costs had been covered, but they were looking for a donated performance space.

Rita agreed to help arrange for them to use the Charlie Chaplin Auditorium at St. Augustine College, a space the college had frequently made available to The People's Music School free of charge for public concerts. In exchange for the venue, the Studentenphilharmonie Tübingen agreed to present a full classical program open and free to the public and to list The People's Music School as the "presenter," in appreciation for their help in arranging for the performance space.

Rita's press notice and her letter to students about the concert highlighted the group's Latino connections. Their conductor, Nicolás Pasquet, was born in Uruguay, and the flutist for the Flute Concerto by Jacque Ibert, Huascar Barradas, was from Venezuela. The concert took place on September 23, with a full house attendance, including many People's Music School students and parents.

As soon as Daniel Barenboim returned to Chicago to begin rehearsals for the opening of the fall season of the Chicago Symphony Orchestra, Rita once again phoned Orchestra Hall. She was familiar with the symphony's rehearsal schedule and knew that while mornings were tied up with rehearsals, and often the mid to late afternoon time period as well, the orchestra generally took a break from approximately noon to three o'clock in the afternoon. The two days when concerts were rarely held were Mondays and Wednesdays. With this in mind, Rita had planned her groundbreaking ceremony for 1:30 p.m. on Wednesday, September 29.

The phone call to the administrative assistant proved discouraging. "The maestro's schedule is tightly booked whenever he is in town, and it is unlikely he will have the time to participate," Rita was told.

"But may I just ask him personally?" persisted Rita.

The assistant resisted for a time, but she finally agreed to arrange for Rita to speak with Henry Fogel. After Rita had outlined the history of the school, its mission, its plans for a new building, and the time set for the groundbreaking, Fogel agreed to discuss the matter with Barenboim.

A few days later, Rita received the reply, "Maestro Barenboim will be happy to join you at the ceremony. Please give us all of the information so that it is on his calendar."

Several days before the groundbreaking, Rita also talked with Barenboim about the details for the day. The two conversed in Spanish.

CHAPTER 47

The Groundbreaking

The morning of September 30, 1993, started cloudy and windy, but by noon the sun was shining brightly on the small lot at 931 W. Eastwood. The ceremony began on schedule at 1:30 p.m. with a short composition for percussion ensemble, performed by students from the school. As the students began to play, a sudden wind gust picked up the music from one of the music stands and threatened to send it scrambling away. Almost instantaneously, Daniel Barenboim rose from his seat, grabbed hold of the music, and secured it on the student's stand. He then leaned over next to the performer, continuing to hold the music in place until the playing had ended.

Following welcoming words from Board President, Blanca Plazas, who was master of ceremonies, Norman Pellegrini, program director of WFMT, Classical Music Radio, formally introduced Daniel Barenboim as the keynote speaker. In recognition of the ethnically mixed audience, Barenboim addressed the crowd in a mixture of English and Spanish, a gesture that brought smiles of appreciation to many faces. He acknowledged the history of the school and its impact on Chicago. He spoke of the importance of this type of musical outreach in communities such as Uptown. The maestro then joined Rita and Lois Weisberg, Commissioner, Chicago Department of Cultural Affairs, in turning over the first shovel of dirt.

The turning of the soil was followed by introductions of several other special guests and comments by some of them, including Sarah Solotaroff from the Chicago Community Trust; Richard Young from the Vermeer Quartet (Appendix II); Nick Rabkin from the John D. McArthur Foundation (Appendix III); 46th Ward Alderman, Helen Shiller; and Victor Marin, whose career as a music teacher had been inspired by his years as a young student at the school.

Few of those present knew how far out of his comfort zone Richard Young was as he delivered his talk. As his wife, Jenni, confided afterwards to a staff member, "He was more nervous about making that speech than performing at Carnegie Hall."

The ceremony ended with a few words from Rita Simó, followed by members of the children's choir leading those present in three choruses of one of their favorite songs, "I Live in the City Made by Human Hands":

I live in the city, yes I do
I live in the city, yes I do
I live in the city, yes I do
Made by human hands.
Black hands, white hands, yellow and brown,
All together build this town.
Black hands, white hands, yellow and brown.
All together make the world go round.

The children repeated the song three times, and by the third time, the whole audience had joined in.

After the groundbreaking, lunch was served at the school, complete with egg rolls, rice and beans, tamales, and even some inexpensive champagne, a very "Rita" kind of party, with food from every ethnic group represented at the school.

CHAPTER 48

An Important Visit

The story of the efforts made by Rita and her Board to build a new school continued to inspire not only those who had attended the groundbreaking, but also many others who had read about it in the papers or seen TV reports of the event, like one that was presented on CBS, WBBM-TV news by Harry Porterfield, or another produced by CNN Headline News on October 18. Some contacted the school with offers of money or help.

Two months after The People's Music School's groundbreaking, on Tuesday morning, November 30, another Chicago cultural institution groundbreaking occurred, this time for the new Museum of Contemporary Art building to be built at 220 E. Chicago Avenue. The keynote speaker for the event was the new Chairman of the National Endowment for the Arts, Jane Alexander. Other distinguished guests present at the ceremony included Lois Weisberg and Chicago's First Lady, Maggie Daley.

As the three women discussed various aspects of the arts culture in Chicago and of the general need for the arts to be accessible to many constituencies, Lois casually mentioned that another groundbreaking had just occurred to the north in Uptown. She talked about the goals and accomplishments of The People's Music School and then suggested to Mrs. Daley that they take their guest on a visit to this "model neighborhood program for the arts."

Congressman Sidney B. Yates, who was standing nearby, and whose Arts Advocacy Award had been presented to Rita several years earlier, joined the group and reinforced the idea of a visit to the school.

Lois Weisberg had alerted Rita ahead of time about the likelihood of a visit. Responsible for Jane Alexander's schedule while she was in town, Lois had tentatively inserted a visit to "a model program" into the chairman's afternoon schedule. The "model program" Lois had in mind was The

People's Music School. Since 1981, The People's Music School had been receiving modest grants from the National Endowment for the Arts. Now, Rita was delighted with the opportunity to meet its new chairman.

The three women and Congressman Yates arrived to a warm welcome from students and teachers, followed by a short "impromptu" student concert. Next, the guests were informed about many aspects of the school and its programs. Finally, the subject of the school's plans to move from its current location came up, giving Rita the opening to review her long search for a site and her current struggles to find money to pay for the new location and building.

Lois Weisberg, feigning ignorance of the details, turned to Rita, "And where is it that you want to build this new school, Rita?"

Like someone following a perfectly rehearsed script, Rita then took the group across the room to the model Paul Gates had created and brought out a map that showed the desired location for the new building. She also showed the group photos of the groundbreaking event. There was discussion of the cost for the lot and how the cost had risen during the time the school was considering the purchase. Rita explained that they were still trying to work out a plan for the purchase, but with anticipated costs for the building, it was going to be a challenge.

Maggie Daley was quiet during the presentation, but thoughts were beginning to circulate in her mind. About a week later, Rita received a phone call from Mrs. Daley.

"Rita, I have talked with some people at City Hall. We may be able to find a way to help you acquire the land on West Eastwood Avenue without paying money. A representative from the city will be contacting you to arrange some visits in order to observe and assess your program."

Two weeks later, a lawyer from the city arrived and spent most of a week observing the school and its students and reviewing various school records. Not long after that, Rita received another call from Maggie Daley.

"We have worked out a plan," she told Rita. "The land will be yours, but not for five years. Our city representative has determined that the value of your program to the city of Chicago is worth $1,000 for every month you are actively engaged in service to your community. As long as you continue to operate as you have been, this amount will deduct on a monthly basis from what you owe the city. At the end of five years, full ownership of the land will be given to The People's Music School. In the meantime, you will need to file regular reports with the city, and occasional visitors from the city will come to observe the school. Of course, if your program does not continue, the land will revert to the city. But I have every expectation that you will continue and grow."

Jane Alexander had also been impressed with what she had observed at The People's Music School. In a letter dated December 15, 1993, she wrote:

> *The visit to the People's Music School was truly a highlight of our Chicago trip. I don't think I exaggerate in saying that you seem to be doing everything right.*

> *Looking at the focus and concentration on the faces of those young musicians was an inspiration. I hope that my energy and commitment will match yours as I try to create an awareness in this great country of the value of arts education, and I trust we will be able, together, to see your school in a new home soon.*

Jane Alexander's already favorable impressions of the school were undoubtedly reinforced by a December 24 letter sent to her by Richard Young, who had also been present during her visit:

> *It was an honor to meet you in Chicago last month at the People's Music School.....*

> *For many young people in that neighborhood, The People's Music School represents their only hope of one day making something of themselves. Regardless of which profession they ultimately pursue, there is no doubt that the lessons they learn there apply to virtually any endeavor......*

> *I'm sure I speak for many artists when I express the view that anything the NEA can do for institutions like this one would provide a long-term investment not only for the arts, but also for America.*

CHAPTER 49

A Trip to Washington, D.C.

Rita's busy schedule sometimes took her out of the city of Chicago to nearby communities. On October 12, 1993, she gave a presentation about The People's Music School at the Center for Urban Affairs and Policy Research at Northwestern University. The story of Rita's efforts in Uptown fit very closely with the conviction of faculty members of the Center like John McKnight and John Kretzmann that urban community regeneration needs to start from within, and that any outside public or private aid is best used in nurturing local grass roots groups whose programs are empowering the citizens and building a positive sense of community.

In their book *Building Communities from the Inside Out: A Path Toward Finding and Mobilizing Community Assets*, McKnight and Kretzmann also recognized the importance of the arts and of individual artists in urban communities, "people who possess creative abilities, who can spur alternative perspectives and solutions to problems leading to neighborhood blight." Through the rest of the 1990s, Rita returned annually to the Center for Urban Affairs at Northwestern to present her story of The People's Music School and its special place and influence within the Uptown community.

Rita's schedule of residency programs in local schools also continued, sponsored by the International Music Foundation and Tribune's Arts Partners. Fall of 1993 through spring of 1994 saw 6-week residencies at Stewart School, Howland School for the Arts, and Manierre School. Rita was pleased at her growing collaborations with the teachers in these schools and with their willingness to incorporate music-related concepts into their curriculum. She was grateful, too, for the funds these residencies provided which she could add to the school's building fund.

Fall also brought visits from a number of Chicago's finest musicians, who talked with students and conducted master classes. Rami Solomonow, principal violist of the Lyric Opera, came to the school on September 20, followed by CSO principal clarinetist Larry Combs on October 4, and CSO principal cellist John Sharp on October 11.

At the end of March 1994, Rita sent the MacArthur Foundation a third report on the matching contributions received to date. Since the matching program had begun January 1, 1993, a total of $96,820 in donations had been received, leaving $53,180 yet to be raised before the end of the year. If the remaining months produced results on the same scale as the first year and a quarter, the goal could be reached, but progress was still slow.

By now the contract for the procurement of the land from the city had been finalized. A request for approval of the purchase, sent to the City Council by the Commissioner of Planning and Development, had been signed by Mayor Daley himself on February 9. In addition, drawings and specifications of the planned building had been sent out for bid to five minority construction companies chosen by the Board. As the bids began to arrive, Rita and her Board became more excited, as they could envision the building outlined in Paul Gate's architectural model becoming a reality. By the end of April, four of the five companies had submitted bids.

Amid all the activity relating to the new building, Rita also made plans for a special trip to Washington, D. C. Through the office of Congressman Sidney Yates, Chairman of the House Appropriations Committee, Rita had been invited to travel to the nation's capital to testify before Congress in an NEA Public Witness Hearing in support of funding for the National Endowment for the Arts. Congressman Yates was proposing a bill for increased funding for the agency, and a massive effort was being made to support the appeal.

Rita's presentation was scheduled for a twenty-minute slot on the morning of May 3. In addition to a personal appeal, Rita had arranged for a vocal demonstration by one of her most talented students, eleven-year-old Marika Christie. Plans had been made by former student Nalini Kotamraju for Rita and Marika to stay in the apartment of one of Nalini's friends in the Du Pont Circle area of Washington. Nalini was currently serving as Deputy Director of Operations for the upcoming 1995 NGO Forum on Women, part of the United Nations Conference for Women to be held in Beijing.

On May 3, the Congressional hearings began at 10:00 a.m. with appeals from flutist Eugenia Zukerman and jazz pianist Billy Taylor. They were followed by a twenty-minute presentation by the Alabama Shakespeare Festival. Rita's twenty-minute presentation began on schedule at 10:40.

Outlining the school's history and mission, Rita eloquently pointed out: "For us democracy means offering everyone the equal opportunity to cultivate their talent through discipline and hard work under quality guidance. Anyone that comes through the door thinking that 'free' means a 'free ride' is set straight pretty quickly."

After stressing the value of the discipline of musical study in every aspect of the students' lives and the value of the outreach of The People's Music School into the larger community, she spoke of the school's special place in the lives of the students.

"For our children, the music school is an oasis in the midst of a neighborhood full of difficulties."

She ended her presentation with the appeal, "Your appropriation of our tax dollars to the National Endowment shows that the nation does value the arts for all."

Marika then stood before the assembly and with great clarity and composure introduced herself, "Hello! My name is Marika Christie. I am eleven years old. I have come to represent the People's Music School in Chicago, Illinois. I have been a student at the Music School for almost five years. At the school, everyone takes one hour of theory class and an instrument or voice lesson each week. Some students are even in the children's choir, like me. On the students behalf, the children's choir would like me to sing a song called 'Listen to the Children' from the operetta *Friends Without Words*, written by a composer from our neighborhood named Hugo Teruel." (Appendix V)

Rita could not have been more proud of her young student than she was that day. Marika's beautiful singing and joyful performance presence had clearly moved the Congressional audience. In a letter dated May 10, Jane Alexander wrote to Rita:

> *Marika Christie's rendition of "Listen to the Children" was poignant and moving. Please tell her that she did something important and she did it beautifully. I am very grateful to you for travelling to Washington to testify at the NEA's Appropriation Hearings.*

CHAPTER 50

Architectural Plans Become Brick and Mortar

On June 2, 1994, Rita was awarded an honorary Doctor of Arts degree from Chicago's Columbia College. The summer that followed brought its usual flurry of activity at the school. As part of the Grant Park Festival outreach program, concert pianist Jorge Federico Osorio and conductor Michael Morgan came to the school to present programs, and students from the school made several trips to the Ravinia Festival for performances sponsored by the festival's outreach program. As always, Rita prepared her students well before these concerts, both musically and on proper concert behavior. She continued to find pleasure in the positive responses of audience members to her well-behaved and musically engaged students and their parents.

At their July meeting, the Board of The People's Music School voted to accept the bid of Mota Construction Company to erect the new building, and announced that construction was scheduled to begin in August, though it was September 28 before the permit process had been completed and Mota could finally begin working on the site.

Unfortunately, most of the construction bids had come in higher than estimated, and the Board now realized that the school was facing a project that would cost at least $1,275,000, up a little more than 30% from their last estimate. With a total of $775,000 in donations committed to date, an additional half-million dollars would need to be raised. But as usual, Rita exhibited her ever-positive attitude when she wrote in the summer newsletter:

> It seems that the longer we wait, the higher the cost gets,
> but we are jumping in. Please jump in with us.

Though new donations were coming in slowly, and generally in modest amounts, major new donations from the Polk Bros. Foundation and the Ira and Leonore Gershwin Philanthropic Fund brought the campaign to an important milestone. On October 3, Rita wrote to the MacArthur Foundation that the matching gift target of $150,000 had been reached with several months to spare. She also told them of the challenge presented by the increased cost estimates, and asked if they might consider an additional $50,000 gift to the capital fund.

By the end of the month, Rita was able to announce in her newsletter that Mota Construction was busy at work on the new building:

> *As of now, the cement foundations are in place and the*
> *walls are beginning to come up. It is scary but fun to see it*
> *all happen. Even the weather has cooperated. It has only*
> *rained on weekends.*

The fall brought additional eminent musicians to The People's Music School to conduct master classes. In September, Vermeer Quartet cellist, Marc Johnson, and his pianist wife, Kathie, worked with students from the school, followed by violinist Joseph Genualdi on October 3, and operatic tenor Frank Little on October 17. Years later in an interview with the Chicago Reader, Richard Young commented, "This community music school can boast about a series of master classes that no other school in the world has. Most of the time the musicians are looking for a way to pay back."

CHAPTER 51

A Thanksgiving Gift

Students, parents, Board members and other friends were continually giving Rita ideas of businesses, foundations, organizations, and individuals that might be willing to make a donation to The People's Music School building campaign. Some resulted in modest contributions, others brought polite refusals, but one proved to be a godsend.

In early 1994, Liska Prochotska Blodgett, a former member of the school's Board, read about a foundation called the Elizabeth Morse Genius Charitable Trust that had recently given a major grant to help fund the exhibit "DNA to Dinosaurs" at the Chicago Field Museum. She called The People's Music School and reached Chris Hodak, a parent of two students at the school, who in 1993 had begun working part time writing grant proposals for the school. Chris passed the information on to Rita, who suggested that Chris check it out further.

Chris periodically visited the Donors Forum in Chicago to research various foundations and other charitable groups. On a visit to the forum soon after she received the phone call, Chris looked for information on the Elizabeth Morse Genius Charitable Trust and learned that since it was a family foundation and very new, the only information the Donor's Forum had on record was the name and address.

Chris decided to call the museum to see if they would share their information. She was told that the trust preferred to keep a low profile and search out their own grant recipients, rather than being deluged with applications. However, Chris was given a name, address, and phone number of a contact. She wrote a letter inquiring about the process for submitting a grant request.

Within a few weeks, Chris received a response with an invitation to submit a proposal. Her proposal went into great detail about the school and its plans. The next response was slow in coming, but when Chris and Rita did hear from the foundation's trustee, James L. Alexander, it was in the form of a letter asking for an appointment to visit the school.

Mr. Alexander came to the school in mid-October, just after Mota had made the hole in the ground at 931 W. Eastwood and was preparing to pour the concrete foundation. After a tour of the school and the site of the new building, he turned to Rita and said, "There is one major problem with your proposal. You didn't ask for any specific amount of money."

"But we didn't know very much about you, " explained Rita. " We didn't know if you were a big foundation or a little foundation. " Then, with a chuckle, she added, "If you are a big foundation, we should ask for the remainder of the money we need, which is half a million dollars. If you are a small foundation, we are happy to accept anything you think you can give us."

"Maybe you shouldn't worry about our size and instead ask for what you need," was the response.

"In that case, we need $500,000," said Rita.

In a December 8 letter to the MacArthur Foundation, Rita happily announced, "Just before Thanksgiving Day, we received our largest gift so far in this capital campaign. The Elizabeth Morse Genius Charitable Trust has pledged $250,000 toward the new school building. The capital campaign has finally passed the one million dollar mark."

Within the same letter, Rita included her official proposal for an additional $50,000 grant from the MacArthur Foundation. With a $15,000 gift the campaign had just received from the Harris Bank Foundation and an expected $50,000 Chicago "Community Development Block Grant," which had already been included in the city's 1995 budget, Rita and her Board calculated that they still needed to raise $169,000. This amount would present a challenge, but reaching their goal had suddenly seemed more achievable.

Thanksgiving of 1994 had truly become a time for giving thanks.

CHAPTER 52

"So What Do You Think? Isn't It Beautiful?"

Along with the successes of the capital campaign in late 1994, there had been disappointments. In early December, Rita learned that a large foundation with which she and Chris had exchanged encouraging communications, and which had made several visits to the school, would not be making any contribution after all. At the same time, anticipated costs of the building project had been raised from $1,275,000 to $1,300,000.

After good weather in the early fall, a rainy period followed, slowing down progress on the construction. Still Rita announced in December:

> *Even with the bad weather of recent weeks, we anticipate we*
> *will be able to move into the new building in August of 1995,*
> *just before our fall term.*

On January 20, 1995, a second concert by the Vermeer Quartet at Wright Junior College raised over $6,000 for the building fund. January also brought a change in leadership to The People's Music School Board. After four years of devoted service as president, Blanca Plazas stepped down and Assir DaSilva, who had joined the Board three years earlier, became the new Board president.

A native of Brazil, DaSilva had worked his way through the University of Illinois at Chicago and had rising through the ranks to become a vice president of Exelon, the parent company of Commonwealth Edison. In gratitude to his adopted country, and especially the city of Chicago, he volunteered his services to a variety of community organizations as a way of "giving something back." DaSilva continued as president of the Board of The People's Music School for three years, through the remainder of the construction, the inauguration, and the period of settling into the new building.

The early months of 1995 brought an increase in efforts to raise the $150,000 needed to complete the building. New proposals were written and sent out. In addition, dozens of the school's young students created personal letters of appeal to be included with various grant proposals.

To further energize and educate her Board, Rita planned a surprise for the January Board retreat. She started the meeting off with a four-page quiz titled, "How Much Do You Know About the People's Music School?" The answers to the quiz's fourteen multiple-choice questions provided a springboard for discussion of many issues and statistics relevant to the campaign, as well as reminding all present of the school's rich history.

On February 1, Rita was one of sixteen women to receive a Chicago Women in Philanthropy Award from the Chicago Women in Philanthropy (CWIP) organization. The awards that year were co-sponsored by Marshall Field & Company, which presented each woman with a monetary award for her organization. Information about each woman and her organization also became part of a traveling exhibit created by Marshall Field's, which was moved from one Chicago area Field's store to another during the year. Awardees were photographed for the exhibit, and personal narratives of their accomplishments were created and posted next to their photos. Once again, the story of Rita's extraordinary efforts in creating and sustaining The People's Music School was spread through the Chicago area.

For several years, Susan Gundlach, an English and social studies teacher at The North Shore Country Day School in Winnetka, had been interested in The People's Music School, and in late March, she and Rita arranged exchange visits for their students. The experience proved to be a very meaningful expansion of horizons for each group. Summaries of the visit written by the students from the Winnetka school contained some of their impressions, including, "This is a very interesting neighborhood to live in because of all the different ethnic groups," "I was amazed by Ms. Simó's knowledge," and "The rooms were old and small and the chairs were squeaky and wobbly, but it had a cozy and happy feel and the shelves were full of music books and instruments."

The students also noticed Rita's unusual accent. When they commented on it, Rita told them that she was glad that her accent was a little different. "It reminds me of where I came from, something I don't want to forget."

It was also at the end of March that Rita met once again with her friends at the MacArthur Foundation, renewing her appeal for an additional grant of $50,000 to help bridge the remaining approximately $150,000 gap in the building fund. Rita was told that the foundation's Board would consider the request at their next meeting. But progress remained slow. Most of the likely funding sources had already made their commitments. A line of credit had been established at the Uptown Harris Bank on North Broadway, and Rita regretfully announced that the school would likely need to activate it soon to meet the current bills.

In contrast to the fundraising efforts, the construction was moving along right on schedule. Rita's June newsletter mentioned that the scaffolding had come off the new building, and MOTA had announced that it would be ready for occupancy by early August. The newsletter reflected her excitement:

Hooray! Hooray! So what do you think? Isn't it beautiful?

CHAPTER 53

Wanted: 1000 People with a Heart

Rita's personal accolades continued to increase. In June 1995, she was the commencement speaker for the Longy School of Music of Bard College in Cambridge, Massachusetts. During the ceremony, she also received the college's Distinguished Achievement Award.

By July 18, the school was continuing to experience mixed results in their fund raising efforts. Rita had received word that the MacArthur Foundation would grant an additional $50,000 to the building campaign, but one by one the other proposals outstanding had resulted in letters of rejection. In fact, that day's mail had brought rejection of a proposal by a major foundation that had seemed promising a few months earlier. Prospects for raising the remaining $100,000 were looking dim.

As she often did when feeling discouraged, Rita decided to take a walk around the neighborhood. These walks always put her back in touch with the heart and soul of the neighborhood and its people and made her feel better. They also helped to stimulate her mind, enabling her to study her problems in new ways.

Some time later, she found herself on Clark Street, near a second hand store that she periodically had visited. Wandering inside, she saw a salesman speaking with a lady, whose faded and ill-fitting clothes suggested that second hand stores were the main source for most of her clothing and household needs. The lady was standing beside a table she was hoping to purchase for her family, so they would have one place to share meals together. When she saw the price of $25 on the table, she turned away to look for something else, explaining that she only had $15.

The salesman followed her for a while and then said, " I don't promise anything, but I could ask the store manager if he would accept less for that table."

A few minutes later he returned and told the woman she could have the table for $15. "See," he said, "you don't know if you don't ask."

Standing nearby, Rita repeated those words over in her mind. She had asked everyone she knew or could think of, individuals, businesses and foundations. Suddenly it dawned on her that in the big city of Chicago there were many others who had not been asked, people she didn't know but who might listen. How could she reach them?

Then she recalled the times when the school had found new friends following stories that had appeared in local newspapers or on television. Why not place an ad in a local paper and frame it in the form of a challenge? Could there be one thousand people in the big city of Chicago who would respond and pledge $100 each to help her meet her goal?

Rita decided to place her ad in the Chicago Reader, partly because she could afford a larger ad in that paper, and partly because she felt that many of those who read the Chicago Reader had "big hearts." Her ad ran in the Reader in late July. It read:

!!WANTED!!

1000 people with a heart to give $100.00.
Be a part of the free music education of
THE PEOPLE'S MUSIC SCHOOL.

We need YOUR help to complete our
building, our mission.

PLEASE CALL RITA SIMO at:
    (312) 784-7032
with your tax deductible donation and for
more information, or SEND your donation
to 4750 N. Sheridan Rd., Chgo, IL 60640.

We are grateful for any size donations.

Next to the ad was a picture of the school's partially completed new building. It wasn't long before donations began arriving, some for $100 and some for less, but others for more.

Responses to the ad continued to arrive through the following months and up until the end of the year. In all, $68,000 in donations and pledges was given to the building fund in response to the ad in the Chicago Reader.

CHAPTER 54

Moving Day and a Giant Music Staff

Rita's life was so busy with the imminent move to the new building that she was unable to accompany Tomás on a late summer book-buying trip to Santiago, Chile, during which he visited their old friend Martín Gárate. Instead, once lessons and classes had ended for the summer, Rita sent out a call for volunteers to help pack up for the move to 931 W. Eastwood. The packing was scheduled to begin on August 14, and Rita announced that the doors would remain open until they were finished.

On Sunday, August 27, at 2:00 p.m. a blessing ceremony was held for the new building. A crowd of several dozen gathered in the front reception area. After an opening prayer and scripture reading, Father Michael Rochford moved through the room with his aspergillum, distributing the holy water. To Rochford, the completion of the building was almost as meaningful as it was to Rita. For many months, he had regularly visited the site, checking on the progress of the dream he had helped support over so many years.

The actual move into the building took place on Monday, August 28. In addition to professional movers, who transported pianos, desks, and file cabinets for half their usual fees, there were also so many parents, students, and teachers who showed up to help that the move was completed by 2:00 p.m.. All who helped with the move were invited to celebrate with a picnic at the new building. Rita carefully wrote down the names of all those who participated. Later she wrote a personal note of thanks to each one.

One of the most cherished items to make the move was a large partition screen, created and donated by graphic artist Kathy Kozan, which had served both as an important room divider and a decorative object at the school's space at the Ecumenical Institute. The screen was transported to the stage of the concert space in the new building, where it continued to serve as a beautiful backdrop for many performances over the years ahead.

An additional special artistic focal point of the new building was a large colorful mural of a giant musical staff and various musical symbols that had been painted on the floor of the concert hall by muralist Curtis Bewley, who operated a business painting murals and faux finishes. The prior year he had created a mural on a newly renovated apartment building on W. Argyle Street as part of an affordable housing project, and through that work he had come to the attention of Suellen Long, chairman of the community development organization Uptown United.

Suellen and her husband, Chip, were strong supporters of The People's Music School. Thinking that Curtis' talents could add color to the school's new building, the Longs introduced Curtis to Rita, who agreed to let Curtis make a plan for a mural. Most of the interior walls of the new school were rough cement block, not good surfaces for a mural, but as Curtis toured the new building in early August, he saw the large smooth cement floor of the concert hall and proclaimed it to be a perfect surface for his artwork.

"Let me develop a plan," he told Rita. "I work best when I am alone in a quiet space. If you could let me into the building tomorrow morning at 9:00 a.m., I will call you when I am ready to show you my design."

Rita was grateful that Curtis wanted to work alone, as she was busy organizing the packing and moving activities at 4750 N. Sheridan Road. In fact, she was so busy the next day, that it was almost 6:00 p.m. before she realized that Curtis hadn't called her. Walking over to the West Eastwood building, she found him putting finishing touches on a huge design that he had sketched out in great detail on the floor.

Rita was thrilled with what she saw, and she told Curtis to begin the painting as soon as he could so that it would be ready before the move into the building. Curtis assured her it would be finished within the following two weeks. Only later did Rita realize that she hadn't asked Curtis how much it would cost. But Curtis had already decided that this project was to be his contribution to the new school, and he refused to accept a fee for his work. He even helped Rita acquire the necessary paint at a discount. In gratitude, Rita had his name added under those of Paul Gates and Andy Elchorn of Mota Construction on a large brass plaque that was installed in the entryway of the new building.

Curtis wasn't the only one to donate talent or materials to the new building. In all, building materials and services worth about $200,000 were donated. Other donors of services and materials who were acknowledged by having their names engraved on the brass plaque in the entryway included Prairie Material Sales, which supplied the concrete and gravel at cost; North American Glass Industries, donors of all window and door glass;

Chip Long, donor of numerous furnishings; Accurate Partition Company, donor of the bathroom partitions; Chicago Faucet Company, donor of bathroom faucets and fixtures; Shaw Industries, donor of carpeting; U. C. Industries, Inc. , donor of the insulation materials; and L & R. Development.

When Rita was asked by a reporter who covered the inauguration of the building how she got all of this in-kind support, she said, "I never beg. Instead, I suggest that they have a special opportunity to be an important part of a wonderful project serving talented young people with limited resources."

CHAPTER 55

A Festive Inauguration Celebration

The September 20 meeting of the Board of The People's Music School was the first to take place in the new building. High on the order of business was the planning for the official grand opening or inaugural ceremony for the building, which had been set for Wednesday morning, November 1, 1995. It was to include as many people as possible who had been central to the history of the school and to the planning and creation of its new home.

Invitations had been sent out, encouraging one and all to: "Celebrate A Dream Fulfilled." It was reported that Daniel Barenboim hoped to be able to attend and that Maggie Daley had responded that she would definitely be present. James Alexander, from the Elizabeth Morse Genius Charitable Trust, and Richard Young, of the Vermeer Quartet, also had accepted the invitation, and both had agreed to say a few words.

Responses were still being awaited from Mayor Daley, Sidney Yates, Jane Alexander, Helen Shiller, and representatives of the MacArthur Foundation. But for Rita, perhaps the most exciting news was that her brother Alfredo and his family would be flying up from Santo Domingo for the celebration, and that her old friend, Ann Kelley, whom she often referred to as "like my sister," would also be present.

Many other issues were addressed at the September Board meeting. Several recent donations to the school had been earmarked for an increase in teachers' pay, and Rita recommended that the pay should be increased from the current $8.50 a lesson as soon as possible. As she had from the beginning, Rita continued to insist that all of the school's teachers must be professionally degreed musicians; therefore, they were teachers who usually received higher fees from their other private pupils. The school currently employed twenty-one teachers, of whom quite a few insisted on volunteering their time for free at The People's Music School, but for most, pay was a necessity.

Any decision on teacher pay raises was postponed, however, as the school struggled with the immediate cash flow demands. Before long, the construction company would need to be paid further installments of their contract, and $210,000 in outstanding pledges might not be received in time. The People's Music School had finally found it necessary to take out a $110,000 loan from the line of credit that had been set up at Uptown Harris Bank, in order to keep current with their bills. There was also pressure to begin a health care insurance program for administrative staff, and an arrangement with Humana was being explored.

Rita told the Board that once all pledges had been received, they would still be about $100,000 short of their goal, though contributions were still arriving from the ad in the Chicago Reader. She once again stressed her determination to make the building debt-free as soon as possible. On a happier note, Rita announced that on September 7, the school had enrolled 225 students, "twenty-five more than last year's fall term."

The day for the inauguration ceremony for the new building began with crisp temperatures but clear skies. By 10:00 a.m. most of the staff, students, parents and guests had arrived in anticipation of the festivities, scheduled to begin at 10:30. Well before the program began, the auditorium was full and newcomers were jockeying for places on the surrounding balconies, many standing several rows deep.

At precisely 10:30, all attention was drawn to young Marika Christie, who had quietly walked on stage. As the audience members shushed each other and focused on the young singer, she began to sing the song that had become central to the identity of the school, "Listen to the Children," (Appendix IV) from the operetta that had been written by Hugo Teruel for the school's tenth anniversary almost ten years earlier.

Following Marika's song, Board president Assir DaSilva welcomed the audience and introduced the master of ceremonies for the day, Harry Porterfield, the veteran news anchor now working for ABC, WLS-TV, whose interest and support of the school had remained constant over the years. Porterfield, in turn, introduced several individuals who gave personal reflections on the school, its history and its place in the Chicago arts community.

Maggie Daley spoke first, telling of her first meetings with Rita and of her great admiration for Rita's vision and determination. Mrs. Daley greatly impressed the audience with her warmth and genuine interest in the school, not only in her presentation on stage, but also during many conversations with students, parents and teachers, both before and after the program.

Next came Richard Young, who reminded listeners that while the day might seem to be marking the end of a remarkable achievement, what was really important was to see the day as a beginning for all the possibilities going forward, possibilities to make a major educational impact on many lives. His eloquent words were deeply moving to all who were there. (Appendix IV)

The third speaker was James L. Alexander, trustee of the Elizabeth Morse Genius Foundation, who also spoke of how he became acquainted with Rita and her mission.

These presentations were followed by a performance by a piano trio composed of three members of the Lee family, all students at the school. Christine Lee, violin; Daniel Lee, cello; and Katie Lee, piano, performed "Allegretto" from *Three Miniatures* by Frank Bridge. Finally, former student Nalini Kotamraju, spoke of the huge impact The People's Music School had made on her life and on the lives of others she had come to know during her years at the school.

The party following the ceremony was the grandest one yet experienced at The People's Music School. Many students, parents and staff members brought food, and, in addition, there were many donations of food, drinks, and serving supplies from area shops and restaurants. Food tables were spread along the walls of both the upper and lower hallways, and people ate standing or sitting, wherever they could find room.

By the next day, Rita was already beginning to write the numerous thank-you notes she would send to the many friends and supporters who had added some special memento or service to the celebration. In addition to thanking those who had played a role in the inaugural ceremony, she wrote notes of thanks to others who had played a big role in the successful completion of the new building, including Curtis Bewley, for his work on the mural and Ted Hearne, for his firm's creation and printing of new brochures for the school at cost.

But for Rita, one of the most meaningful gifts to the new building came from Frances Holtzman, the retired teacher friend who, along with Jim Duignan, had joined with her to form the school's first Board, and who had offered to share her apartment when Rita first moved to the Uptown area in the summer of 1975. Fran had sent a plant for the school's lobby, and along with it she had sent a personal note, which read, "Keep Dreaming." Rita's deep appreciation was evident in her letter of thanks to her old friend:

We have realized our dream - a permanent home for The People's Music School! It couldn't have happened without the foundation you helped to lay nearly 20 years ago. That is why I am so glad you were able to join us for the Grand Opening. Saturday, November 18, will be our first concert in our new home. You have been there for all of our 'firsts.' I do hope that you will be able to attend this one as well.

The building's grand opening generated a great deal of media interest, with spot news segments running on many Chicago area television channels and numerous articles, many with pictures, in the local papers. The Chicago Tribune ran a long feature article on the school in its Chicago Metro section, complete with several pictures of the new building. Melita Marie Garza, the reporter who wrote the November 2 article, had visited the school on Halloween, the day before the inaugural ceremony. In the article she noted how Rita, seemingly oblivious to the pressures of the busy day ahead, had playfully joined her young students in celebrating the holiday: "She strode through the building in black gym shoes with Bugs Bunny faces on the ankles, black stretch pants, and an orange sweatshirt emblazoned with a giant black-widow spider."

In late December, Rita's annual year-end letter reflected the continuing excitement felt by all:

Greetings for the Holidays! "It's a magical, mystical world that we're living in." These are the words of one of the songs the children's choir has been singing. We feel that this year has been really magical for all of us at The People's Music school.

CHAPTER 56

A New Year and a New Beginning in a New Home

A five-page January 1996 article on The People's Music School in the national publication *American Music Teacher* spoke of the great ethnic diversity served by the school in its new home. The publication quoted the school's new brochure which stated that 37% of the students were Latino, 30% African-American, 16% Asian, and 17% white.

But, as Rita pointed out, those figures were divisible into many sub-categories, and included students with Vietnamese, Cambodian, Arab, American Indian, East Indian, and East European heritage. Many had immigrant parents. During the prior decade, the neighborhood had experienced growing populations of Polish, Bulgarian, Russian, and Bosnian immigrants, and while there had been few students with these backgrounds in the early years of the school, recently their numbers had grown.

The People's Music School celebrated its 20th anniversary on Saturday, February 24, 1996, with a recital by faculty and guests at the new building. Richard Young again volunteered his talents, this time as first violin in the Quintet in E-flat Major by Robert Schumann. Two weeks later, the celebration of the 20th year continued with the awarding of the school's "Fred Fine Democracy in the Arts Award" to author, legendary radio personality, and Uptown community friend, Studs Terkel.

In April, Rita Simó received a letter from Jesse Woods, Chairman of the Advisory Board of the Chicago Department of Cultural Affairs asking for permission to submit Rita's name to Mayor Daley for membership on the advisory board, a group of twenty-one citizens representing major cultural institutions in the city. Rita served as a member of the Cultural Affairs Advisory Board for the next fourteen years.

Several other notable awards and events highlighted the first year at 931 W. Eastwood. During the spring, the new building was one of three finalists for the Chicago Building Congress's "Merit Award for Construction Under Five Million Dollars." In April, the school was featured in the "Coming Up Taller" project of President Clinton's Committee on the Arts and Humanities, a report created to draw attention to outstanding programs across the country that were successfully reaching and inspiring at-risk youth. Finally, in September, The People's Music School was selected as a workshop site for the 4th International Congress on Educating Cities, whose focus for the current year's conference was "The Arts and Humanities as Agents for Social Change." The workshop held at the school was titled "Urban Regeneration Through the Arts."

Spring of 1996 also brought a visit from a very special and inspirational guest, internationally celebrated jazz trumpeter and bandleader, Winton Marsalis, in conjunction with a late March performance engagement at Chicago's Symphony Center. Marsalis had recently been named the first Director of Jazz at Lincoln Center in New York City. During the following year, he would be awarded a Pulitzer Prize, the first jazz musician to win the honor, for his jazz epic "Blood on the Fields."

With his typical low key and wry humor, Marsalis gave the audience of over a hundred children a basic class in "How to Listen," bringing students up to the stage to illustrate his points. Afterwards, he stayed on at the school to talk with students and answer their questions. He then presented the school with a complete sound system, complements of Harmon Industries International. Many photographs were taken of students with the jazz artist, photos the students and their families would certainly treasure for many years to come.

Less heralded, but also very significant and appreciated, were the master classes conducted by many other major international and local musicians at The People's Music School during 1996. Among them were: Michael Henock, CSO oboe; Rachel Barton, violin; Sylvia Wang, piano; the Ying Quartet, strings; and, as in many previous years, Rita's former student and dear friend, soprano Mary Frances Lubahn, who was visiting from Graz, Austria.

CHAPTER 57

Debt Free!

The early months of 1996 brought continuing donations and fulfillment of pledges to the building campaign fund, and in mid-April, Rita proudly walked into the Uptown Harris Bank and presented a check for $110,000, plus $6,197.36 in interest, fully repaying the loan the school had taken out at the end of the prior summer. Though the final payment to MOTA was past due, the construction company kindly offered to withhold interest payments on the balance through the remainder of 1996. Rita very much appreciated this offer, and vowed to make the final payment as soon as possible.

As expected, the school's new facilities were much more suitable for sharing public concerts and recitals with the Uptown community than prior locations. Designated funding had been received for the school to continue to celebrate the 20th anniversary at special events throughout the year, and during June and July, outdoor concerts were presented at 6:00 p.m. every Thursday on the second floor open performance deck. If weather threatened, the concerts were moved inside into the new building's concert hall. Most were happy, however, when the concerts could be held on the performance deck, from which the sounds of the music could travel throughout the neighborhood, in many cases to nearby neighbors who found it difficult to leave their homes.

For the 1996 fall term, 275 students were registered at the school, the highest enrollment to date. While the building was designed to accommodate up to 400 students, Rita and the Board agreed to expand enrollment by no more than twenty-five students per semester in order to maintain the school's high standards of instruction while keeping the budget in check.

Of course, this resulted in a lengthy waiting list of prospective students. Registration day at the school had become a challenge, as applicants and their parents or guardians lined up many hours before the doors opened. Rita continued her firm belief in a "first come, first served" policy as long as teachers were available in the area of interest to an applying student. Once admitted, however, students had to honor the strict rules of attendance, practice, and volunteer service in order to hold their spot.

As a finale to the 20th anniversary year, The People's Music School Board held a new fund-raising event, a "benefit brunch," on Sunday, October 27, at Cafe Pastiche on North Clarendon Avenue. Participants enjoyed a gourmet meal and a musical program featuring Terrance Gray, violin, and Justin Wilson, cello. A successful silent auction coupled with profits from the brunch tickets and additional donations from those unable to attend raised $20,000 for the school, setting a high standard for future benefit events. The three Board members who planned and managed the benefit, Peggy Ross, Tom McLaughlin, and Jeff Kelly, were roundly thanked for all their work.

In addition to the funds raised through the October 27 brunch, the fall also brought further fulfillment of earlier pledges that had been made to the building campaign, and on October 30, exactly one year after the inauguration celebration at 931 W. Eastwood, Rita happily wrote a final check to MOTA construction for their work on the building. The People's Music School's new home was now totally debt free. After all expenses were tabulated, the final total cost of the new building was $1,318,270.40. It was only after all other bills had been paid that Paul Gates would accept payment for his work.

Along with the pleasure of knowing the new building would soon be completely paid for, Rita had also been excitedly anticipating a special evening at Orchestra Hall. On Friday, October 11, at 9 p.m., Daniel Baremboim on piano, Rodolfo Mederos on bandoneón, and Hector Console on string bass presented a concert of music from their recently released CD "Tangos Among Friends," Daniel Barenboim's nostalgic return to the music of his Argentine childhood. Rita had received a personal invitation from Barenboim to both the concert and the reception that followed.

The festive reception included musicians playing many of the Argentine tunes and rhythms that Rita had known and loved from her earliest days. After enjoying drinks and a buffet, some of the guests began dancing and singing to the tunes. At one point, Rita began quietly singing to one of the less well-known songs. Soon she found Barenboim beside her, joining in. As the crowd around them quieted, the two continued singing, becoming more demonstrative and playful as they sang. Finally, someone in the crowd piped up, "It's a good thing you two decided to be professional pianists and not professional singers!"

CHAPTER 58

Growth and New Challenges

By the end of 1996, Rita and the Board of The People's Music School were realizing that building ownership and program growth meant major new challenges beyond monetary ones to the school. Beginning with the founding of the school in 1976, Rita had been not only the general administrative director, but also the director of all artistic and educational activities of the school, as well as piano teacher to a full load of students.

While Rita relied heavily on loyal staff, especially on Hazel Leukaufe, who was capably running the front office, as well as on helpful volunteer parents and students, she could see that the increased demands of managing a building along with the challenge of a growing student enrollment was becoming too much for one person. In October 1996, the school began a search for a new general manager, to take over general administrative and fund-raising responsibilities.

Rita was to continue to supervise all educational and artistic planning and activities. In 1995, she had expanded the faculty jury review system to include an evaluation of all vocal and instrumental students, and this and other programming enhancements were taking increasing amounts of her time at the same time that general administrative commitments were increasing.

In November, the Board hired Cynthia Thomas as the new general manager, with duties including development, financial oversight, and building maintenance. Cynthia immediately set to work on a number of issues including the installation of new FAX and phone lines, the purchase of new computer software, and the streamlining of communications with students and parents. She also began to solidify contacts with key funding sources.

On January 1, 1997, the Board met for their annual retreat to create both specific plans for the year ahead and also a general plan for the longer future. Though everyone rejoiced that the school was able to maintain a balanced budget while fully paying for the new building, several Board members suggested that it would be wise to build on the current enthusiasm and momentum and to begin plans for a more secure financial future. It was time to begin thinking about creating a permanently endowed reserve fund that could help secure the success of the school in the years ahead.

Cynthia Thomas suggested that the Board might be able to receive help in this planning from the Chicago Arts Business Council, which often advised on such projects. In the meantime, the Board voted to set up a separate short-term reserve fund of $50,000 to cover any unexpected building operation expenses.

The Board also felt it was time to review and tighten up Board structure and the clarification of the scope and obligations of its committees. To that end, they asked Pam Moore, from Management Cornerstones, Inc., to attend the retreat and to prepare a management analysis to help the Board move forward. By the end of January, Pam had prepared a report summarizing the retreat discussions and setting forth proposed objectives for the future, titled "From Dream to Reality--Building From the Inside Out."

CHAPTER 59

21 Years Old: The People's Music School is an Adult

On February 22, 1997, The People's Music School celebrated its 21st anniversary with a faculty recital in the new building. As Rita enthusiastically announced in a playful reference to the anniversary year, "The school has progressed through its childhood and adolescent stages, and has become an adult. We should now serve as an inspiration and model to the community, and in order to do that, we must never stop striving to be the best we can be."

Yet obstacles remained. At the Board meeting the following week, Board treasurer, Ann Murray, reported on her attendance at a recent meeting at the Chicago Donor's Forum. A bleak picture of the future of arts funding had been presented, especially for smaller arts organizations. Government funding for the arts had been decreasing, and foundations and other major donors were directing more of their contributions to the larger arts and cultural institutions. The path ahead would not be easy for smaller organizations like The People's Music School.

In the meantime, Rita's impact on music education in Chicago was being recognized in ever-widening circles. In April, she received an invitation to become one of fourteen people on a newly formed board for the Civic Orchestra of Chicago, the training orchestra for the Chicago Symphony Orchestra. Knowing of the Civic Orchestra's active educational programs in Chicago schools, she happily accepted.

Amid much excitement, on May 1, the People's Music School welcomed composer and conductor Marvin Hamlisch, composer of the Broadway musical *A Chorus Line*. Hamlisch was accompanied to the school by several Chicago dignitaries, including Lois Weisberg, who had helped arrange the visit, as well as reporters from PBS, WTTW-TV, and the Chicago Tribune. Both WTTW and the Tribune subsequently ran news segments about the event.

In his interview with the Chicago Tribune, Marvin Hamlisch spoke eloquently about the advantages gained by children whose educational experiences include substantial immersion in the arts. He bemoaned the current cutbacks in many public school arts programs, especially in lower income neighborhoods.

"It's the average public school kids that I'm most worried about," he told the Tribune reporter. "The really talented and wealthy kids who get to be in special programs will be fine. It's the other kids we've got to worry about."

He continued, "Safe havens of music, theater, dance and visual arts programs have proved particularly potent in stemming violence and drug abuse and in keeping students from dropping out of school. You've got to give kids a dream."

He confessed that he, himself, had been an unruly student in early years. Instead of recommending severe punishment, a wise teacher had chosen to give him access to a school piano. For him, that decision had made all the difference.

At the end of May, representatives from local Channel 50, WPWR-TV, visited the school and on June 14 from 7:30 to 8:00 p.m., the station aired a half-hour program on The People's Music School as part of their series titled "The Power to Make a Difference." Hosted by Jeanne Sparrow, the program talked about the school and the new building, but it also focused on the growing registration lines.

In fact, handling registration was a growing problem for the school. As the existence and quality of The People's Music School had become more widely known, increasing numbers of people were arriving for registration day, and they were arriving at an earlier hour. With a longer waiting period, some would periodically leave their place in line to feed a parking meter or attend to a restless child. Confusion sometimes resulted as they tried to return to their place in line. In other cases, people claimed to be saving places in line for close friends who later joined them, irritating those in line behind them. It was decided that in order to minimize problems in the future, numbers would be passed out one to a family, as people arrived ahead of the opening of the building.

By mid-summer the school was once again without a general manager following the resignation of Cynthia Thomas, who had found the many evening commitments at the school to be too difficult. Rita suggested that the building operations and the grant writing function be separated, as the fund raising function needed to be pursued on a strict time schedule, which was often at odds with the sporadic and often unpredictable demands of attending to the management of the building. The fund raising position could be a part-time job. Once again, the school's Board began the search, this time for a general manager and also for a part-time development director. In the meantime, Rita once more took over coordinating all duties, administrative, artistic and educational.

At the same time, Rita's responsibilities with administering residency partnerships in area schools was continuing. During winter and spring of 1997, residency series had taken place at Brenneman and Stewart schools under the sponsorship of the International Music Foundation. In the fall, Rita began an educational series at a new school, Medgar Evers School, on South Lowe Avenue.

Rita's cooperative relationship with the Chicago Symphony Orchestra continued to develop during the summer of 1997. On the evening of July 23, the CSO held one of its series of "Town Hall" meetings at The People's Music School. CSO President, Henry Fogel, attended, accompanied by members of the Chicago Symphony Women's Board. Almost 200 people from the neighborhood came to hear the presentation and to participate in a discussion of how the orchestra could better reach and serve the wider community.

The summer ended on a sadder note when Rita learned that Management Cornerstones, Inc., which had been so helpful to the school over the preceding five years would be moving their offices to Milwaukee to be closer to their primary customer base. On Saturday, August 9, Rita invited the Board to a goodbye party at her home for two people who had not only guided the school wisely, but had become friends of many at the school, Pam Moore and Pat Wyzsbinski.

Groundbreaking Day at 931 W. Eastwood
September 30, 1993

Building architect, Paul Gates

Rita with Daniel Barenboim and
Lois Weisberg

Rita, Barenboim and the percussion ensemble

At the inauguration of the new building, 931 W. Eastwood, 1995;
from left to right: Richard Young, Harry Porterfield, Assir DaSilva,
Maggie Daley, Rita Simó, James Alexander

With brother Alfredo

Curtis Bewley's floor painting

Marika Chrisie   Carter Hoyt

Rita accompanying a master class with Mary Frances Lubahn

The Bricolage Project, 2011

Rita receives the
Mountblanc de la Culture Arts
Patronage Award, 2005

The People's Music School El Sistema Inspired Youth Orchestras

Deborah dos Santos with YOURS Project students

New instrument day for YOURS students at
Hibbard Elementary School

A young YOURS student takes a turn at conducting

A surprise reunion with former student Eleanor Hodak, 2013

Executive Director Bob Fiedler, Rita, and Alan Pierson, October 2013, against the backdrop of the partition screen created by Kathy Kozan

CHAPTER 60

A Children's Choir CD

On Sunday, September 21, 1997, Rita Simó traveled to Northfield, Minnesota, to receive an honorary degree from St. Olaf College. The degree ceremony took place on Wednesday, September 24, as part of a morning convocation in Boe Memorial Chapel. Rita had arrived in Northfield on the prior Sunday in order to spend Monday and Tuesday engaged in classroom and other activities with students in the college's music, Spanish, education and women's studies departments.

While she was at the college, Rita was especially pleased to have a chance to visit with friend Jeanine Grenberg, who had lived in second floor rooms in the Beacon Street house some years earlier. Jeanine was now a professor in the St. Olaf philosophy department.

Shortly after Rita returned to Chicago, on Sunday, September 28, the school's second fall benefit brunch was held, this time at Pasteur Restaurant, on Broadway. In addition to gourmet food, the celebration once again featured a raffle and a tour of the new building. Everyone was delighted when Peggy Ross, the benefit chairman, announced that the event raised $19,000, only a little below the record-breaking first benefit brunch held a year earlier.

On October 1, Chris Hodak, the parent who had helped Rita make contact with the Elizabeth Morse Charitable Trust, was hired as the school's new general manager. Several years earlier, Chris had left her part-time job at The People's Music School for a full-time job, and now she was glad to be returning to the school as a full-time employee. Her job involved not only organizing the campaign strategy for the special reserves fund and engaging in general fund raising activities, but also building and payroll management and public relations. Hazel Leukaufe continued to have her hands full with running the office and supervising the volunteer commitments of the school's students and parents.

Since the building on West Eastwood was now in its second year of operation, maintenance issues were cropping up with increased frequency, and Chris found her new responsibilities very challenging. Her first report to the Board on October 15 listed installations or repairs in process or recently completed to, among other things, window blinds, bathroom hand dryers, lights in the pit area, and the school's elevator.

During the fall, Rita reported that a new string chamber ensemble under the direction of Terrace Gray had been formed for the school's growing number of intermediate and advanced string students. Meeting weekly, this ensemble gave students an opportunity to have a small orchestra experience along with their individual lessons and theory classes. The chamber ensemble gave its first performance at the spring concert at the end of the school year.

Rita was also pleased with the growing professionalism and recognition of the school's children's choir. After school began for the fall term, several people suggested to her that the choir should be recorded, and arrangements were made for a recording with Hinge Studio.

Another recording received brief attention about this time. In the process of unpacking boxes after the move to the new building, teachers had uncovered the reel-to-reel tape recording that had been made of Rita's piano concert in Milwaukee, Wisconsin, in 1966. After listening to it, several teachers suggested that Rita should have the performance transferred onto a CD and used as a fund raising project. Rita was flattered but made no effort to pursue the idea, and the tape was once more packed away.

Violinist Rachel Barton visited the school in October to present a program of compositions by 18th and 19th century black composers. Rachel had just made a recording of this music with the Encore Chamber Orchestra for Cedille Records, a disc that had generated much interest among educators and musicians around the country. She was eager to share both the music and the information she had learned in her research about early black composers, especially with minority music students.

Rita was pleased with her students' response to the program. As she observed, "They realize that if those people could do it, so can I."

CHAPTER 61

A Plan to Secure the Future
"Music is a Gift: Pass It On"

In November 1997, the Board of The People's Music School began planning in earnest for the development of a permanently endowed reserve fund to ensure the future health of the school. The finance committee, under chairman Jeff Kelly, worked with Chris Hodak to arrange for Ed Buckbee, a development officer from the Chicago Symphony Orchestra, to speak to the Board on reasons and strategies for building such a fund.

At the November Board meeting, Buckbee said that having a permanent reserve fund set aside against future challenges not only made good business sense but also aided in annual fund solicitations, because it proved the school had a dedicated institutional vision for the future. Jeff said that the finance committee, with Chris's help, would prepare a proposal for moving ahead which the Board could discuss at their January retreat meeting.

In another matter discussed at the meeting, it was decided that the school was finally in a financial position to raise teacher pay from $8.50 to $9.50 per lesson, as Rita had long hoped. It was the first time teacher pay had been raised in many years. In a final action taken at the November meeting, after three years of leadership, Assir DaSilva stepped down as president, and Mary O'Connell became the new Board president.

Plans for a campaign to raise money for the new permanent fund to endow the future of the school were roughly outlined at the January 17, 1998, Board retreat. It was agreed that a time frame needed to be set and a kick-off event planned. Chris Hodak pointed out that the 25th anniversary of the school would occur in 2001, and it might be good to target that year as the culmination point of the campaign, though several Board members questioned whether the goal could be achieved by then. They noted that final pledge contributions were still being received from the capital campaign for the building.

Regarding a campaign monetary goal, Board members agreed with the advice they had received from the Chicago Symphony representative, Ed Buckbee, that the goal should approximate the school's annual budget. Since the annual budget was currently around $250,000, that figure was suggested for a campaign goal. The idea resonated with the Board, considering that the school was approaching its 25th anniversary.

In March, the Board made its first step toward the new goal by transferring $100,000 from general operating funds into a new separate accounting category called "special reserves," to distinguish it from the "general reserves" that had been set aside the prior year. At the same time, it was agreed to continue to maintain the general reserves fund for use in temporary emergencies, such as unexpected building repairs. That fund was to be maintained at a figure equal to three months of operating costs.

It was also at the March meeting that Board member Joe Sterling asked whether the school might be interested in kicking off the campaign with a fundraising event in connection with a November concert engagement featuring world famous pianist, Ivan Moravec, who was scheduled to perform the Ravel G Major Concerto with the Chicago Symphony in Orchestra Hall. Joe, a well-known photographer, had provided photographic covers for a number of Moravec's record albums, and the two had become friends. The idea was met with great enthusiasm, and Joe agreed to investigate the possibility and come up with a plan.

The Board also agreed that an attractive and convincing fund raising brochure would need to be created. New Board president, Mary O'Connell came up with a suggested tagline that was immediately embraced by all: "Music is a Gift: Pass It On." It spoke both to Rita's original dream and to the ongoing mission of the school. It was also a perfect way to invite others to help continue passing on the gift of music by making a gift.

A timeline for the special reserves fundraising campaign was set up in May. Solicitations for the private phase of the campaign were scheduled to begin as soon as possible, with the public phase beginning in the fall at a special event, hopefully in connection with the Ivan Moravec concert, if all developed as Joe Sterling hoped. It was also firmly agreed that the campaign should be structured to culminate in 2001, the 25th anniversary year of the school. A separate steering committee was set up for the campaign, chaired by Jeff Kelly.

By June, Joe Sterling had confirmed that Ivan Moravec was willing to stay on an extra day after his four concerts with the Chicago Symphony in

November, and that he would be willing to perform a benefit concert on Monday, November 16, for the school's campaign.

While plans for the Moravec event and the special reserves fund campaign progressed, Rita continued her active personal schedule. On April 25, she received a Thomas Jefferson Award for Public Service, a national award presented through the committee's local sponsor, NBC, WMAQ-TV. On June 3, she played the piano for a reception preceding a luncheon of Chicago public school principals at which First Lady Hillary Clinton was the guest speaker.

The summer of 1998 brought an exciting and important new partnership between The People's Music School and the Chicago Symphony Orchestra's "Echo" educational outreach program, funded by the Joyce Foundation. It was a collaboration that would greatly enhance educational experiences both for students of the school and also for the wider Uptown community in the years ahead. The partnership was launched by a performance of Chicago Symphony Orchestra (CSO) musicians at Truman College on West Wilson close to the school. Many of the students from The People's Music School as well as neighborhood residents attended.

As part of this new collaboration, beginning in fall, the CSO woodwind quintet became "woodwind quintet in residence" at The People's Music School, giving flute, oboe, clarinet and saxophone students the periodic opportunity of studying one-on-one with CSO musicians. Woodwind players who were especially generous in sharing time with the students included Alex Klein, principal, oboe; Richard Graef, assistant principal flute; Larry Combs, principal clarinet; John Bruce Yeh, assistant principal clarinet; Dale Clevenger, principal French horn; and Burl Lane, saxophone.

Through the partnership, the school also received performances by chamber ensembles from the Civic Orchestra of Chicago, the training orchestra supported by the CSO. The first of these performances took place on November 2. This important partnership between The People's Music School and the CSO and Civic Orchestra continued for many years.

Officials at the Chicago Symphony Orchestra, in acknowledgement of all that Rita had accomplished, invited her to become a member of their Board of Trustees. At the October 5, 1998, installation of the new Board members, Rita was the only woman among the six nominees. To her great delight, she found that James L. Alexander, her friend from the Elizabeth More Genius Charitable Trusts, also was joining the CSO Board. For many years, Rita participated in the work of the Chicago Symphony Orchestra Board of Trustees, especially in areas of policy and programming for education and community outreach. In 2010, she was honored with the title of Life Trustee.

CHAPTER 62

A Glorious Evening with Ivan Moravec

A record number of 320 students was admitted on fall registration day of 1998 at The People's Music School. At the same time, late summer brought several unexpected problems. Rita had known she would need to hire a new voice teacher and a new teacher for class piano, and she had been busily interviewing candidates. Then at the last minute, a Suzuki violin teacher quit, and Rita needed to fill that position, as well. On top of everything, the school's air conditioning was not working properly, adding to frayed tempers and nerves.

Efforts relating to the creation of the new special reserves fund were progressing well, however. Several months earlier, The People's Music School Board had unanimously agreed on investment guidelines for the fund that reflected their overall mission. This included avoiding investments in companies that (1) did not respect human rights and equalities, (2) were involved in production or use of weapons, (3) were engaged in racist, sexist, or other discriminating labor policies, or (4) were engaged in activities that resulted in pollution or other kinds of harm to the environment. Now it was time to hire an investment manager for the fund.

After considering several investment managers, the Board decided to hire Michael McGullicuddy, a financial planner and broker who had left the investment firm in which he had been a vice-president to form a new company, Responsible Investment Group, whose investment goals were similar to those of The People's Music School. Michael continued to manage the school's investments for many years.

Plans for the kickoff concert with Ivan Moravec also were progressing smoothly. The concert was scheduled for Monday evening, November 16, at 7:30, in the Preston Bradley Hall of the Chicago Cultural Center. Tickets to the concert were $60. Under Peggy Ross's competent direction, publicity, food, and artist arrangements were being planned and "save-the-day" cards had been mailed. In order to maximize focus on the event, no fall brunch and raffle fundraiser was planned.

Two days before the Moravec concert, Rita performed a piano recital at the Mexican Fine Arts Center Museum on West 19th Street. Following the program, she was presented with the Sor Juana Inés Medal, given in remembrance of Sor Juana Inéz de la Cruz, a 17th-century female Mexican playwright, philosopher, mathematician, and poet, who became a nun when other educational opportunities for women were blocked to her. Some refer to her as the "first feminist of the Americas."

The benefit concert evening was as wonderful as everyone had hoped. Board members arrived at 6:00 p.m. to be sure all details were in place and the welcoming table fully staffed. Soon, guests were streaming into the beautiful hall with its stained-glass dome.

Before intermission, a capacity audience enjoyed Mr. Moravec's performances of three Mozart compositions: *Rondo in D Major, K.485; Fantasy in c minor, K. 475; and Sonata in B-flat Major, K. 333.* After intermission, Moravec performed all *24 Preludes, Op. 28* of Fredric Chopin. As a finale, the enthusiastic audience was treated to encores of Chopin's "Mazurka in c-sharp minor" and Debussy's "Ondine." The evening's printed program spoke of Rita's deep appreciation of the Chicago Symphony's donation of the use of their Steinway Grand piano for the performance.

Following the concert, several students from the school went on stage and presented Mr. Moravec with an enormous card of thanks on which all students, faculty, staff and Board members had placed their signatures. A few words of greeting and thanks by Rita and members of the Board were followed by champagne and a buffet of sweets. Thanks to the generosity of Joe Sterling and Mr. Moravec, a large number of the pianist's records and CDs were given to the evening's attendees, among whom there were many prominent Chicago citizens. After expenses, the concert raised a significant profit for the new special reserves fund.

Though unable to attend, Maestro Daniel Barenboim sent his best wishes and confirmation of his continuing support for the school. His words were shared in the evening's printed program:

> *The People's Music School knows that the greatest value in music is in its making. It brings discipline, beauty, and joy into the daily lives of many people.*

CHAPTER 63

A Nationwide PBS-TV Special: Seeking Solutions

After the excitement of the closing months of 1998, 1999 began with a more normal schedule of activities at The People's Music School. That didn't mean things were quiet at 931 W. Eastwood. Students continued to benefit not only from their classes and lessons, but also from the many programs generated by the ongoing partnership with Chicago Symphony and Civic Orchestra musicians, as well as the continuing involvement of Richard Young and his friends and fellow musicians. On February 20, the school's 23rd anniversary was celebrated with a faculty recital.

In March, the school received two special visits. New Orleans jazz and blues pianist Henry Butler presented a master class and performance on March 18, and two days later the Northfield Youth Choir from Northfield, Minnesota, came to present a program. For one of the numbers in their program, members of the children's choir from The People's Music School joined them. On April 9, another jazz artist, Panamanian pianist and composer Danilo Perez, visited the school, for a performance and conversations with the students.

The school's residencies in Chicago public schools continued with an integrated educational and performance series at Dodge School in May and June. But it was in the fall of 1999 that Rita began an especially important new residency at Hibbard School in Albany Park, starting a unique partnership that a decade later would produce a groundbreaking new program with significance not only for The People's Music School and Hibbard School but also for the entire city.

On Wednesday, September 22, The People's Music School received wide national attention, when it was featured in a PBS program titled "Seeking Solutions," which was produced and reported by Pulitzer Prize-winning journalist Hedrick Smith. The two and a half hour program, which was broadcast coast-to-coast, aired from 7:00 to 9:30 p.m. local time. It focused on six locations across the nation which were attempting to turn their communities, which were marked by low incomes and ethnic diversity, into areas of cohesion and mutual support. One of those communities was Chicago's Uptown.

As Smith reported, "We plan to reach beyond the soul searching and finger pointing to show how ordinary grassroots heroes are confronting and overcoming problems of crime and violence."

Regarding Uptown, Smith observed:

> *Uptown is a tough-looking neighborhood. But in this gritty arena, jam-packed with diverse peoples from all walks of life, the violent crime rate is surprisingly low. The secret lies within Uptown's powerful community spirit and the scores of active civic groups that ensure all who live here are accepted and supported. Tucked within this urban mosaic are extraordinary people like Rita Simo....*

As a participant on one of the panels for the show, Rita spoke of some of the things that make the Uptown community unique. She recalled examples which showed how even those with little money had exhibited their pride in being part of the community. As one illustration, she cited a homeless woman who came into the school during the fund raising for the new building and proudly contributed her three dollars, saying she wanted to feel a part of the effort to improve the neighborhood and suggesting that she might even "come in and learn something."

Rita stressed the importance of people knowing and connecting with their neighbors, stating that most people are too isolated. If instead, people made it a point to know a number of their neighbors, it would both build trust and also develop a protective human shield, as potential troublemakers would hesitate to bother citizens who are well-known in the neighborhood. She pointed to Uptown as a community that has promoted this kind of friendly interaction among neighbors.

But Rita's final comments, near the end of the panel, resonated with the entire group, which responded with approving chuckles and applause: "I think in the neighborhoods in which we have so many difficulties, we need to learn how to celebrate. There is nothing that builds community more than breaking bread together.....life is full of problems, but once in a while, let's live it up."

CHAPTER 64

Moving Toward the 21st Century

On Sunday, October 17, 1999, The People's Music School held its third benefit brunch and raffle, with all profits going to the special reserves campaign. Titled "Food for the Future," the event was held at Julie Mai's Le Bistro restaurant on North Clark Street. The brunch and raffle raised $17,500 for the campaign. In addition, a marathon run organized by Board member Jeff Kelly in the fall of 1999 brought in more than $1,200, also earmarked for the special reserves fund campaign.

Fundraising for the campaign had gone well enough by April of 1999 that the school's Board raised the goal to $300,000. By September, they had determined that $500,000 was reachable, and the goal was raised again. In October, Bret Ruiz was hired as the new general manager and development director, replacing Chris Hodak, who retired from the position to follow a passion for playwriting, along with part time freelance grant writing.

A fall concert titled "Autumn Fest" took place at the school on Sunday, October 30, featuring duets by Richard Graef, Chicago Symphony Assistant Principal Flutist, and his wife, Emily. All through the preceding year, both had given generously of their time working with woodwind students at the school. In the years to come, they would continue presenting programs and working with the students at The People's Music School.

As the year ended, progress in the special reserves fund campaign continued to be slow but steady. In mid-November, just after the benefit brunch, the total stood at $183,335. By the end of December, the amount in the fund was $199,338, or, as Rita's ever-optimistic perspective put it, "just a few dollars away from $200,000."

At the January 16, 2000, annual retreat meeting of the Board, two retiring long-time Board members were given special recognition for their many years of productive service to the school. Thomas McLaughlin had served faithfully in many capacities since the school's inception, including a number of years as Board president and also as head of the capital fund raising money for the building on West Eastwood. Peggy Ross was also recognized for her loyal years of service, including the chairmanship of many benefit events.

Amid the excitement of the turn in the century, Rita and Tomás made plans for a trip Rita had long desired, a journey through the Panama Canal. In February 2000, they flew to Acapulco, Mexico, where they boarded a cruise ship that, after stopping for a rain forest visit in Costa Rica, proceeded through the canal. Photographs from the trip confirm Tomás' claim that Rita spent most of her waking hours on the observation deck of the boat as it passed through the canal, abandoning her post only long enough to eat and sleep. The trip concluded with stops in Cartagena, Aruba, and San Juan.

Rita and Tomás returned to Chicago just in time for the school's 24th anniversary faculty concert made up entirely of music by J. S. Bach, in commemoration of the 250th anniversary of his death. On Saturday, March 11, the faculty presented another concert, this time featuring all women composers in honor of Women's History Month.

CHAPTER 65

The School Welcomes Lilly Torres

For almost a decade, Hazel Leukaufe had been a dedicated and capable office manager and assistant to Rita at The People's Music School. Early in 2000, she informed the Board that she was planning to retire at the close of the spring term in May. Now past 65, she was finding it more challenging to meet the time demands and other responsibilities of her job at the school, and she told them it was time to hire someone younger with more energy.

A search began for her replacement, but finding the right person proved a challenge. Some prospective candidates were looking for more pay, others for more regular hours. Still others did not seem to be quite the right match for the unique family culture of The People's Music School. Rita felt it was important for Hazel's replacement to speak reasonably good Spanish, as a number of the Hispanic students' parents were limited in their ability to converse in English.

In the summer of 2000, a young bi-lingual woman named Lilliana (Lilly) Torres was unhappy with her job as an executive administrative assistant in Chicago's Loop and was looking for new employment. In early August she walked into an agency that helped Latinos in their job searches. Lilly was sitting in the lobby waiting for an interview when a woman who had been walking back and forth through the lobby approached her and struck up a conversation.

After conversing for a while, the woman evidently was impressed, because she told Lilly that she was on the Board of a school called The People's Music School which was looking for a new office manager. She suggested that Lilly apply for the position.

Lilly soon discovered that the woman, whose name was Alba Aranda Suh was not only on the school's Board but was also the director of the employment agency. She had been walking back and forth through the lobby on her way between appointments.

Though The People's Music School was located at least a half hour's drive from her home, Lilly had enjoyed her conversation with the employment agency director and was curious to learn more about this unusual school. Within a few weeks, she was on her way to a three o'clock interview appointment with Rita Simó, whom the agency director had described as a wonderful woman but a little eccentric.

Though she had allowed plenty of time for the trip, traffic was unusually heavy, and then, adding to her frustration, Lilly took a wrong turn and got lost. Realizing she would be about a half-hour late for the appointment, Lilly phoned the school. Rita responded, with some annoyance in her voice, that Lilly would have to wait until five o'clock for the interview, as now Rita was busy with her teaching schedule and would not be able to meet with Lilly until then.

Lilly's interview began at 5:00 p.m. with Rita and Iguill Guillermo, a former student who was serving as interim office manager during the summer, following Hazel's retirement. From the beginning, Lilly was impressed, and she immediately liked Rita's no-nonsense, no-pretense ways. But she wasn't sure about Rita's reaction in return. Lilly had dressed in a business suit for the interview, while everyone else at the school was dressed casually. Rita had made a comment about how "fancy" Lilly was dressed. She went home thinking the interview had not gone well, so she was pleasantly surprised when three days later the school's general manager, Bret Ruiz, called and offered her the job.

Lilly reported for work on the first day of the school's 2000 fall term, this time dressed neatly but casually. The first thing Rita asked her to do was to clean the school's bathrooms. By now, Lilly was beginning to take a clearer measure of Rita, and she quickly realized she was being tested. She cheerfully picked up the bathroom cleaning supplies and proceeded to her task, proving once and for all that she was not "too fancy" for The People's Music School.

While she found the hectic and unpredictable schedule especially challenging during the early months, within a year Lilly had decided that this was the place she wanted to stay for as long as the school wanted her. She was deeply impressed with how Rita treated everyone with the same respect and appreciation for work well done. Famous guests visiting the school were treated in the same manner as the newest parent or other local resident coming in off the street to find out about the school. All were greeted warmly and with respect. Yet, Rita wasn't a "soft touch." Lilly saw that Rita demanded maturity, consideration, and adherence to rules from all, even the youngest.

Lilly's greatest joy at The People's Music School, however, was the pleasure of watching new families blossom as they became part of the school family. Immigrants, shy at first, would become leaders in planning bake sales and receptions following concerts. Babies accompanying their mothers and siblings to lessons would later become students at the school themselves. Lilly was awed by the dedication and energy Rita inspired in everyone in service to the school.

"I had never seen anything like it," she marveled.

CHAPTER 66

"It's Time to Go"

Even before her trip to the Panama Canal, Rita had been thinking that it was time to begin planning for her retirement as executive director of The People's Music School. In early 2000, plagued by controversy, Paul Vallas, Chicago Public Schools Superintendent and CEO, had publically announced, "It is time to go." Rita whimsically decided to take that on as her mantra, and in April of 2000, using those words, she announced her decision to her Board. While most Board members hated to think of the school's leadership no longer being in the hands of the dynamic lady who had inspired its success for so many years, all had to agree that Rita deserved more free time to travel and pursue other pleasures and interests.

For several months Rita met with Board members to work out details of the transition, which was planned for the end of the 2001 spring term. After examining all of Rita's responsibilities, the Board could see that two people would need to be hired to cover them all, an executive director to oversee all aspects of the school and a separate director of music and education. By the time Rita announced her retirement in an October 2000 public letter to the larger school family, plans were already well underway toward hiring a music and education director. Filling the executive director position proved more challenging.

October was a busy month for Rita. On October 12, she received the "Outstanding Achievement in the Arts" award from the YWCA of Metropolitan Chicago. Three days later, she was on an airplane to Bolivia on an assignment from the U. S. State Department to evaluate the music program of the Conservatorio Nacional in La Paz, which had been receiving funds from the agency.

While in La Paz, Rita not only observed the school's activities and interviewed its faculty but also conducted several master classes with conservatory students. During her visit, Rita became acquainted with David Handel, conductor of the Bolivian National Symphony, who subsequently came to Chicago to conduct the Chicago Symphony Orchestra.

When asked by her new Bolivian friends if she had any special requests before heading home, Rita told them she had always wanted to visit Lake Titicaca. Her visit to the beautiful legendary lake, immortalized in Incan mythology, was everything she had imagined it could be. She even made friends with a resident llama and had her picture taken with the animal and its Bolivian tender.

In January 2001, Vincent Centeno was hired as the director of music education and programs at The People's Music School. It was a position he would continue to hold until August 2008, when he left to pursue a PhD in music theory and choral conducting at the University of Oregon.

Vincent had moved to the Uptown neighborhood from the Philippines in 1972, when he was nine years old. He had studied piano in his native country, but once in Chicago, family finances did not allow for the purchase of a piano, let alone lessons.

"It was too early to benefit from The People's Music School," he observes.

After a few years, Vincent was able to resume piano studies with an aunt and, subsequently, with a Northwestern University student. In 1981, he entered DePaul University, where he studied piano with Melody Lord and Mary Sauer.

He learned about The People's Music School from friends who taught at DePaul and who introduced him to Rita Simó. Vincent was immediately attracted to the school's philosophy and the sense of community it engendered. In 1998, he was hired to teach piano at the school, so by the time he became director of the school's music education programs, he was quite familiar with both the school and the people who worked and studied there. In addition, he had often performed piano duets with Rita in public concerts.

CHAPTER 67

A Magnificent 25th Birthday Bash

Beginning in the fall of 2000, planning began for a special celebration in recognition of the 25th anniversary of The People's Music School. The event was scheduled for Friday, February 16, 2001, at Symphony Center. Board and staff members exchanged ideas for creating a particularly memorable "birthday" party, and there was optimism that major progress could be announced in the campaign for the special reserves fund, which everyone hoped would meet its goal by the end of the anniversary year.

In going through files and looking for historical information or items to incorporate into the celebration, school staff once again ran across the reel-to-reel tape Rita had made many years earlier in Milwaukee. Replaying the tape, Rita was dismayed to find the recording filled with background noises and static. A young friend of the school, Jim Ginsburg, who had recently founded Cedille Records, happened to be in the school at the time, and he walked into the room where Rita was playing the tape. As Rita joked about the bad condition of the recording, Jim was hearing something else.

"Who is the pianist?" he asked. "That is really good playing. I'd like to take that recording to my studio to see what I can do with it."

Rita deflected the question about the performing artist, but told Jim he was welcome to take the tape. At his studio, Jim worked diligently on the recording until he had eliminated virtually all of the background noise and static, except for the first two movements of a Bartok Sonata, in which the noises had proved too overpowering. He transferred the remaining parts of the concert to a CD, and within a few weeks brought it back to Rita.

When Jim played the CD for her and once again queried her on the identity of the artist, Rita confessed that she was the pianist and told him the story of its origin. Jim went back to his studio and soon made a box full of copies of the CD, which he presented to Rita. It was decided to give one of the discs to each person who attended the 25th anniversary party, as well as all current donors to the school.

Rita chose to title the CD with the phrase Mary O'Connell had suggested for the fundraising campaign, "Music is a Gift; Pass It On," words that had become the unofficial motto for the school and its mission. Perhaps when she spoke those words, Rita was also thinking of the ants on the guava tree in San Francisco de Macorís.

In the years that followed, Jim Ginsburg made hundreds of additional copies of the CD at Cedille's expense, as his contribution to the school. Rita's performances on the CD, of works by Bach, Beethoven, Bartok, Schumann, Chopin, Prokofiev, and Catalan composer Frederic Mompou, were so outstanding that many who heard the recording commented that the performances compared favorably to those of the world's premier pianists.

The 25th anniversary celebration on February 16, 2001, was truly a magnificent affair. The evening began with a tapas dinner in the Grainger Ball Room at Chicago Symphony Center, followed by a CSO performance with Daniel Barenboim conducting music of Spain and Latin America. The maestro then joined the group for a champagne reception following the concert.

During the reception, the Fred Fine Democracy in the Arts award was presented to Nick Rabkin, Rita's supporter and friend at the John D. and Catherine T. McArthur Foundation, who was now Director of the Center for Arts Policy at Columbia College. In a letter Nick wrote Rita ten days after the event, he spoke of his great admiration for all she had achieved and the manner in which she had achieved it:

> You, dear Rita, have always been at the top of the list. No one has been more deeply committed to the democratic spirit in the arts than you. No one has succeeded at building a grassroots organization that is more dynamic than yours. And no one has remained truer to their best utopian impulses than you.

Nick went on to say that it was because he held Rita in such high esteem that the award meant so much to him.

Once again Rita realized that many of her students and their families could not afford the benefit evening at Orchestra Hall, but she didn't want them to miss out on the festivities. A second 25th anniversary celebration took place on Saturday, February 24, as Rita said, " to celebrate here at the school with our neighborhood friends. It will include a faculty concert and a reception."

CHAPTER 68

Mary Ellen McGarry: A New Chapter Begins

By its June 20, 2001, meeting, the Board still had not identified a candidate for executive director of The People's Music School, though it was announced that several promising candidates were being interviewed. Rita agreed to continue in the position until the right person could be found. It was also announced that on Saturday, June 23, Rita would be among a small group of arts innovators in the city honored as one of the "Queen of Hearts of the Arts" by the Boulevard Arts Center at the DuSable Museum in Chicago.

The July 18 Board meeting brought the good news that a strong candidate had been identified among the applicants for executive director. Mary Ellen McGarry, formerly head of the theater department at the Chicago Academy of the Arts, knew Rita through St. Thomas Church. When Rita approached her about applying for the job of executive director, she hesitated. Though her background had involved some music, including work with a small opera troupe, her main focus had always been theater.

But once she walked through the door of the school, she later recalled, "I knew I wanted to be there."

Members of the personnel committee of the Board who interviewed Mary Ellen were impressed with her history in arts management and educational program planning, and in July the Board voted to offer her the position, which she happily accepted. On August 4, during a small reception at The People's Music School, Mary Ellen was introduced to the teachers and staff. By September 1, she had begun work as executive director.

In her August newsletter to friends of the school, Rita announced the hiring of Mary Ellen McGarry and spoke of her appreciation for all the support she had received since the opening of the school. She also announced her plans for the future, which included a change of residence:

My life after September 1st will be just as hectic as before.
Tomás and I are selling our house on Beacon Street and moving
to a condo. Our new address after September 15 will be:
4343 N. Clarendon, 60613. The phone remains the same.
Please call anytime. I will be practicing. I want to learn all of
the 48 preludes and fugues of the Well Tempered Clavier.

I want to tell you how grateful I am to all of you for your friendship
and support of me and all the projects of the school throughout the
years. I hope you will continue your commitment to our mission.

The August 2001 newsletter was the last of Rita's handwritten letters to The People's Music School family. Rita had hoped to announce that the school was close to its $500,000 goal for the special reserves fund, but progress in the campaign had been slow for a number of months and reaching the goal by the end of the year was looking less likely. At the July 18 Board meeting, Jeff Kelly announced that the fund total stood at $340,437. While Rita remained hopeful, the burst of the "dot-com bubble" in early 2000 had taken its toll on fundraising.

At that point, no one could foresee that less than two months into the future, a world-shaking terrorist event would throw the U.S. economy into an even greater tailspin. By fateful coincidence, The People's Music School made plans to introduce the new executive director to the Uptown community at a lunch and reception on Tuesday, September 11, 2001. The guest list included people from Uptown businesses, schools, churches, and other community organizations. By noon, the tragedy unfolding in New York, Washington, and a farm field in Pennsylvania preempted all other activity, and amid the confusion, the lunch was cancelled, as people around the country focused in horror on the events of the day.

Early that afternoon, Rita, Mary Ellen, and Vincent discussed what to do about the lessons and classes planned for the rest of the day, and decided to go ahead with the schedule as usual, even though some students might be too upset or fearful to come. To their surprise, almost all of the students and faculty showed up. Students took their classes, practiced, and performed. Parents completed volunteer chores or waited quietly nearby, some watching the TV that was set up in the lobby.

Several people mentioned that they had come because they felt safe in the school and wanted to be with a group of friends. Others said they felt a need to experience the healing powers of music. Many local businesses, including the local McDonald's closed for the day, but not The People's Music School.

CHAPTER 69

Keeping in Touch with "Counter Point"

Though Rita had retired as executive director of The People's Music School, she remained an active presence at the school. She continued to teach many of her former piano students and often served as substitute teacher when other piano faculty members had to be absent. Though she originally refused an invitation to join the school's Board of Directors, feeling it was important for Mary Ellen to first establish her pattern of leadership, she finally succumbed to pressure from her faculty and Board friends and joined the Board in early 2002.

On Saturday, October 27, 2001, Rita joined Vincent Centeno and Richard Young, along with others, in a recital at the school titled "Faculty and Friends." Among other works, the musicians performed three and four keyboard concerti by J. S. Bach. For Rita, it was a pleasant return to the pieces she had practiced so diligently in preparation for the inauguration of the Palacio de Bellas Artes in Santo Domingo in early 1956.

Mary Ellen McGarry appreciated the efforts Rita had made to bring monthly updates to the wider school family through her personally written letters, but she chose a new way to communicate. In October 2001, the first issue of a new four-page printed newsletter titled Counter Point was mailed. Along with news of the school, the newsletter contained a calendar of events for the month and scattered photographs and other graphics. It also announced the hiring of Nathan Rosser as the new general manager, replacing Bret Ruiz, who had resigned several months earlier to become director of the Anita H. Martinez Ballet Forlórico.

In this first issue of the new newsletter, Mary Ellen encouraged people to submit their writings about music, "whether it be educational in nature or just to share personal insights about music or a composer. Everyone's point of view is important and welcome."

She also started a tradition of honoring a "volunteer of the month," someone who had gone beyond normal expectations in serving the school. The first volunteer honored was Hugo Morales. The choice of Hugo surprised no one. Hugo was always the first to respond to a problem with a confident, "I can fix it."

The November issue of Counter Point spoke of two programs presented by visitors from Spain. On September 29, classical guitarist Rafael Serrallet, from Valencia, Spain, gave a concert of Spanish music ranging from the Renaissance to the present. On October 2, pianist Sylvia Toran presented a program of Spanish, Latin American, and French music. Her performance of a Ginastera sonata drew an especially enthusiastic response from the audience. The People's Music School concert hall was filled to capacity for both of these programs.

The December Counter Point honored two faculty members who between them had taught at the school for over half a century. Carter Hoyt III was entering his 26th year of teaching guitar and adult theory at the school, and Judith Johnson-Brown was close behind him with 25 years of teaching flute as well as general music theory classes.

As 2001 drew to a close, The People's Music School's special reserves fund campaign was still quite a bit short of its goal. Then, in February 2002, news was received of an unusually large bequest to the school. Weldon Hall was an Uptown resident who had lived frugally for many years. At one point he had studied piano with Rita Simó, and he told her that though he had studied piano as a youth, he now was now finding pleasure in his piano studies for the first time.

In 1998, Mr. Hall had died and left his assets in a trust to take care of his sister. When she died in late 2001, his will provided for distribution of his remaining assets, including a $100,000 gift to the music school, which the Board voted to add to the special reserves fund. With that generous gift, the school moved closer to achieving its $500,000 goal..

There was another part to Mr. Hall's will that was especially meaningful to Rita, and that provided the school with something Rita had long desired. At the sister's death, Mr. Hall's carefully maintained Steinway baby grand piano was given to The People's Music School.

CHAPTER 70

"Rita Simó Way"

The year 2002 brought significant new recognition to Rita. In January, she was named one of *Chicago Magazine*'s "2001 New Centurions." The January issue of the magazine contained a long article on Rita and the school.

Rita was also the honored guest at the 26th anniversary celebration of The People's Music School on Saturday, February 23, 2002. A faculty ensemble performed Ravel's *Mother Goose Suite*, arranged by Vincent Centeno, which included narrations by some of Rita's special friends, including Harry Porterfield, Henry Fogel, Onnie Darrow Assir DaSilva, and Nick Rabkin. These and many other longtime friends joined Rita at a post-concert dessert and beverage reception, during which all toasted Rita Simó's twenty-five years of leadership of The People's Music School.

Vincent explained his choice of the Ravel piece in the concert program: "Mary Ellen and I have been envisioning The People's Music School as a fairy-tale musical garden 'grown' by Rita. We thought that the *Mother Goose Suite* with its last movement titled Enchanted Garden, would be the perfect piece for this year's anniversary."

The most exciting moment of the afternoon, however, was yet to come. Following the concert, Mary O'Connell, retiring Board president; Jeff Kelly, new Board president; and Alderman Helen Shiller invited Rita to the stage. A large draped object was uncovered to reveal a metal sign reading "Rita Simó Way." On the prior October 31, Helen Shiller had sponsored an order in the Chicago City Council for "authorization for installation of a 'Rita Simo Way' honorary street sign" for the block of West Eastwood fronting the school, a proposal that had received unanimous approval from the Council.

Soon after the anniversary celebration, the sign was installed at the corner of Eastwood and Sheridan Road, where it is to remain in perpetuity. A duplicate sign was given to Rita, who placed it on the windowsill of her condo on Clarendon Avenue.

CHAPTER 71

Music Everywhere

Three days after the 26th anniversary celebration, The People's Music School hosted a mini-performance and lecture by internationally renowned violinist Gil Shaham as part of the partnership with the Chicago Symphony Orchestra. Shaham was in town rehearsing with the orchestra for performances of concerti by Stravinsky and Mozart to be performed in early March. A capacity audience filled the school's concert room to hear the young Israeli violinist play and to hear him speak. Shaham commented that he always felt like he was coming home when he visited Illinois, as he was born in Urbana while his parents were fellowship students at the University of Illinois.

Other outstanding performers also graced the school's concert stage during early 2002. February brought a concert by the Bella Voce Singers, and on March 21, members of the Chicago Symphony Orchestra Chorus presented a program.

On March 23, the Genesis Opera Ensemble performed Gian Carlo Menotti's *The Thief and the Old Maid*. The group's director was Bereniece Jones, a voice teacher at The People's Music School. CSO sponsored master classes with Emily Graeff, flute, and Burl Lane, saxophone, also took place in the late spring.

During the summer of 2002, The People's Music School was invited to participate in a new project, Music Everywhere, jointly sponsored by the Chicago Department of Cultural Affairs and the Chicago Office of Tourism, with additional financial support from Exelon. The project was designed both to provide a pleasing atmosphere for visitors to some of Chicago's most popular tourist destinations and to showcase Chicago artist groups. Students and teachers from the school performed on Saturdays, from

11:00 a.m. to1:00 p.m., beginning June 8 and continuing through the summer.

The project's kick-off program at City Hall on June 8 involved the school's orchestra and choruses in concert with other groups. On June 29, the flute ensemble and clarinet and recorder students performed at the Adler Planetarium. On July 6, piano and violin students performed with their teachers on the north steps of the Field Museum. A performance by the percussion students with teacher Dominique Louis took place at the Shedd Aquarium on July 13, followed by one by the guitar ensemble on July 20. The final performance of the series took place on August 31, featuring all the choral ensembles. These performances not only brought the school more visibility, but it also gave the students experience performing in exciting new venues, building up their confidence for performing in public.

During the summer, the school also collaborated with the Chicago Department of Cultural Affairs and the Shedd Museum in the production of a musical puppet show titled *A Mermaid's Tale*. Inspired by the Hans Christian Anderson tale, *The Little Mermaid*, the production featured original music composed by Vincent Centeno, some of which was sung by students from the school. Students also operated the puppets.

Mary Ellen McGarry wrote the narration for the show, which was staged in the Claudia Cassidy Theater of the Chicago Cultural Center on Friday, July 19, and Saturday, July 20. The puppets used in the performance were made by students from The People's Music School, under the guidance of master puppeteer, Bill Hubner.

CHAPTER 72

Spain, and a Visit with Pedro Lerma

During the spring of 2002, while the city of Chicago was making plans to showcase its artists through the Music Everywhere project, Illinois was once again facing budget problems, and Governor Ryan had proposed across-the-board 5% cuts to all agencies, which included dropping the Illinois Arts Council's 2002 budget of $20.6 million to $19.6 million for 2003. Once the Governor's budget reached state legislative bodies, an additional $8 million cut was proposed.

Students, faculty, and friends of The People's Music School were strongly encouraged to write their state legislators in protest. On April 17, all were invited to join a busload of arts supporters on a trip to Springfield for an "Arts Advocacy Day" of protests. Ultimately, the budget cut to the Arts Council held at 5%, a cut but not the draconian one that had been feared.

It was fortunate that the year of 2002 brought record corporate and foundation support to the school's operating budget, because at the same time financial markets were continuing to weaken, affecting the school's investment funds, especially those of the special reserves fund. Even with the major addition in February of the money from the Weldon Hall bequest, the fund's value was down significantly.

The increase in the operating budget, however, did allow for an increase in teachers' pay, which had continued to be far below the norm. In mid-2002, the pay per lesson was raised to a level necessary to retain and attract the best teachers, though it was still significantly below the fee commanded in the private market.

In the fall of 2002, Mary Ellen announced the hiring of a new "business manager," a new title for the position formerly called general manager. The position included building and payroll management, public relations, and assistance in fundraising. Aubree Weiley was hired for the position following the departure of former general manager, Nathan Rosser, for Los Angeles. At the same time, The People's Music School announced that 396 students, a record number, had been enrolled for the fall term.

In October, Rita and Tomás traveled to Barcelona for the LIBER Spanish book fair. During the trip, they also went to Madrid to visit friends. Their Madrid host, Manoli Martinez, mentioned to Rita that Pedro Lerma, who was now in his mid-eighties, was still living in the city and teaching at the Royal Conservatory of Music. When he asked if Rita would like to connect with her old piano teacher from her years in Santo Domingo, she responded with great enthusiasm.

The next day, while Tomás was meeting with some of his publishing contacts, Manoli drove Rita to the conservatory. The reunion between former student and teacher was full of lively conversation and laughter. When Rita told Pedro about all the twists and turns of her life and of the creation and development of The People's Music School, his response was, "That's all very wonderful, but Rita, please tell me you are still spending time playing the piano."

CHAPTER 73

An Abundance of Musical Gifts

Many performance groups and other special guests visited The People's Music School during the fall of 2002. On September 26, a Hungarian dance and instrumental group gave a program, followed by an October 17 concert by singers from Music of the Baroque and, on October 22, a rousing program by a group of African musicians. On October 15, WFMT radio program host Carl Grapentine gave a presentation on J. S. Bach.

The partnership between the school and the Chicago Symphony Orchestra was further enhanced when the two joined forces on November 7 for a benefit and awards event titled "Reach for the Stars." The celebration, which ran from 5:30 to 7:30, began with master classes by clarinetist John Bruce Yeh and flutist Emily Graef. It then proceeded with the presentation of the first annual Partnership Award to Charles A. Lewis, Vice Chairman of the Board of Trustees of the Chicago Symphony. Cocktails, a buffet, and a silent auction followed. All were pleased when it was announced that the evening cleared $34,498 in profits.

The People's Music School also continued its close ties with The Merit Music Program. In the summer of 2002, Merit had lost its talented and much loved artistic director, Anne Monaco, who was killed in a tragic accident. On November 7, The People's Music School dedicated its fall student recital to Anne's memory. Duffie Adelson, executive director of Merit, attended.

January 2003 saw a continuation of the busy schedule at the school, beginning with a new series of monthly concerts by chamber ensembles from the Chicago Civic Orchestra. Then, on January 30, a People's Music School trio, composed of Rita on piano, flutist Judith Johnson-Brown, and guitarist Steve Vazquez, presented two programs for students from several Chicago Public Schools at Preston Bradley Hall, sponsored by the International Music Foundation. Their program, interspersed by narrative, took students on a musical journey through Latin America.

On January 19, twelve-year-old violinist Kristina Cooper performed Vivaldi's *Four Seasons*, accompanied by piano teacher Sarah Renberg, at a concert in the Preston Bradley Hall of the Chicago Cultural Center. The program was organized by the Chicago Consortium of Community Music Schools, a new collaboration among ten independent music schools in the Chicago metropolitan area that had been formed to increase awareness of music education opportunities throughout the area.

Rachel Barton was the emcee of the event, in which she also performed. Kristina Cooper's performance of the Vivaldi and her determination to become a professional violinist moved Rachel deeply. In the years that followed, she continued to aid Kristina's violin study, first through the instrument loan program and later through educational grants from her Rachel Elizabeth Barton Foundation.

At the January retreat meeting of the Board, Jan Feldman, an attorney and partner in the firm of Perkins Coie, took over as Board president. One of his first announcements concerned a generous new unrestricted gift of $100,000 from the school's longtime supporter, the John D. and Catherine T. MacArthur Foundation. This gift was in addition to $60,000 the foundation had previously granted to the annual operating budget of the school. The Board unanimously voted to add the new unrestricted donation to the special reserves fund.

As thrilled as she was with the generous gift from the school's longtime supporter, Mary Ellen McGarry also continued to acknowledge the generous efforts made by many others on behalf of the school. The February issue of Counter Point told the story of a young girl who had asked her friends to send a monetary gift to The People's Music School instead of bringing presents to her birthday party. The girl studied cello, but neither she nor her teacher was connected with the school. She had just read about it and been inspired.

Mary Ellen went on to point out the many ways in which students, parents and teachers also went beyond what was expected in serving the school: "Often our students, who must volunteer two hours a month, willingly extend those hours to complete a task, and to do it in a way that shows their pride in the school."

CHAPTER 74

"From Sea to Shining Sea"

Music Director Vincent Centeno decided to devote the spring semester of 2003 to a focus on contemporary music at The People's Music School. On February 22, the anniversary concert by the faculty kept true to that goal, with performances of compositions by Gershwin, Bernstein, Schönberg, Crumb, Schuller, Bartok, Cage, and Ives, as well as the school's own Steve Vázquez. As a further extension of the theme, the school received visits from two contemporary composers, representing two very different kinds of music, Augusta Read Thomas, composer-in-residence for the Chicago Symphony Orchestra, and Coleridge Taylor Perkinson, film score composer.

In April, Rita participated in a program featuring music from a very different time period. During Holy Week, the Vermeer Quartet performed Joseph Hadyn's *Seven Last Words of Christ* in the Rockefeller Chapel of the University of Chicago. In an effort to mirror the work's original performance in 1787, the chapel was almost dark except for two small lamps positioned near the performers. Also in keeping with the original performance, the event included not only the music, but also spoken commentary.

Instead of mini-sermons, as had occurred in 1787, however, local theologians and professors, joined by journalist Don Wycliff and Rita Simó, gave short meditations on the seven last lines spoken by Christ on the Cross. Rita interpreted the words, "Woman, behold thy son. Behold thy mother," as "an invocation for all of us to be compassionate companions to each other, not just when it is easy, but especially when it is hard."

Over the years, performing Hadyn's *Seven Last Words of Christ* continued to have special significance for the Vermeer Quartet, and they performed it many times in various venues in Chicago and around the world.

Young spoke of the spiritual solace each player received from performing the work, "We have never talked about it, but I think each of us responds in his own, deeply personal way to what lies beyond the notes on the page."

The May meeting of the school's Board brought wonderful news. After months of downward movement in the financial markets, the tide had turned, and the special reserves fund was showing positive growth. With the increase in capital value, coupled with the MacArthur gift, the fund had finally crossed the target of $500,000. During the following months the fund continued to post gains, and by December 31, 2003, the total in the account had risen to $581,213. The future stability of the school seemed assured.

The May issue of Counter Point announced that once again students from the school would be taking part in the city's Music Everywhere project on three summer dates at the downtown Museum Campus. The school also had received funding from Exelon for the creation of a new production incorporating puppets, musical ensembles, and narration. By the end of May, the students were busy preparing for their latest show titled "From Sea to Shining Sea," and subtitled "What America Means To Me." The two performances of the show, given on Saturday, June 21, in the Claudia Cassidy Auditorium of the Chicago Cultural Center, were so successful that it was videotaped for future presentation on cable television.

A further highlight of the summer, was a trip sponsored by Ravinia Festival's outreach program on June 6 to the Chicago premier performance of composer John Adam's new opera/oratorio *El Niño* at Ravinia Park. The work was performed by the Atlanta Symphony Orchestra and Chorus, with the addition of the Chicago Children's Choir. On the night before the performance, Ravinia artists visited the school and presented a lecture which included musical highlights. The students who attended the performance were deeply moved by this retelling of the Christmas story using a variety of texts and poems for inspiration. Many of the texts were in Spanish.

Throughout the summer, a large group of African immigrant youth spent Friday afternoons at The People's Music School. Business Manager Aubree Weiley was a member of the Board of the Sunlight African Community Center, a non-profit organization that assists immigrant children from African nations as they acclimate to their new country. She felt the children would benefit from an afternoon at the music school, and she designed a class for them.

By the end of the summer, Aubree happily announced, "We have worked on learning solfège, ear training, rhythm, listening skills, notation, singing, and characteristics of western classical instruments. The children have been very attentive, engaged, and wonderfully responsive."

Once again, The People's Music School was participating in a broad community outreach effort. This one was truly in the spirit of "from sea to shining sea."

CHAPTER 75

A Classical Fall

With a freer schedule, Rita was now finding it easier to make more frequent trips back to the Dominican Republic. This was important to her for two reasons. First, she always enjoyed returning to a simpler, more relaxed way of life, accompanied by the taste of foods and the smell of flowers she had loved as a child. But she also felt a need to check in periodically with her brother Alfredo, who was now living alone in Santo Domingo. In August of 2003, Rita and Tomás went to Santo Domingo, where, in addition to visiting with Alfredo, Rita conducted a series of master classes at the Conservatorio Nacional de Música.

At The People's Music School, the number of applicants for enrollment continued to grow. Beginning in the fall, the Board and staff, wanting to ensure that students were putting forth sufficient effort to justify keeping their place at the school, decided to institute a new policy for monitoring student progress. Within the first three levels of proficiency, upward movement to the next level was expected of a student after a maximum of four semesters. If a student did not meet the test, his or her situation was evaluated by a committee that included the teacher and the Music Director. If it was felt to be to the benefit of both the student and the school, the student's contract with the school was terminated. The policy did not generally apply to more advanced students who had complied with all the other requirements of the school.

Focusing on a specific historical period in music had worked so well in the spring, that Vincent Centeno decided to continue the idea through the 2003-04 school year. Fall was devoted to music of the classical period. One of the first concerts scheduled was a performance by artists from Music of the Baroque on November 1, followed by a performance of Mozart's one-act opera *The Impresario* by Genesis Opera, under the direction of Bereniece Jones. The fall faculty recital also featured music of the classical period.

Another fall event at the school was a second recital in a new program of outreach to amateur musicians in the community titled "For the Love of Art." Instituted in the summer of 2002, the program was designed to provide a public performance opportunity for talented local musicians who had continued singing or playing an instrument while pursuing other careers.

The first to perform in the series, on August 1, 2002, was flutist Trent Santonastaso, a biologist with the Brookfield Zoo. On November 8, 2003, dentist Dr. Cary Adams gave a piano recital in the school's concert hall, the first of several recitals he would give at the school in the years ahead.

Everyone was pleased with the improving conditions in the financial markets and the effect on the special reserves fund. Beginning in the fall of 2003, it was decided that the school could once again increase the amount faculty members were paid per lesson. The Board had set a goal of bringing teachers payments in line with a benchmark that had been established by the Consortium of Chicago Music Schools, and the raise brought them closer to that goal. The school's payments per lesson were no longer one uniform amount but varied depending on the tenure and experience of the teacher.

At the same time, to assure the continuing strength of the operating budget, the Board decided to limit fall enrollment to 350 students. It was felt that this balance between number of students and faculty salaries was necessary to maintain the school's high quality of instruction.

The second annual "Reach for the Stars" benefit in partnership with the Chicago Symphony Orchestra took place on Thursday, November 6. Phil Ponce, host of the Chicago Tonight program on PBS, WTTW-TV, was emcee.

The Partnership Award was presented to Assir DaSilva, in recognition of his many years of service to the school. In his acceptance remarks, DaSilva made the observation that The People's Music School now had over 4,000 alumni, most of whom would never have had the opportunity for private music study without the school.

Also contributing to the festive evening were John Bruce Yeh, Teresa Reilly, T. Daniel, and Laurie Willets who performed, and master chef Gale Gand, who donated the desserts and a "goodie bag" for each person attending the benefit to take home. Profits from the evening were $36,317.

The year ended, as usual, with a holiday concert. But this year, the concert included a special musical treat. Challenged by their teacher, John Elmquist, students in the advanced theory class had created an opera about cockroaches to present at the program. The concept, writing, and performance of the opera were all done totally by the students.

As one boy told his teacher, "I never thought that writing music would be so much fun."

CHAPTER 76

A Romantic Spring

Carrying on with the idea of concentrating on a specific historical period of musical composition, the spring semester of 2004 at The People's Music School was dedicated to music of the romantic period, music mainly written in the last half of the 19th century and the early part of the 20th century. The faculty's 28th anniversary concert on Saturday, February 21, featured compositions from that period.

The world of opera was also visited beginning on March 23, when radio station WFMT's Carl Grapentine gave a lecture titled, "A Funny Thing Happened to Me on the Way to the Opera." Mr. Grapentine had the audience in fits of laughter as he told of historic operatic disasters. His presentation was followed a few weeks later by an opera workshop conducted by two members of the Chicago Symphony Chorus, Rae-Myra Hilliard and Daniel Henry, who met with students in the Tuesday general music theory class and soon had them in costumes acting out their own versions of operas.

As a final event connecting to the world of opera, students from the school were invited to Orchestra Hall for a concert conducted by Daniel Barenboim featuring German mezzo-soprano Waltraud Meier, renowned for both her concert and operatic performances, who met with the students after the program and answered their questions.

In late spring, Rita entered into rehearsals with the Chicago Symphony Wind Ensemble as a narrator for several presentations of Prokofiev's *Peter and the Wolf*. While the instrumentalists played, Rita told the story in both English and Spanish. The group's first performance was given at The People's Music School on Saturday, June 5, at 1:30 p.m. to a capacity audience. A second one followed shortly after at St. Pius V Church on South Ashland for students of St. Pius V School. Tomás Bissonnette provided the Spanish translation that Rita delivered.

Following the *Peter and the Wolf* performances, Rita and Tomás left for a long anticipated trip to Alaska, which included stops at Fairbanks, Anchorage, and Denali National Park, where, on an unusually clear day, they saw great Mount McKinley in all its glory. At Seward, they joined an Inner Passage cruise, along the way viewing much wildlife, including many grizzly bears.

In the meantime, back at The People's Music School, a new summertime performance series had begun titled "Thursdays at Six." On July 29, First American Bank sponsored the final concert in the series, a program by instrumentalists and singers from Music of the Baroque. The concert consisted of a number of English madrigals, and featured early instruments, including a classic lute and its larger relative, the theorbo. Donors and other supporters of the school were honored guests at the performance.

The school also began a new summertime fund-raising tradition when it held its first "Andante Walk-a-thon" on a warm, sunny Saturday, July 24. While most of the participants were connected with the school, many community residents joined in, as well. The walkathon began at the school and ended four blocks away at Truman College, where the Uptown Unity Fest was in progress. Participants wore t-shirts decorated with music staffs and the word "Andante," underlining the fact that this was a "walk" and not a "run." Some carried flags; others sang, played their instruments, or blew on kazoos. At one point, the group was led by student Dorian Morningstar, playing his flute and joyfully marching along like the legendary Pied Piper.

Once at Truman College, the instrumentalists gathered to form a small band led by Carter Hoyt, which continued to play a wide variety of songs. The walkathon was a financial success as well as an uplifting community event, and it resulted in over $3,500 in donations for the school.

After arriving home from Alaska, Rita celebrated her 70th birthday on Friday, August 6, 2004, by inviting many friends to a party in her apartment on North Clarendon. The party invitation made one strict demand. Guests were to bring no birthday presents.

When all the guests had arrived, Rita quieted everyone and announced, "Ever since we moved here from our big house, I have had too much stuff. I didn't want any of you bringing me any more. Instead, I have collected together things that have had special memories for me. They are now ready to find new homes. My one request is that each of you remember me and this night by choosing one of the gifts from the bed in the guest room."

She then led the group into the guest room where an array of books, jewelry, and various useful and decorative items were spread on the bed. No one was allowed to leave that evening without a "reverse gift" to celebrate Rita's birthday.

CHAPTER 77

"Working at Playing"

In the fall of 2004, Vincent Centeno announced that the focus for the semester would be on the music of France. In keeping with the theme, music performed on the October 30 faculty concert featured only music by French composers.

Under Vincent's supervision, the school also initiated new guidelines and policies during the fall that were aimed at making the transition from a beginning student's introductory theory lessons to a musical instrument smoother and more meaningful. All instrumental and vocal teachers were required to have a detailed familiarity with the content of the introductory theory curriculum and were then to carry those ideas and specific vocabulary over into their private lessons with the students. Musical vocabulary sheets with definitions and examples were provided to parents, and they were encouraged to help reinforce their child's learning.

A special guest came to the school in late November, as part of the partnership with the Chicago Symphony. Pinchas Zukerman, internationally renowned violinist, violist, and conductor, made a visit between concerts at Orchestra Hall, during which he both conducted and performed with the Chicago Symphony. Following a short performance and demonstration of string techniques on the school's concert stage, Zukerman talked about his own early years of study and what his life was currently like as a busy performing artist.

The third "Reach for the Stars" benefit in cooperation with the Chicago Symphony took place on Thursday, November 4, with two honorees. This time the honorees were two organizations. The first was the Ravinia Festival, which for decades had sponsored many visits by students from The People's Music School to programs, educational lectures, and exchanges with the festival's performing artists. In addition to acknowledging Ravinia

Festival President and CEO Welz Kauffman, and Director of Education Christine Taylor, a special award was presented to Margaret Harris, the Ravinia Women's Board volunteer who had made the first contact with The People's Music School many years before.

The second honoree of the evening was radio station WXRT, which, in addition to making a $55,000 donation to The People's Music School earlier in the year, had also run hourly messages about the school on its station over a three-month period. Once again the evening included performances by a number of well-known artists and a wonderful dinner.

The emcee for the evening was Rick Kogan, senior feature writer for the Chicago Tribune and WGN radio host. Rick was so impressed with the school and its history that the following January he interviewed people from the school for his "Sunday Papers" radio show and also wrote an eight-page cover story for the Sunday Magazine section of the Chicago Tribune, which ran on January 23, 2005, titled "Working at Playing." Many students and their stories were presented in the article, along with photos and a general history of the school.

The first segment of the article highlighted the experiences of two student violinists, fourteen-year-old Kristina Cooper and fifteen-year-old Kevin Fahey, both students of Terrance Gray and both now playing in the Chicago Youth Symphony Orchestra. Kristina's and Kevin's mothers told stories of how each had shown early interest in music by making pretend instruments out of everyday items around the house. Though Kristina lived in Wrigleyville, Kevin's home was on the South Side and his trips to the school involved a ride on the "L," plus a skateboard trip from the Wilson Avenue station. Both mothers spoke about the importance of the school in their children's lives and in their goals for the future.

The second student profiled had a very different story to tell. Though college educated, Dorian Morningstar, aged 58, had ended up homeless after a series of personal setbacks. In his early years he had played several woodwind instruments but had sold them as his financial situation deteriorated. In 1981, he discovered The People's Music School.

"I was just walking down the street and heard the music," he says.

Drawn to the sounds, he went in. Now, several decades later, he spoke of how the school saved him by becoming an inspiration for turning his life around. Once again playing several woodwind instruments, he talked about how he now performs in various venues around the neighborhood.

Seventeen-year-old Dawuan Weatherly was featured in the third profile. At age 7, he had read a biography of Beethoven through a project at his school and found it inspiring. Once home, he told his mother that he wanted to play the piano. His mother did some investigating and learned about The People's Music School. Now, ten years later, Dawuan's talent as a pianist and budding composer was being recognized.

He spoke of how he considers the school to be his second home, "Even when I have no classes I hang around. I wouldn't be where I am today if it wasn't for the atmosphere here to grow and experiment," he observed.

A fourth story continued to point out the contrasts within the student body of The People's Music School. Herman Andalcio had immigrated to the United States from his native Trinidad in his twenties. Through hard work, he had achieved four of the five goals he had set for himself in his new country, including a university education, a family, home ownership, and a productive career, but he had never had the opportunity to pursue the fifth: to learn to play a musical instrument. Herman had always loved music and felt he had a talent, but his life had been too busy. In his 50s, he learned about the school from a friend and began guitar lessons. Not only did he become proficient on guitar, but he soon was pursuing a new dream.

"Back in Trinidad I have started a steel drum band school," he reported. "There are a few adults in it, but more important, already there are forty-five kids."

Following a divorce and the resulting depression, Terry Bakowski, the story's fifth subject, abandoned his successful computer career and moved to a small Uptown apartment. He learned about The People's Music School through an article in the newspaper Streetwise. First enrolling as a voice student, he later began studying violin. By the time of the interview, he was playing in a band called the Chicago Jam Club.

Yet, he spoke of being interested in all genres of music. "I like classical; I am discovering Bach and etudes. But I am also interested in country and jazz fiddle."

The sixth subject of the article, Tracey Marino, whose picture was featured on the magazine's cover, had always wanted to play the piano, but fate had conspired against her. Born with shortened arms and legs, she had learned to be content with playing the clarinet as she grew up in the public schools. When she heard about The People's Music School, she thought she would see if there was a way to learn to play the piano, something she had always dreamed of doing, even though it meant an hour commute each way from her home in Bensonville. She appreciated the school's special efforts in creating a seating arrangement that allowed her to reach the piano keys. Currently finishing a degree in elementary education at Roosevelt University, Tracey was looking forward to sharing her love of music with her future elementary school pupils.

The final segment of Kogan's story focused on the six members of the Menendez family, five of whom were taking lessons at the school. Both the father and mother had changed their job schedules to accommodate their lessons. Oldest son, Josh, studied percussion; younger son, Isaac, studied French horn; and daughter, Monique, studied violin. The family especially enjoyed times of making music together. The youngest family member, Tiana, often accompanied the others to the school. "Very soon she will be playing an instrument, too," reported her father.

At one point in the article, Rick Kogan quoted the late M.W. Newman, the award-winning, longtime urban affairs reporter for the Chicago Daily News, who had described the school in 1992 as a "community school with professional standards. But first of all, it is a place of the spirit."

CHAPTER 78

The Montblanc de la Culture Arts Patronage Award

The People's Music School had begun a new partnership with the Chicago Opera Theater in the fall of 2004. As part of this new alliance, members of the company conducted workshops with a group of the vocal students at the school, and on March 19 and 20, 2005, many of those students joined the opera company in three performances of Tchaikovsky's one act opera, *Iolanta*, at the Vittum Theater. Though their roles were primarily as members of the crowd in the king's court in the opera, the students did join the cast in several choral numbers and admirably executed their movements around stage as they had been directed. For most of them, it was their first experience on a stage with professional singers.

Though she was retired as executive director, Rita continued to be very active at the school. In addition to serving on the Board, she regularly took part in the piano juries at the end of each term, and she often conducted theory class sessions or served as a substitute piano teacher when the need arose. She also continued to receive major awards for her accomplishments.

In 1992, Montblanc, maker of luxury pens for over a century, established the Montblanc Cultural Foundation with the aim of identifying programs and individuals "who have played a crucial part in the health of the arts through their passionate commitment." Through their Montblanc de la Culture Arts Patronage Award program, they began giving awards to artists and cultural projects around the world. In 2005, ten awards were given. Rita Simó was one of the awardees and the only one from the United States.

With all expenses paid by Montblanc, Rita and Mary Ellen McGarry traveled to New York City to receive Rita's award. Tomás also accompanied the group, along with Board members, Mary O'Connell and Jan Feldman, and former Board member, Jake Fisher. Chicago Symphony Orchestra President and CEO Henry Fogel also made the trip.

Several of Rita's friends and relatives currently in New York were present at the ceremony as well, including brother Alfredo and childhood friend Inocencia Berges and her family. Lee Koonce, former director of community relations for the Chicago Symphony and now executive director of Opus 118 Harlem School of Music in New York, also attended.

The festivities took place at noon on Tuesday, April 19, at the new Jazz Center at Lincoln Center. Author Salman Rushdie presented the award, assisted by Brazilian composer, singer, and guitarist, Chico Buarque. Rita was the only award recipient at this ceremony, as those from other nations had received their awards at locations in their home countries.

Others among the guests included Derek Gordon, the new Executive Director of Jazz at Lincoln Center, and Juilliard President, Joseph Polisi. As a special tribute to Rita, Polisi had helped arrange for the ceremony to include a performance by a Juilliard piano student. During her stay in New York, Rita also was treated to a luncheon at Juilliard, hosted by Polisi and the school's alumni director.

The Montblanc award included a gift to Rita of one of only ten exclusive Pope Julius II 18K solid gold pens and a contribution of 15,000 euros to The People's Music School. Though Rita was honored to receive the pen, she observed that it was very foreign to her style of living.

"I admired it for a few days and then put it away in a very safe place," she told friends upon her return.

A few years later, however, Rita decided to put the pen to use. Visitors to her condo on Clarendon Avenue found that before leaving, they were asked to leave a signed message in a guest book kept on the piano. For writing the message, the Montblanc Pope Julius II pen would suddenly appear. Rita wanted as many of her friends as possible to have the experience of writing with the Montblanc pen.

CHAPTER 79

An NBC "Today Show" Broadcast and a Resignation

On Thursday, June 9, 2005, a four-minute segment on The People's Music School was broadcast on the NBC Today Show. Taped in early May, the presentation was hosted by Bob Dotson and was beamed throughout the world. It featured interviews with Rita and several students and included many scenes of activities at the school. The school enjoyed much positive feedback from the worldwide exposure.

Rita's Juilliard friend, Lily Siao Owyang, was among those who viewed the show. Now retired from her position as dean for academic affairs and professor of music at Emmanuel College in Boston, Lily had moved to California. With eager excitement, she located Rita's phone number and gave her a call, delighted once again to be establishing connection with her former classmate, duo-pianist, and fellow dreamer of grand music education plans.

Lily was not the only one to reconnect with Rita as a result of the broadcast. Many other former friends, colleagues, and students wrote or called her, offering their congratulations and sharing in the joy of a dream fulfilled and still growing.

At the end of June, as the summer term was beginning, Mary Ellen McGarry resigned unexpectedly from her position as executive director of The People's Music School to become head of the drama department at the Louisa May Alcott School, a return to the drama teaching she had always loved. A search immediately began for her replacement.

To help bridge the gap until a new director could be hired, Board members Mary O'Connell, Ann Murray, Jan Feldman, and Assir DaSilva generously stepped in to coordinate all administrative activities. Their responsibilities were increased when Vincent Centeno fell ill and had to severely curtail his time at the school, leaving music and educational planning and decisions to the volunteers, as well as building management, fundraising oversight, and other general management chores.

The extreme commitment of time and energy made by these Board members over the four-month period without an executive director at the school speaks eloquently to the extent to which volunteer engagement can go when individuals are devoted to the mission of an organization.

Several staff members gave extra time, as well, especially Lilly Torres and Iguill Guillermo, who had taken over as general manager when Aubree Weiley left in the fall of 2004 on a two-year leave of absence to participate in a Peace Corps project at a school in Lesotho, Africa.

In spite of the disruption in leadership at The People's Music School, the summer "Thursdays at Six" programs continued as scheduled, to the delight of students and their families, as well as area residents and guests. The final program of the series was a donors' appreciation concert featuring the rarely performed Mozart one-act comic opera *Bastien and Bastienne*, a work composed when Mozart was twelve years old. Soloists from Music of the Baroque included Kathleen and Peter Van De Graaff and Christopher Lorimer, accompanied by Edward Zelnis. All who attended marveled at the amazing talent exhibited by the composer at such a young age. One of those in attendance was a young man named Bob Fiedler.

Not long before, Bob had attended a party at the home of a friend, where he had fallen into conversation with Jan Feldman, who earlier in the year had become the president of the Board of The People's Music School. Jan had talked about his involvement with the school, and when Bob showed an interest, Jan invited him to attend the "Thursdays at Six" concert featuring the Mozart opera.

Jan also casually mentioned that the school was looking for a new executive director, but as he later recalled, he definitely wasn't thinking of Bob Fiedler as a candidate. Bob has always looked much younger than his years, and Jan assumed he was quite young and inexperienced.

But for Bob, within a few minutes of talking to Jan, he felt a flash of recognition that this was exactly the kind of position he had long dreamed of finding, one that combined his passion for music (as a longtime guitarist) with his dedication to service. At the school for the "Thursdays at Six" program, he found himself totally captivated by what he saw, and he became excited at the prospect of joining the school's staff. He decided to speak to Jan Feldman about becoming a candidate for the position of executive director of The People's Music School.

CHAPTER 80

Bob Fiedler Becomes Executive Director

In late July of 2005, Rita and Tomás left for San José, Costa Rica, where Rita had been invited to conduct a master class at the Conservatorio Nacional de Música. While in Latin America, they travelled to Nicaragua, where they visited with their friend Father Joe Mulligan, who had married them in 1978. Father Mulligan was now living in Managua and had become a missionary and advocate for human rights in Central America. With Father Mulligan, Rita and Tomás took a side trip to Lake Managua. They then returned to Chicago in mid-August.

As school began in the fall of 2005, the Board still had not filled the executive director position. During September and October, four promising candidates were interviewed. Bob Fiedler was one of them. After much discussion and review of references, on October 25, a motion made by Mary O'Connell and seconded by Ann Murray, was unanimously approved to offer the position to Fiedler. The new executive director was introduced at the November 16 meeting of the Board, two days after officially starting his new position.

Bob Fiedler had started his career in the private sector after having earned a degree in electrical engineering. After seven years, he began to feel that he wanted to work in an area that more directly benefitted people. Working with a career counselor, he became even more committed to working in an area of human service in the nonprofit sector. In this way he could combine his business skills with his passion for philanthropy.

His first new position was with the Muscular Dystrophy Association (MDA), where he became executive director of the Chicago chapter. After five years at MDA, he decided he would prefer to work for a more grassroots organization, which led him to a local homeless service agency called REST, where he served as development director for five years.

Destiny then intervened when he met Jan Feldman at the summer party and subsequently attended the Mozart opera concert at The People's Music School. When he contacted Feldman about his interest in the executive director position and revealed his age and years of experience, Jan happily added him to the list of potential candidates for the position.

Having lived and worked in the Uptown neighborhood for many years, Bob had actually known a fair bit about the school and the important impact it was making within the Uptown community. He had even crossed paths with Rita at various events around the neighborhood. He was deeply honored and excited at the prospect of following in the footsteps of someone he very much admired.

Bob's challenges were great from the beginning, however. During the prior two years, government, corporate and foundation support of the school had all been deteriorating, and the transition in leadership had caused hesitation even among some of the school's longtime, loyal funders. For the first time, the Board had been forced to take money from the endowment reserves to meet budget.

For Rita and many others on the Board, who had made every effort to spend no more than the current year income, this reality was troubling. Much work would be needed to re-establish ties and revitalize programs and bank balances. One bright spot on the horizon, however, was everyone's excited anticipation of the school's 30th birthday in early 2006.

CHAPTER 81

30-Year Anniversary Celebrated at Orchestra Hall

As early as spring of 2005, the Board and staff of The People's Music School had begun planning for the school's 30th anniversary in February of 2006. The Chicago Symphony had graciously offered for the event to be celebrated at Orchestra Hall, and Excelon had agreed to be lead corporate sponsor. Since there had been no benefit event the prior November during the transition of leadership, major support was anticipated for this 30th birthday party.

The celebration, titled "Musicians in the Making," began at 6:00 p.m. on Saturday, February 25, with a pre-concert buffet supper in the Grainger Ballroom on the second floor of Orchestra Hall. Special honorary awards were presented to two longtime friends and major supporters of the school, Suellen Long and Onnie Darrow. The guests then took their seats for the evening's program of Mozart's *Piano Concerto No. 25* and Schoenberg's symphonic poem, *Pelleas and Melisande*. Daniel Barenboim conducted the Chicago Symphony Orchestra, and Alfred Brendel was soloist in the Mozart.

A post-concert reception followed the program, once again in the Grainger Ballroom, with Maestro Barenboim attending and talking with the guests. The school's birthday was toasted with champagne, as guests enjoyed the buffet tables filled with pastries by chef Gale Gand.

Emcee for the evening was Assir DaSilva, who had graciously agreed in January to once again serve as the president of the Board. In addition to providing a memorable evening for all who participated, the celebration was a successful fund raising event for the school.

Soon after the February 25 event, a second birthday party was held at the school. Once again, Rita was determined to make all members of the school family part of the celebration, even if they could not afford a ticket to the concert benefit evening.

Registration day for the 2006 spring term had confirmed that there were many who desired to be "musicians in the making." Even with the cold winter temperatures, people began to line up the evening before, some bringing tents and camping out. Word had circulated that there would be forty-two openings for new students. By the end of registration day, twice that number of prospective students had been turned away, with many families vowing to come earlier for the next registration.

For the spring term, the number of students stood at 326. Of that number, 40% were male and 60% female; 34% were Latino; 24% were African or African-American; 21% were Caucasian; and 15% were Asian.

Almost ten years earlier, the school had started passing out numbers during the early hours of the day of registration, so people wouldn't have to wait in a line. Now people were coming early and waiting in line to get the numbers. But Rita was determined to see that places in the school would continue to be allotted on a first-come, first-served basis.

"No one is better than anyone else," Rita had told Bob Dotson on the Today Show the prior June. "If the Pope comes, he has to wait in line like everybody else."

CHAPTER 82

Swimming in the Nile

Spring of 2006 brought further visits from Chicago Symphony Orchestra musicians. On March 7, the Icarus String Quartet, under the leadership of violist Max Raimi, gave a concert at The People's Music School, and on April 12, Scott Hostetler presented a lecture/demonstration on the oboe and English horn.

In late April, Rita and Tomás traveled to Santo Domingo, where Rita once again engaged in master classes at the Conservatorio Nacional. Their most anticipated trip, however, lay ahead. Through the inspiration seeded by her third grade geography teacher, Rita had always dreamed of visiting all three of the world's greatest rivers. She had found a way to visit the Mississippi River while at Sinsinawa Mound, but at almost seventy-two years of age, she still had not seen either the Nile or the Amazon.

In June, Rita and Tomás boarded a plane for Egypt. Beginning in Cairo, they explored Saqqara and Alexandria before joining a small group for a boat trip down the Nile, with stops in Abidus, the Karnak temple complex, Luxor, Qena and the ruins of Dendera, the Valley of the Kings and Queens, Kom Ombo, the Aswan Dam, and Philae, a holy island in the Nile River. They then flew to Abu Simbel with its temples of Ramses II.

Rita enjoyed sightseeing and taking photos of Tomás astride a camel, but all through the early part of the trip, she had something else on her mind. Though it was not part of the schedule of the tour, she finally convinced one of the tour guides to let those in the group who were interested take a swim in the Nile. For Rita, it was a mystical experience as she submerged herself in the waters that had flowed past so many centuries of significant world history.

Back on West Eastwood, the six summer "Thursdays at Six" programs continued to celebrate the 30th anniversary year. All were especially well attended. The first four programs featured performances by blues artist Fernando Jones, Fifth House Ensemble, L'Aquarelle Piano Quartet, and the Chicago Chamber Choir.

In late July, Rita's former student and special friend, Mary Frances Lubahn came to stay with Rita for a few days, and, as she often did during those visits, she gave a concert as part of the "Thursdays at Six" series. Her July 27 program featured music by Kurt Weill. Vincent Centeno was her accompanist.

The culminating program of the series, on August 3, involved members of the chorus and orchestra of Music of the Baroque performing works by Purcell, Bach, Handel, Mozart and Vivaldi. During the evening, Board president Assir DaSilva paid special tribute to Jan Feldman, Mary O'Connell, and Ann Murray who were honored for the significant roles they had played in the school's transition in leadership during the prior year.

At the September meeting, Bob Fiedler informed the Board that enrollment at the school was now at 340. Bob also announced several new projects and programs. The Chicago Symphony had made five scholarships available for students from The People's Music School in their Percussion Youth Ensemble program. Entry to the program was contingent on level of proficiency and teacher evaluation. The CSO had also generously agreed to donate all pre-sale ticket profits from the first concert of their 2006-7 season to the school, and they offered discounted tickets for selected concerts to students, parents and faculty.

Also in the fall of 2006, a new partnership began for the school, arising out of the formation of a new Chicago organization of young musicians called International Chamber Artists (ICA). In 2005, the group had formed under the artistic and administrative leadership of pianist and composer Patrick Godon with the mission of: "presenting performances of the highest quality while supporting communities and organizations whose activities supported the growth of classical music audiences." Patrick had served as principal pianist for the Civic Orchestra of Chicago for a number of years, and through that orchestra's partnership with The People's Music School, he had often performed at the school with various Civic musicians. It was therefore natural for him to think of the school as one of the new organization's first partners.

The first public concert to come out of this new partnership took place on September 24 at St. Gregory the Great Church on North Paulina in Andersonville. The concert was free to the public, but the printed program included a short history and description of The People's Music School, and audience members were encouraged to leave a contribution for the school.

During the year that followed, concerts were presented on an almost monthly basis by the ICA. With each concert, a portion of the proceeds was donated to "TPMS" the acronym that had now officially been adopted for The People's Music School. A number of students from TPMS, including pianist Sabriah Wiedman, clarinetist Jonathan Fullman, and brother and sister pianists Rebecca and Hugh Yeh, ages seven and nine, were invited to participate in some of these concerts.

By November, Bob Fiedler was pleased to report that the financial situation had improved, and that it looked like the school would make it to the end of the year with a much smaller budget deficit than in the prior few years. He also announced that through the continuing partnership and support of the International Music Foundation, The People's Music School had provided outreach programs for seventeen different Chicago public schools during the year. On another positive note, audiences for the annual winter concert had increased greatly over the years, and beginning in December 2006, the venue was changed to the People's Church, several blocks to the north, which contained a large auditorium.

The 30th anniversary year ended with a return to the tradition of a year-ending benefit event. On the evening of Friday, December 15, the school celebrated at a "Beethoven's Birthday Bash" at the Hokin Gallery of Columbia College. The night featured hors d'oeuvres and drinks, a musical performance by teachers and students of TPMS, and a silent auction.

As Beethoven had provided an innovative musical bridge between the classical and romantic musical periods, The People's Music School was soon to help create a bridge into new territory in its ongoing commitment to the music education and inspiration of students from Chicago's lower income backgrounds.

CHAPTER 83

Planning for a New Strategic Vision

Shortly after the beginning of the spring term, on January 27, 2007, the Board of The People's Music School held its annual retreat. The prior summer, a committee led by Board members Bob Ford and Patricia Lasley had addressed issues of "resource mobilization." While their focus had been primarily on fundraising efforts, their overriding maxim had been that non-profit organizations that do not change do not survive.

With this maxim in mind, in January Assir DaSilva challenged his Board to "look towards a new strategic vision" for the school. The retreat began with a new quiz, like the one Rita had designed twelve years earlier, examining Board members' knowledge of the school and its history. It was followed by a challenge to members to deepen their commitment to the school in the year ahead. This commitment included both exploring collective dreams and giving creative thought to the school's mission and how it could best be realized in the years ahead.

Early in 2007, Bob Fiedler reintroduced the quarterly newsletter Counter Point to The People's Music School family. In the spring issue, three people were the focus of a section titled "Who's New." The first was Aubree Weiley, who had returned as the school's business manager after her two years in the Peace Corps. The second was Angel Nava, a recent graduate of Columbia College's Arts in Youth and Community Development (AYCD) program, hired as the Aubree's assistant for development and communications. The third was a young Brazilian violinist named Deborah Wanderley dos Santos, hired as a string teacher.

Deborah dos Santos had begun the study of violin at the age of ten in her native Brasilia, Brazil. Like Rita Simó, she studied in a free music school, the Escola de Musica de Brasilia.

"The school was my refuge from a troubled and financially challenged home life," she explained.

As a result of tremendous talent and determination, by the time she was eighteen, Deborah was playing in the Porto Alegre Symphony, one of Brazil's top symphony orchestras. One year later she joined the Youth Orchestra of the Americas, and it was while she was touring with that orchestra that she came to the attention of the Chicago Symphony Orchestra's former principal oboe, Alex Klein, who was also Brazilian by birth. Immediately recognizing Deborah's talent, Klein also realized that she would benefit greatly from further professional instruction, which he learned she could not afford.

In 2005, Klein invited his longtime friend, violist Richard Young to Curitiba, Brazil, to participate in a chamber program. While Young was in Brazil, Klein told him that there was a young violinist he needed to hear. Richard Young was soon sharing Klein's excitement about Deborah dos Santos and wondering what he might be able to do to help her further her career. Back in Chicago, Young approached North Park University with a proposal. If they would enroll Deborah as a full scholarship student, he would join the faculty, teach dos Santos for free, and arrange a free benefit concert with Klein and award-winning Brazilian pianist Ricardo Castro to raise funds to put toward Deborah's living expenses.

Richard Young had a further idea for helping Deborah finance her American studies. He recommended her for a teaching position at The People's Music School. Though Deborah was still officially an undergraduate student, and TPMS generally required that its teachers have a professional degree or certificate, Richard convinced the school that Deborah's performance and teaching skills were outstanding enough to warrant an exception. Little did Richard Young know that his generous act in support of Deborah's education would lead within the following year to a revolutionary development within The People's Music School as it moved forward looking for new ways to carry out its mission.

In the meantime, spring of 2007 brought its usual abundance of visiting speakers and musicians to the school. On February 17, the Chicago Symphony's Creative Director of the "Beyond the Score" project, Gerard McBurney gave a talk, complete with video examples, on the importance of understanding the stories and musical principles behind compositions before they are heard in the concert hall. Ensembles from the Civic Orchestra of Chicago came to the school and gave concerts on March 10 and April 14.

The Chicago Symphony Orchestra also continued its generous sharing of major visiting artists with TPMS. On March 24, the young Chinese pianist Yuja Wang, in town to perform the Prokofiev Second Piano Concerto with the CSO, came to the school to talk with students, faculty and friends.

Special programs telling about the school continued to appear on local television as well. In late May, both CBS, WBBM-TV and local PBS station WTTW-TV aired profiles highlighting the activities and accomplishments of the school.

The 2007 summer "Thursdays at Six" series once again brought excellent free programs to TPMS and its surrounding community. The lineup for 2007, beginning June 28 and ending August 2, included the International Chamber Artists, pianist Mark Valenti, Genesis Opera, and the Chicago Chamber Choir. For the fourth year in a row, the culminating program of the series was presented by artists from Music of the Baroque, the outstanding Chicago early music organization which generously continued to provide a memorable summer evening of music for the Uptown neighborhood. As had become customary, the performance was followed by a reception honoring donors and volunteers of The People's Music School.

CHAPTER 84

Moving Toward a New Strategic Vision

As Deborah dos Santos gave violin lessons to children at The People's Music School, she began talking with Rita about an exciting program she had discovered several years earlier. Upon joining the Youth Orchestra of the Americas (YOA) in 2005, she had become aware of one of its sponsoring organizations, the youth program El Sistema (Appendix VII), a Venezuelan youth orchestra project begun in 1975, that had transformed the lives of over a million at-risk children.

While traveling and performing in Venezuela with the YOA, Deborah had talked with El Sistema's founder, José Antonio Abreu, and with one of his disciples, a rising young conductor named Gustavo Dudamel, and she was struck by the connections between what the El Sistema project was trying to accomplish and what she had experienced in her own childhood. She also took to heart Maestro Abreu's challenge to: "help bring this human development project using music to all corners of the world."

Deborah wondered if the El Sistema concept could be applied in Chicago. Though her earlier life had been focused on music practice and performance, Deborah's friendship with the socially conscious Richard Young coupled with her new admiration for the El Sistema program in Venezuela had expanded her musical horizons in ways beyond performance.

"Richard taught me the importance of both social and personal responsibility," she said. " He opened my mind to the possibility that just as my own life had been transformed, I could also help transform lives through music."

Rita was quite aware of El Sistema and had also quietly wondered if there would ever be a place for the innovative instructional method within The People's Music School's range of activities. She could see that in many ways El Sistema was a logical extension of the philosophy and mission behind TPMS. Both sought the development of human potential through the musical education of children from economically challenged backgrounds.

As instructional methods, however, they were basically different. Students at TPMS began with theory followed by private instruction on an instrument. Ensemble playing came later. In El Sistema, the ensemble, or orchestra, came first, developing a social as well as musical community or partnership from the beginning. Rita encouraged Deborah to share her thoughts with Bob Fiedler.

At first, Bob was dubious. Rita had told him a little bit about the program, so he was vaguely aware of it, but he thought it might be another of a series of passing educational fads. In addition, his hands were already very full with the administrative and financial challenges the school was facing. Though impressive headway had been made in the area of corporate and foundation funding, Bob had just learned that cuts in the Illinois Arts Council budget would mean that the school's grant for the year would be cut in half.

In addition, the building on West Eastwood, now ten years old, was experiencing a series of maintenance and repair problems, several of which would be costly. The school also was facing storage problems and Rita and some Board members were eager to explore the possibility of adding the third floor that had been anticipated in the original architectural plans. Bob could see that amid all these pressures, pursuing Deborah's dream could be very expensive.

On the other hand, as he listened to Deborah and Rita and furthered his own research into El Sistema, Bob's interest grew. He could envision a compelling story to give potential funders to excite them with the idea of making Chicago one of the first cities in the United States to develop an El Sistema youth orchestra program. He learned that El Sistema projects were already being considered in New York City, Los Angeles, and Baltimore. He also saw that exploring the potential of El Sistema could be a good opportunity to foster partnerships with major Chicago music institutions, as well as the Chicago Public Schools system.

But most important, Bob Fiedler could see that the El Sistema mission was virtually identical to that of The People's Music School: free music instruction for at-risk youth, to help them develop not only a musical skill, but also a discipline and a vision for a better life.

When Deborah expressed an interest in traveling to Venezuela in the summer of 2007 to spend two months learning in more detail about the El Sistema philosophy and methodology, Bob encouraged her and did what he could to help. Though The People's Music School could not supply funds for Deborah's travels, Bob helped her secure sponsorship through Eduardo Mendez, director of FESNOJIV, an organization coordinating El Sistema efforts in Venezuela.

Soon after Deborah returned to Chicago from Venezuela, even more deeply motivated about El Sistema than before, she, Rita, and Fiedler began planning how they should proceed. It was clear to all three that in order to start an El Sistema project it would be helpful to have partners within the Chicago music and educational communities.

Fortunately, Bob was scheduled to meet with representatives of the Chicago Symphony Orchestra's education department within a few weeks, and he raised the subject with them. Chicago Symphony management debated the issue and agreed to help explore the possibilities for a Chicago El Sistema program. Bob then approached officials at the Chicago Public Schools Office of Arts Education, who also expressed an interest.

CHAPTER 85

"A Bountiful Harvest of Talent"

Beginning with fall 2007 classes, The People's Music School instituted a new policy regarding entering students. In the past, too many had signed up for an instrument they thought they liked but without much experience or knowledge of the instrument they had chosen. When they began lessons on their instrument after four weeks of beginning theory, they often changed their minds and also, in too many cases, were not sufficiently prepared in music theory basics. This caused great disruption in teachers' schedules as well as a need for teachers to do much remedial theory work.

The new policy required all new students without previous instruction in music theory to complete a full semester of beginning theory before starting lessons on their instrument. During that semester, students were required to sit in on private lessons involving three different instruments that interested them before making a choice. Then they were required to pass a basic elementary theory test before proceeding with lessons on the instrument of their choice. Under this new system, students who were less committed were weeded out before enlisting the time of a teacher. Once a student chose an instrument, there was a better chance that he or she would stick with it.

Even with more strict requirements for new students, however, the registration line for the fall term of The People's Music School was longer than ever. Equally troubling was the fact that the line had begun to form two days ahead of the registration day. While there had been no serious incidents, many of those connected with the school began to worry about the safety of the families waiting in line.

The fall schedule of special events was as full as ever. In addition to an International Chamber Artists concert at St. Gregory Church on September 23, which again involved students from TPMS, many professional groups performed at the school. The week of October 8 alone saw three outstanding events, including a performance by The Pintele Trio on Monday; another by

245

the Brazilian Guitar Quartet on Wednesday, made possible by a partnership with the Ravinia Festival; and a harpsichord workshop on October 13, sponsored by Ars Musica Chicago. After their workshop, Ars Musica Chicago left a harpsichord on permanent loan to the school.

While Rita's thoughts were focused on the many activities surrounding The People's Music School, some students of the school from years past were thinking about Rita and the impact she had made on their lives. In October 2007, Rita received an envelope in the mail with a very familiar name in the upper left-hand corner. It was from Marika Christie, the young student who had accompanied her to the Congressional hearings in 1994. Inside was a card with a message which touched Rita deeply:

> *Dear Rita,*
> *In celebration of my 25th birthday, I purchased a pack of 20 cards imprinted with flowers on the cover and decided to give them to the 20 people who most have shaped my life. After my mother, you were second on my list.*
>
> *You don't know the impact you have had on my life. Thank you so much for pushing me the way you did. I now see that you weren't trying to discourage me, but that you were molding the gifts you saw in me.*
>
> *Again, thank you for your presence in my life. Much of who I am today is because of you.*
> *Marika*

It was also in the fall of 2007 that Bob Fiedler began talking in earnest with the school's Board about the possibility of becoming involved in an El Sistema project. The Board agreed that the idea was worth exploring and encouraged Bob to continue his discussions with the Chicago Symphony and the Chicago Public Schools, so long as no major expenses were incurred or definite commitments made without Board approval. Bob agreed to keep new Board president, Kate Evert, informed of progress.

The fall benefit, titled "A Harvest of Talent," took place at The People's Music School on Sunday, November 4. Rita performed at the benefit along with honors students from the school. It had been a difficult health year for Rita, as she had experienced a series of respiratory ailments. Everyone was happy to see her in good health for the benefit.

One month later, in December, the Jane Addams Senior Caucus honored Rita with their Certificate of Appreciation.

CHAPTER 86

Rita in Los Angeles with Whoopi Goldberg and Susan Sarandon

In February 2008, representatives from the Chicago Symphony and the Chicago Public Schools attended a gathering in Los Angeles to learn more about the El Sistema method. Experts from Venezuela's El Sistema program had been brought in to lead the meetings. As part of the Chicago Symphony Orchestra's "innovation challenge team," on which he had been asked to serve, Bob Fiedler was invited to join the trip. The group returned enthusiastic about what they had learned and agreed to continue talking about a possible collaborative project making use of El Sistema principles.

Rita, in the meantime, was looking forward to a trip that would complete her longtime dream of visiting the world's three major rivers. In late April, she and Tomás left for a cruise along the Amazon River, visiting many ports on the way. At one of the stops, Rita found an opportunity to take a quick swim in the mighty river. Once again, the experience made her feel a deep, almost metaphysical connection with the entire globe and its interconnecting waterways.

At The People's Music School, a new summer event was being planned that everyone hoped would bring in funds for the school and also be an enjoyable time for neighborhood families. On Saturday, August 9, the school held a street festival.

Beginning early on the day of the festival, the block in front of the school was closed to traffic, and a number of booths and tables were set up with food and games for all ages. A temporary stage was erected for musical performances given by students, faculty, and several other performing groups. Roaming clowns and various street performers added to the festive day. Though the event ran a small deficit, all agreed that the festival had been a wonderful mingling event for the school's families and the surrounding community, and it was decided to repeat the festival the following summer with more careful planning designed to make it profitable.

In August, guitar teacher Carter Hoyt received recognition from the Chicago Sun Times in its series "50 People Who Make Chicago A Better Place." Carter, who had begun teaching at The People's Music School following graduation from Roosevelt University, was now in his 32nd year as a teacher at TPMS. He estimated that during that time he had taught more than a thousand students between theory classes and guitar lessons. Throughout the years, his dedication to the school and its mission had remained as strong as ever.

As he told the Sun Times reporter, "Music has given so much to me. Teaching here is a way to give back."

August also brought the resignation of Music Director Vincent Centeno. Vincent had been accepted into the doctoral program in conducting at the University of Oregon beginning with the fall term, and he was eager to continue his education. Bob and the Board decided that Aubree Weiley's music education background qualified her to take on Vincent's responsibilities, and she was promoted to the position, which was now called "program director." In her new position, Aubree was given responsibility for all educational and artistic initiatives of the school.

Chicago's Uptown community had long appreciated the significant impact that Rita and The People's Music School had made in the lives of its residents. In September 2008, the Uptown Chamber of Commerce honored Rita with a Lifetime Achievement Award. At the presentation ceremony, Rita was referred to as "a brilliant gem shining within the Uptown community."

Also, as a past recipient of the Montblanc de la Culture Arts Patronage Award, Rita was invited to travel to Los Angeles for the September 11 presentation of the award to the 2008 recipient, actress Susan Sarandon, at the Angel Orensanz Center. As new chairman of the Montblanc Foundation, pianist Lang Lang was present to greet the crowd. The main highlight of the afternoon for Rita, however, was the mistress of ceremonies, Whoopi Goldberg, whose stories and other humorous observations had everyone in gales of laughter.

CHAPTER 87

El Sistema Begins in Chicago

As the summer of 2008 progressed, the likelihood of The People's Music School working with the Chicago Symphony and the Chicago Board of Education on an El Sistema project was evaporating. Officials at the CSO had decided to move ahead with a different youth initiative that they felt would reach more students across the city, The Institute for Learning, Access and Training. One part of the new initiative was a biennial festival to be called the Chicago Youth in Music Festival. As a member of the innovation challenge team of the CSO, Bob Fiedler was helping to plan the festival. Budgetary pressures were also cooling the interest of the Chicago Board of Education in an El Sistema project.

For all concerned, the timing could not have been worse. Financial markets had begun a slide toward what would become their worst tumble in many decades. In the nonprofit world, as well as in businesses at large, existing programs and projects were undergoing great scrutiny and new ones were being postponed or eliminated. Many foundations were either cutting their levels of funding or delaying their funding decisions.

For several years, The People's Music School's operating budget had been running a modest deficit and the school had needed to draw money from the special reserves fund. Now the value of those reserves was falling along with the financial markets. It was agreed that enrollment for the school in the fall should not exceed 300 students. There would be very little money in The People's Music School budget for an El Sistema project. Bob Fiedler told Deborah dos Santos that without other institutional support, it appeared their hopes for an El Sistema project would have to be put on hold.

Deborah dos Santos was not to be deterred. She enlisted the help of a Brazilian classmate from North Park University, Sara Gomes, and by late summer the two of them had lined up a group of fellow music students from North Park who had agreed to volunteer their time to teach in a program if one could be started.

Deborah and Sara next began a search for musical instruments to use in the program. They were greatly aided in this search by Richard Young, who contacted his friends in instrument dealerships, including Kenneth Stein, Carl Becker, and Shar Music. He asked them to check their inventories of "trade-in" or beginner instruments to look for some they might be able to donate, and he assured them of the legitimacy of Deborah's project and her credentials to make it succeed.

Notices in various publications and through the North Park University communications lines produced other donations both of instruments and money toward the purchase of instruments. The People's Music School also had a cache of instruments in its storage closet that were made available.

Buoyed by Deborah's enthusiasm and success in gaining support, Bob Fiedler agreed to help her investigate possible locations around the city willing to become a "nucleo" or educational site for an El Sistema pilot project. A partnership with a location offsite would be necessary, since The People's Music School's own building could not accommodate an El Sistema-sized orchestra. An offsite location would also fit into the school's commitment to serve and partner with the wider community whenever possible. As their part of the collaboration, the institutional partner would need to supply a venue and, hopefully, at least a little financial support.

By late summer Bob and Deborah had three positive responses: the Robert R. McCormick Boys and Girls Club on North Sheridan; Cornerstone Community Health Outreach Center, a homeless services organization a few blocks west of the school on Clifton; and William G. Hibbard Elementary School, which for almost a decade had participated with TPMS in educational residencies sponsored by the International Music Fund.

It was decided that initial "nucleos" would be set up at each of the three locations and would begin in early October. Much of the work would have to be done by Deborah, Sara, and their teacher recruits, however, as Bob Fiedler was deep into activities for the beginning of the fall term at The People's Music School. To add to Bob's busy schedule, he had been serving as chairman of the Chicago Consortium of Music Schools during most of 2008.

By the end of the fall term, a decision was made to discontinue the El Sistema efforts in both the Boys and Girls Club and Cornerstone Outreach Center and concentrate resources on one location, Hibbard Elementary School. Deborah's teachers were finding that there were too many conflicting activity choices at the Boys and Girls Club, resulting in students beginning the orchestra only to drop out as another activity captivated their attention. At Cornerstone, the highly transient nature of their clients made the program too challenging.

CHAPTER 88

The YOURS Project at Hibbard School

Two months into its El Sistema program, Hibbard Elementary School, located in Albany Park, was proving a perfect fit. For one thing, it was very close to the North Park University campus, making access easy for the volunteer teachers Deborah and Sara had recruited. For another, there were few competing after-school activities, and many of the school's students had working parents who were very happy to have their children involved in a creative after-school program.

Most of all, Deborah could not have found a more welcoming home for her fledgling project. Hibbard's principal, Scott Ahlman, was not only a strong believer in the power and necessity of the arts in young lives but was also the father of several children studying at The People's Music School. He was deeply devoted both to Rita Simó and to the school. He was also eager to expand opportunities for his young students, among whom ninety-six percent were from low-income families. Ahlman was ready to do anything he could to help make the project work.

Because of Rita Simó's long association with Hibbard School through the IMF-sponsored educational residencies and because of Deborah's great respect for Rita, the Hibbard School project was named "YOURS," for Youth Orchestras Uptown (subsequently changed to "Urban" and even later to "United") Rita Simó.

In the fall of 2008, Deborah and Sara recruited thirty-five Hibbard students for the YOURS orchestra, with plans to meet three days a week. The first day of the program, each student was presented with his or her own instrument and given careful instructions on how to take care of it as if it were a special new friend.

In the meantime, financial constraints had resulted in a need for The People's Music School to take a new look at its enrollment demographics. As the January 2009 registration day approached, serious discussions took place regarding the admission policy and programs for adult students. From the beginning, Rita had been deeply committed to the idea that all should be treated equally, and that meant applicants of all ages. Funders, however, were more receptive to the idea of shaping young lives.

In December 2008, the Board made a strategic decision to focus more resources and efforts on children and voted to limit adult instruction to theory classes and group lessons in piano, guitar, percussion, and voice. All adult instruction would take place on weekends.

The school didn't accept any new students in January of 2009, and total enrollment for the spring term was reduced to 240. The financial crisis, now global in its reach, was hitting its lowest point, and along with much of the world, The People's Music School was "battening down the hatches."

Despite all of this, the YOURS Project was thriving. By the second semester, the number of students involved in the program had doubled to almost 70, and they were making impressive progress under their conductor and principal on-site coordinator, Milan Miskovic. Pleased by the increase in the numbers and the enthusiasm of the participants, Deborah and Milan decided to expand the Hibbard YOURS Project from three days a week to five. On May 11, a cover story in the Chicagoland Extra section of the Chicago Tribune spoke of the project's great success and the important social as well as artistic mission it was serving.

The progress being made by the YOURS students was amazing to everyone who came to observe and hear them. On March 20, the YOURS students gave their first concert at North Park University, which included music by Beethoven and Rossini. It was an especially proud moment for parents of the Hibbard students in the orchestra. For most of them, it was the first classical music concert they had ever attended, and it was being performed by their own children.

For the first two semesters of the program, Deborah and her YOURS Project teacher assistants worked almost exclusively as volunteers. It was several years later that Richard Young learned that in order to make ends meet, Deborah had sold her blood, sometimes as much as twice a week. She kept it secret, knowing that Young and her other friends would object and worry about the effect of this practice on her health.

When queried about it later, Deborah responded with a shrug, "Sometimes you just have to do what you have to do. People don't need to know the details."

Richard Young could not help but make a comparison between this determined young lady and the Dominican woman at the helm of The People's Music School, whom he had grown to love and admire.

CHAPTER 89

A Visit from José Antonio Abreu

Rita Simó's schedule in early 2009 was a busy one. In addition to helping with the YOURS orchestra at Hibbard, she had been invited by the Chicago Consortium of Community Music Schools to emcee their January 25 concert at the Chicago Cultural Center. To ensure that the school would incur no costs, she and Tomás also hosted a celebration of the 33rd anniversary of The People's Music School at a "birthday party" at their home on North Clarendon on Saturday, February 21.

Along with everything else, Rita and Aubree Weiley had been meeting for a number of months with a group of individuals working to establish a Chicago High School for the Arts. The idea had begun several years earlier with James Alexander and other representatives of the Elizabeth Morse Charitable Trust, who had observed a lack of ethnic diversity in mid-sized as well as large arts organizations in Chicago. It was felt that part of the reason was the absence of a public arts academy or school within the Chicago system to attract and nurture individuals from a variety of backgrounds.

A group of Chicago arts educators known as the Diversity Working Group (DWG) was formed to begin pursuing the idea, in cooperation with the Chicago Board of Education and the Renaissance 2010 program for establishing charter public schools. Rita and Aubree were members of DWG.

In the fall of 2007, approval had been received from the Chicago Board of Education to proceed with plans for a high school that would be structured to provide both an education focused on the arts and also a comprehensive college preparatory program. With the school scheduled to open in the fall of 2009, the work of the DWG was accelerating.

In March, Bob Fiedler was pleased to report that a student from The People's Music School, Coren Warden, had been accepted into the new Chicago High School for the Arts for the coming year. The process had been very competitive, with only sixty students having been accepted into the music program at the school.

Plans were also accelerating for events within the Chicago Symphony Orchestra's new Institute for Learning, Access, and Training. The first Chicago Youth in Music Festival took place in April 2009. Spread over a six-week period, the festival's centerpiece was a three-day visit by Gustavo Dudamel and the Simon Bolivar Youth Orchestra of Venezuela, which performed several concerts at Orchestra Hall during their visit and also participated in various community outreach projects.

Altogether, the festival involved activities and events with fourteen community arts and school groups across the greater Chicago area, including The People's Music School. One of the school's clarinet students, Jonathan Fullman, was selected to perform in a special youth orchestra with Gustavo Dudamel at Symphony Center on April 11. Members of the Simon Bolivar Youth Orchestra also gave a performance at The People's Music School during their visit.

Among those traveling to Chicago with Dudamel and the orchestra was José Antonio Abreu, founder of El Sistema. As part of his visit, and in conjunction with the festival, Abreu paid a visit to The People's Music School and to the Hibbard YOURS Project. Abreu was so deeply impressed that he declared himself "part of The People's Music School family," and he invited Deborah dos Santos to be an honorary member of El Sistema.

CHAPTER 90

The YOURS Project Becomes a Formal Program of The People's Music School

At the February 2009 Board meeting of TPMS, it had been announced that through a relationship cultivated by Board members Kate Evert and Michael Weis with members of the Student Advisory Board of the Northwestern University Bienen School of Music, a new event was being planned to raise money for The People's Music School. On May 1, a Music Marathon event began on the Evanston campus and lasted over 24 hours. The entire marathon was broadcast over local radio.

Performers signed up to perform for periods of either fifteen or thirty minutes and were required to raise pledges of $100 for each fifteen-minute slot. Audience members were charged a $5 entry fee. The repertoire ranged from Rachmaninoff to Radiohead, and when all proceeds were tabulated, $17,000 had been raised and donated to The People's Music School through the event's planning committee chairman, Russell Rolen.

Through the spring of 2009, Deborah dos Santos had been busy with a project beyond the Hibbard YOURS orchestra and her studies at North Park University. Again working with fellow students and administrators at North Park and other area musician friends, she founded and directed the city's first "Music for Peace Festival," through her involvement with the Chicago Build the Peace Committee.

Chicago had celebrated its first official Peace Day in 1978, four years before the United Nations established its International Day of Peace, and the city had actively continued the tradition in coordination with the United Nations observance. In 2008, an expanded Chicago Build the Peace Committee was formed to plan and carry out Peace Day activities in the city.

While the official Peace Day, as designated by the United Nations, was September 21, 2009, the Chicago Build the Peace committee supported Deborah's plan for a special week in the spring focusing on music as both an international language and a path for creating more purpose-inspired, peaceful citizens among the world's most troubled youth. Though the general goal of the festival was to spotlight various creative ways in which musicians and educators could make a difference in young lives through music, the more specific focus was on the El Sistema method as a tool for fostering the positive socioeconomic development of underserved youth. The YOURS orchestra was featured as a premiere model.

The Chicago Music for Peace Festival took place from May 11 through 16. Deborah dos Santos was artistic director of the festival. Her advisory committee included Rachel Barton Pine, Richard Young, Alex Klein, Rita Simó, and Ann Murray. Many other prominent Chicago musicians joined in the planning and participated in the festival including Dale Clevenger, Yukiko Ogura, Tage Larsen, Roger Chase, Jennifer Gunn, Stefan Hersh, Mathias Tacke, Alvaro Sagastume, Gilson Carnelho, Jasmine Lin, and Andres Lopera. Also joining the group of Chicago musicians were twelve members of the Youth Orchestra of the Americas and several members of the Simon Bolivar Youth Orchestra.

The week's events included workshops, demonstrations, and concerts in a variety of venues around the city. All events were free admission. One of the concerts took place on May 13 at The People's Music School, featuring violinist Rachel Barton Pine and CSO trumpet player Tage Larsen. On Sunday, May 16, the Hibbard YOURS orchestra performed at Symphony Center as part of the festival.

In the meantime, tightened standards at The People's Music School, with increased expectations and structure for both theory education and performance, had brought notable results. Following the May juries, several judges commented that they were highly impressed by the significant progress they had observed among the young students.

As a result of the increased visibility TPMS had been receiving, in the summer of 2009 the school entered into a contract with the George S. May Foundation for the Arts to start music education programs in two Chicago Public Schools, Stephen F. Gale Community Academy in Rogers Park and Circle Rock Charter School in the Austin neighborhood. The programs began during the summer with twenty students in each location, two days a week.

Once again, The People's Music School sponsored a street festival in the late summer. Since the 2008 festival had not turned a profit, there was hope that new organizational procedures would help the 2009 event be more financially successful. Though this second festival was also an enjoyable community event, it resulted in only a minor profit. Given all the work needed to organize the event, it was decided not to repeat the festival in the near future.

In August, Rita and Tomás traveled to Ecuador, where they once again visited with Sonya Rendón and Patricia McTeague. They were pleased to find the Nuevo Mundo school still thriving in its service to children of Guayaquil. While in Ecuador, Rita and Tomás traveled to Coca, where they took a boat to Yarina Lodge in the Ecuadorian section of the Amazon, thus exploring the origins of this mighty river from its western side.

In the fall of 2009, with a strengthening of the school's operating and reserves funds, Bob Fiedler announced that 100 new students had been admitted to TPMS, sixty children and forty adults, raising total enrollment from 240 in the spring term to 308. Of major concern, however, was the continuing development of longer lines waiting for registration to begin. Bob observed that some people had slept outside for three nights.

The Board and staff began to consider whether there might be a better way to deal with this situation while still keeping the enrollment equitable. At the September Board meeting, it was voted to limit registration to once a year, in late August, when the weather was more hospitable, and to add new students in January from the waiting list.

At this Board meeting, the school also voted to formally adopt the YOURS Project, which had previously been considered a pilot project, as an official program of The People's Music School. This meant that significantly more funds would be available to the program, most notably to pay teachers.

Bob was also pleased to announce that the two new educational programs at Stephen F. Gale Community Academy and Circle Rock Charter School had gone well and support for them through the George S. May Foundation would continue into the fall. By early 2010, the foundation was providing funds for similar programs in two additional sites around the city.

CHAPTER 91

The Women's Board of the Ravinia Festival and the REACH Orchestra

Beginning in the early 1970s, the Ravinia Festival Women's Board had created and funded outreach projects designed to bring a more diverse audience to the music festival and to increase accessibility for those with financial or mobility challenges. For several decades, students from The People's Music School had attended numerous Ravinia concerts through these outreach programs and had enjoyed workshops and visits with Ravinia artists as well as pre-concert lectures by area educators. Some of these exchanges were held at the school and others on the festival grounds. Rita Simó often had been asked to present educational pre-concert talks, both in connection with TPMS visits and as a guest lecturer for other participating organizations.

In the fall of 2008, the outreach committee of the Ravinia Women's Board was asked by Chairman Jane Casper and her executive committee to begin looking for a new project that would have "great impact on music education in the greater Chicago area," for which the Ravinia Women's Board would supply major financial support. The co-chairmen of the outreach committee, Patty McGrath and Caroline Huebner, visited a number of sites engaged in innovative music education projects in locations ranging from the south side of Chicago north to the Wisconsin state border.

In May of 2009, Patty McGrath with two staff members from Ravinia's education department, Christine Taylor and Isaac Sinnett, paid a visit to Hibbard Elementary School and a YOURS orchestra rehearsal. Patty was greatly moved and inspired by what she saw and heard. She immediately conveyed her enthusiasm to Caroline, and the two returned a few weeks later for further observation and with many questions. Both were soon convinced that this was an innovative educational project well suited to Ravinia Women's Board interests and resources.

Through the summer and into the fall, the two organizations discussed options for collaborating. During that time, Patty and Caroline gave several presentations on the YOURS Project to their board and encouraged members to visit Hibbard School to observe for themselves. Many did visit and returned with enthusiastic stories.

At Hibbard, the YOURS orchestra had reached impressive maturity and the time had come for the more advanced students to "graduate" into a higher-level orchestra. A new group of beginners was being formed into an entry-level orchestra. As they learned of the growing numbers of children interested in participating, Patty and Caroline began to think that this beginning orchestra would be a perfect focus for a new outreach effort.

By late 2009, the various stumbling blocks had been worked out and approval of an El Sistema collaboration had been reached. Within the Ravinia family, it was decided that the project would begin exclusively as a Ravinia Women's Board initiative. If all went well, it could become a partnership between The People's Music School and the education department of the Ravinia Festival at a later date.

As part of the planning for the new orchestra, teachers from the YOURS Project began instructing Ravinia staff and teachers in El Sistema theory and methodology. Along with providing financial support, Ravinia Women's Board volunteers planned to facilitate other needs of the program, especially the acquisition of instruments.

Beginning in January 2010, the Ravinia Women's Board officially assumed sponsorship of the new beginning orchestra at Hibbard, which was named the REACH orchestra. The orchestra that was entering its second year at Hibbard would continue to be called the YOURS orchestra, and the entire program would continue to be referred to as the YOURS Project.

Rita Simó and Bob Fiedler greatly appreciated this new collaboration with their longtime friends from Ravinia and the increased visibility and financial support it brought to the El Sistema project at Hibbard. With the new funds, 72 students joined the REACH orchestra, bringing the participation in both orchestras to 140 students.

Even with that large increase in total numbers, 200 eager Hibbard students remained on the waiting list for the program. Participating in the YOURS orchestras had clearly become associated with both prestige and having fun. While in many Chicago schools, children involved in sports were the ones the others admired, at Hibbard the "cool" kids were the El Sistema kids, and everyone wanted to be part of one of the orchestras.

Adding to the positive spirit at The Peoples Music School, for the first time in half a dozen years the school not only was meeting budget but also was slightly exceeding budgetary goals. New foundation support, proceeds from the Northwestern Music Marathon, a large estate bequest gift and careful cost containment measures by the staff had come together to result in a $157,000 budget surplus at the end of the year, allowing the school to replenish both general and special reserves funds and to plan more aggressively for the future.

CHAPTER 92

Worldwide Recognition for the YOURS Project

In early January of 2010, Bob Fiedler was pleased to announce that for the first time since the new guidelines had been established requiring students to successfully complete a full semester of theory before choosing an instrument, all children admitted in the fall had passed the rigorous requirements and each had selected an instrument. In order to accommodate this influx in new eligible students, three new teachers had been hired.

Great excitement accompanied the inauguration of the new REACH El Sistema orchestra at Hibbard School on January 25. WGN-TV cameramen were present to record the passing out of new instruments to the 72 REACH students in the new orchestra. Also on hand to help with the festivities were Ravinia CEO Weltz Kauffman, and a dozen women from the Ravinia Women's Board. In addition to an instrument, each student received a blue and white jacket with "REACH" written on the front.

"It was like Christmas with no wrapping paper," exclaimed Ravinia Women's Board outreach committee co-chairman, Caroline Huebner.

On February 20, 2010, The People's Music School celebrated its 34th birthday with a concert and party at the school. Among the highlights were a performance by the YOURS orchestra, and a visit from Dario Ntaca, a virtuoso pianist, conductor and founder of the Greater Buenos Aires Youth Symphony. The day concluded with a special tribute to Board members Ann Murray and Jeff Kelly, who had given the school so many years of dedicated service. In a memorable ceremony, the library of TPMS was renamed in their honor.

Awareness and acknowledgement of the central role being played by The People's Music School in the growing El Sistema movement in the United States continued to build as the year progressed. Four teachers

261

from the YOURS Project attended a training session in Miami during January and shared stories of their experiences with others in attendance. In February, Bob Fiedler and Deborah dos Santos participated in a symposium and concert dealing with El Sistema at Carnegie Hall in New York. About the same time, Bob was invited to join the El Sistema USA Steering Committee based at the New England Conservatory of Music, which had become the center for El Sistema training in the United States as well as the administrative center for El Sistema efforts around the country.

Originally established with funds that El Sistema founder, José Antonio Abreu, had received when he won the TED prize in 2009, the Abreu Fellows Program had begun at the New England Conservatory in the fall of 2009 with its first ten students or "fellows," selected through competition. In each of the subsequent five years, the program was designed to educate ten more students in a rigorous one-year course of study in El Sistema philosophy, theory, and methodology. The last class of ten Fellows was scheduled to begin in the fall of 2013. In the end, a total of fifty young musicians would receive the intensive training in El Sistema as Abreu Fellows, following which they would be ready to contribute to the development of new El Sistema nucleos around the country.

As a further testament to the growing awareness across the country of TPMS and its pioneering El Sistema program, in early March, Bob Fiedler reported that the school had been invited to join a nationwide network created by the Berklee College of Music in Boston. Designed to promote the life-changing role that a contemporary music education can play in the lives of underserved youth, the Berklee City Music Network's goal was to reach out to organizations across the country that were committed to these ideals.

The partnership with Berklee brought many benefits. Students from within the network were offered scholarships for summer study programs and were given priority access to Berklee College admissions and financial aid. Member organizations of the network were given access through computer to a wide variety of interactive educational tools, workshops, and other program aids. Among these was the Berklee PULSE music method, which related elements of traditional theory and ear training to contemporary popular music styles like jazz, rhythm and blues, rock, and hip-hop, as well as to the more classical musical traditions.

As a result of the media publicity surrounding the Hibbard El Sistema project and the additional efforts of the Ravinia Women's Board, the YOURS and REACH orchestras had been receiving contributions of a significant number of music instruments. In early March, Bob announced that these donations had made it possible to add 25 new children to the Hibbard School orchestras. There would now be a REACH A and a REACH B orchestra, providing an additional level of proficiency for the students.

On March 3, the YOURS orchestra joined the North Park University Orchestra in a concert in Anderson Chapel at North Park. Members of the two orchestras joined forces for compositions by Vivaldi, Beethoven, and John Williams. Playing side by side with their older mentors, the young students performed well, according to their university counterparts. In April, the YOURS orchestra gave concerts at both North Park University and VanderCook College.

On April 6, world-renowned violinist Julian Rachlin visited Hibbard School, where he performed and talked with the YOURS and REACH students. The violinist was in Chicago as conductor and soloist for a Symphony Center concert with the chamber orchestra of the Academy of St. Martin in the Fields. Rachlin was quite familiar with the El Sistema movement. Two months earlier, he and fellow violinist Joshua Bell had performed the Bach Double Violin Concerto with the Youth Orchestra of the Americas in Carnegie Hall. The program had included a few remarks by José Antonio Abreu.

As part of the study of music theory, the students of The People's Music School had always been encouraged to experiment with composing their own music. In March, a special competition was announced, open to all students of TPMS between ages eight and eighteen. Deadline for submissions of student compositions was April 1. To help students who had ideas but little experience with turning them into readable musical scores, theory teacher John Elmquist conducted a composing workshop in late March. Composer and saxophonist Amos Gillespie and Duane MacDowell, owner of Music Unlimited, served as judges for the competition.

On Saturday, May 1, the winners were showcased performing their compositions. Student winners included pianists Jovad Uribe, Joyce Matangulhan, Alessandra Cruz, Megan Gary, and Inga Blalach; guitarist Coren Warden; and the grand prize winner, Andre Nguyen, whose composition "Promenade" was performed by teachers Michelle Morales, cello, and John Elmquist, piano.

On the last day of April 2010, students from the Bienen School of Music at Northwestern University once again staged a Music Marathon on the Evanston campus. This year the event was streamed live over the Internet, in hopes of gaining support from alumni and friends nationwide. Proceeds raised for TPMS were just under $15,000.

Throughout the spring, The People's Music School was visited by many individuals from organizations either in the process of starting or hoping to start an El Sistema project, including representatives of groups from as far away as London, England. In early May, Bob Fiedler, Deborah dos Santos, and Milan Miskovic attended an El Sistema symposium in Los Angeles sponsored by the Youth Orchestra of Los Angeles. Over 200 participants from seventeen states and six countries worldwide gathered in Los Angeles for the three-day event, and upon returning, Bob reported, "We received a great deal of acknowledgment of our work."

As summer approached, it was becoming apparent to many that when all regularly-occurring outreach programs of The People's Music School were tabulated, the number of students involved in these programs exceeded that of the school's on-site population. Since the school's goal had always been to reach as many people as possible through the gift of music, this change was considered a positive evolution in the development of the school.

CHAPTER 93

A Reunion with Joel Sheveloff

Exciting news arrived at The People's Music School in late spring of 2010. Patrick Slevin, a percussion teacher in the YOURS Project, had been accepted as one of ten participants in the Abreu Fellows Program at the New England Conservatory of Music for the 2010-11 year.

During the remaining three years of the Abreu Fellows Program, three other teachers from TPMS and the YOURS Project would be among the final total of fifty Fellows. The class of 2011-12 would include YOURS violin teacher Julie Davis, and the final group of ten El Sistema Fellows in 2013-14 would include YOURS string teacher and composer Ayriole Frost and Aubree Weiley, Program Director of The People's Music School. Though participants in the El Sistema training program had originally been called Abreu Fellows, José Abreu insisted on having the name changed midway through the five years to El Sistema Fellows, modestly asserting that it was the method, not the man that should be honored.

In April, Rita received a letter saying that by "special invitation," Joel Sheveloff, her former dissertation mentor at Boston University, had invited her to attend his retirement party. Rita had always felt a deep connection to Sheveloff, not only as a friend and teacher but also because of their mutual admiration of J. S. Bach. Sheveloff had been quoted as saying, "Bach is our Shakespeare, our Pushkin, the greatest mind ever to write music."

In June, Rita traveled once again to Boston for the ceremony. Sheveloff was delighted to see her and asked numerous questions about her "peoples" school. He was pleased to learn how well it had fulfilled the ambitious dreams she had shared with him many decades before. As always, when she was in Boston, Rita reconnected with longtime friends in the city. While Chicago was now Rita's home, Boston, like New York, was still an important part of her life's journey.

CHAPTER 94

YOURS Students Travel to Turin, Italy

During the summer of 2010, two public concerts were scheduled at The People's Music School, Gaudette Brass Quintet on July 21 and VOX 3, a Chicago vocal music group, on August19. As always, both concerts attracted a wide audience from the Uptown community.

Members of the YOURS and REACH orchestras received a special summer treat when they were provided with pavilion seats for a July 13 concert at the Ravinia Festival featuring world-famous violinist Joshua Bell. Ninety-five students, parents, and teachers attended the concert. Following the performance, three violinists from each of the three Hibbard orchestras met backstage with Bell, who signed programs, posed with the students for photos, and shared stories about his early days studying violin. At one point, Bell became the one to ask the questions.

"What is it about learning to play the violin that you like best?" he asked young Freddi Mercado.

The answer came quickly and enthusiastically, " I like the sound...it's so good!"

An especially proud moment for The People's Music School came during July when piano students Rebecca and Hugh Yeh, gave a beautiful piano 4-hands duet performance before thousands of people on the stage of the Pritzker Pavillion in Millennium Park. The pre-concert musicale was organized by the Chicago Consortium of Community Music Schools and featured outstanding students from several Chicago youth music programs.

On fall registration day, August 2010, only 54 new students were accepted into The People's Music School. With growing expenses in the YOURS Project, it was decided that this time no new adults students would be added, while the young student population would remain about the same as in the former year.

Once again, families of prospective students began lining up and camping out three days ahead hoping for one of the available spots. This year, camera crews from local PBS station WTTW-TV were on hand to film the event as part of their preparation for a major story on the school for their Need to Know series, which they hoped to broadcast in early 2011. Over the following months, WTTW reporters and camera crews made several more trips to the school to shoot additional footage for the presentation.

As more resources were being directed into the El Sistema and other outreach projects at The People's Music School, there was some discussion among teacher and administrators about whether some of the beginning instrument lessons could be conducted just as effectively through small group instruction, rather than through the traditional one-on-one teaching. Several major educational studies had pointed out the positive aspects of small group teaching, as students learned from each other as well as from the teacher. Group teaching would also allow the school to expand its ensemble instruction and perhaps enroll more beginning students. Most important, the school had seen the positive results of group instruction in the YOURS Project. It was decided to try the group method in a few carefully selected areas.

With growing programs and increased demands on the budget of the school, Bob was delighted to announce two major late summer fundraising events. On August 6, TPMS was selected as beneficiary of a Platform One "Dare to Dream" Lollapalooza Aftershow at the House of Blues featuring the popular group MGMT. Several students from The People's Music School were invited to perform in an opening act at the concert, a thrilling experience for all who participated.

The second fund raising event occurred on Wednesday, September 22, when the school participated in a Whole Foods "5% Day." Five percent of all sales made on that day in five Whole Foods stores stretching from Lakeview to the South Loop were earmarked for TPMS, resulting in a donation of over $27,000 to the school.

An informal new intern training partnership was formed in the fall of 2010 between the El Sistema-inspired Youth Orchestra of the Americas (YOA) and the Hibbard El Sistema orchestras. Under the agreed-upon arrangement, YOA paid to send some of its musicians to help with the Hibbard project. In exchange, TPMS arranged for housing for the interns. Many were guests of teachers and Board members of the school, including Rita and Tomás.

During October, Rita and Deborah dos Santos were each presented with a Cook County "Award of Excellence" by Cook County Treasurer, Maria Pappas. Also, in the fall of 2010, Rita finished her fourth three-year term as a Trustee of the Chicago Symphony Orchestra, and the orchestra honored her with the title of Life Trustee. As a Life Trustee, Rita continued to attend CSO Board meetings and to participate on various committees, guaranteeing that her influence within the organization would be ongoing.

In late October, three boys from the YOURS Project flew to Turin, Italy, to perform at the biannual Terra Madre Festival, an event attended by over 5,000 people. With all expenses paid by the festival, the boys joined other students from around the world in the Pequenas Heullas Orchestra, a group of young musicians dedicated to making music in support of world peace.

Teacher Milan Miskovic, who had taken over most of the day-to-day leadership in the YOURS program at Hibbard School, accompanied the young students. The trip was a great mind-expanding experience for the young students, none of whom had ever traveled so far from home nor into such a different culture. When they returned, they had exciting tales to share with their orchestra classmates.

One of the boys who made the trip, 7th grade oboe player Alejandro Luna, summed up the experience: "Being part of the YOURS Project has taught me discipline and responsibility, and I now get much better grades. I can't believe I went to Italy! It has changed my life."

CHAPTER 95

The People's Music at 35 Years

In early December of 2010, The People's Music School was again selected as the recipient of funds from a Platform One "Dare to Dream" Lollapalooza Aftershow, this time in connection with a December 4 concert at the House of Blues by the popular group Roots. As before, students from the school were given the exciting experience of performing on the House of Blues stage as an opening act. Attracting an even larger audience than the MGMT concert in August, the event resulted in a significant contribution to the school.

New educational collaborations with two nearby Chicago public schools had been in the planning stage during the fall of 2010, and in early 2011, teachers from TPMS began providing music instruction at Nettlehorst Academy in Lakeview (percussion and choir) and Clinton School in Rogers Park (strings). The two programs served over 500 students. Funding for both projects was provided from the public schools' own budgets, attesting both to their conviction of the importance of music in their curriculums and to their faith in the quality of the instruction resources provided by teachers from The People's Music School.

Students from the YOURS Project continued to perform in various local venues in early 2011. The YOURS orchestra performed at Navy Pier on January 4, playing music from the movie *Star Wars*. They repeated the performance on February 18. Both times Deborah dos Santos conducted. On January 23, YOURS orchestra members performed at the annual concert of the Chicago Consortium of Community Music Schools in Preston Bradley Hall of the Chicago Cultural Center.

On January 31, students from the YOURS and REACH orchestras attended a chamber concert at Symphony Center as part of the kickoff of the "CSO Citizen Musician" project, a new initiative inspired by cellist Yo Yo Ma and implemented through the symphony's Institute for Learning, Access, and Training. The purpose of the project was to inspire local professional musicians to wider community service and to acknowledge those musicians who had used their love of music to benefit the larger community. Rita Simó and Deborah dos Santos were among those cited as examples of CSO Citizen Musicians.

The performing artists for the concert in addition to Yo Yo Ma were pianist Emanuel Ax, and clarinetist Anthony McGill, who had grown up in Chicago and was now first chair clarinet in the Metropolitan Opera Orchestra. Since the Hibbard School students were seated on the stage with the musicians during the concert, they were able to watch them closely. Afterward the students met with the performers for conversation and pictures.

Early in February, Bob Fiedler had an exciting announcement. The People's Music School had been accepted into the Chicago Community Trust's "Smart Growth Program," an initiative designed to support small arts organizations serving underrepresented Chicago communities. The honor came with a three-year grant of between $20,000 and $50,000 annually, with the specific amount to be determined later.

At the same time, Bob mentioned that camera crews and interviewers from PBS, WTTW-TV, were continuing to visit The People's Music School and the YOURS Project at Hibbard in preparation for their special feature on the school and its programs, now scheduled for airing in late spring.

In the meantime, planning for the 35th birthday celebration of the school was underway. The festivities took place on Friday, February 25, 2011, in the Chicago Cultural Center's Preston Bradley Hall. After a reception and gourmet dinner, guests were treated to performances by violinist Rachel Barton Pine and guitarist Steve Vázquez. Also performing during the evening were students from the Hibbard School YOURS Project, People's Music School piano student Hugh Yeh, and the school's piano trio composed of students Hulya Alpakin, Anna Pastrana, and Rosalia Atilano.

Following the program, three people key to the ongoing success of The People's Music School received special awards. Carter Hoyt was honored for his 35 years of service teaching at the school, and Richard Young was thanked for the numerous ways in which he had personally and through the recruitment of friends added to the success of the school.

The third honoree was Alderman Helen Shiller, acknowledged for her long support of the interests of the school and for her efforts over the years to make the school an integral part of the neighborhood and city. In her personal comments to the audience, Helen recalled the year she stood in line at the school hoping to register her granddaughter for lessons.

When asked by several others standing nearby why, given her position of authority, she was waiting in line, she replied, "When Rita makes a rule, she sticks to it. There are no exceptions!"

CHAPTER 96

A "Bricolage" Mural

In early April of 2011, Deborah dos Santos participated in a panel and performance at Harvard University. She was accompanied by YOURS Project teacher Kassie Lord and two girls from the YOURS orchestra, Rebecca Vazquez and Sheila Esquivel, who played in the concert. One of the girls returned wearing a sweatshirt with "Harvard" emblazoned across the front and excitedly told Bob Fiedler and Rita that she was hoping to go to Harvard University for college some day. Rita and Bob both marveled at this aspiration, which most likely would have been unthinkable without the student's YOURS Project experiences.

On the weekend of May 7, Kassie Lord escorted two other girls, Diana Romero and Cindia Dejesus, to Baltimore to perform in another El Sistema concert, while Kassie participated in the accompanying symposium. On Friday of that same weekend, Hibbard School was the site of a symposium held as part of the CSO Chicago Youth in Music Festival that featured three education experts discussing El Sistema projects and social change. A performance by the Carlos Chávez Youth Orchestra from Mexico was the opening event for the symposium. Members of the YOURS and REACH orchestras were invited to join the Mexican orchestra for part of the program.

Soon after the symposium, on May 10, the advanced orchestra in the Hibbard School YOURS program won the highest grade awarded at the 19th annual Chicago Public Schools Elementary School Music Festival. The "honors superior" ratings from all of the judges equated with a perfect 100% score. Over two dozen of the top elementary school orchestras in the city participated in the festival. One of the members of the audience at the festival was the principal of Monroe Elementary School in Logan Square. After the performance of the YOURS orchestra, he approached Bob Fiedler and expressed interest in having an El Sistema orchestra at Monroe. Bob told the principal that they would first have to explore local funding to support part of the cost of the program. It was agreed that if funding could be found, the two would discuss the possibility further.

In the spring of 2011, The People's Music School sponsored a second competition for young student composers. On April 29, winners were honored and their compositions were performed. Winners included Bao Tran Le, Daniel and Maricarmen Villanueva, La'Shenna McConnell, Lucia Lopoez, Theresa Pham, Anna Ingerson, and Joyce Matanguihan.

It was on Friday, April 29, that the long awaited PBS, WTTW-TV, profile of the school was broadcast on the station's "Need to Know" program. The show's tag line stated:

> *From Muddy Waters to The Smashing Pumpkins, to Kanye West,*
> *Chicago's rich and varied musical tradition is well-known to most*
> *Americans. There is, however, at least one aspect of that tradition that*
> *is less famous -- but no less important. In an age when so many*
> *communities are forced to cut music education programs, The People's*
> *Music School has become a lifeline. The tough part? Getting in.*

During the ten-minute program, interviewer Karla Murthy first talked with Rita about her motivations for starting the school and then spoke with students excitedly preparing for a recital day. The majority of the program, however, followed activities of the previous fall registration, with parents and prospective students waiting in line hoping to get one of the open enrollment spots. Current students and parents, who were now helping with the registration process, talked about their earlier experiences waiting in line and their conviction that it had been worth the inconvenience.

Four public concerts took place at The Peoples Music School during the summer of 2011. Spektral Quartet and Vox3 performed in July and Gaudete Brass and Blagoj Lamnjob in July. When the weather permitted, programs were given on the school's open second floor deck. To add to the excitement surrounding these concerts, the deck was undergoing a dramatic transformation, which summer audiences watched with great interest.

Earlier in the spring, Denise McCracken, the development director at the school had approached representatives of the Green Star Movement, an organization promoting public art projects, which had received support from Maggie Daley's After School Matters program in creating public art murals around the city. Denise thought it would be fun for The People's Music School to have a bricolage mural project on the outside of their building. Green Star agreed, and a design was created. Soon, work on the bricolage began on the open second floor deck of The People's Music School.

By mid-summer, the wall behind and along side the elevated bleachers was coming alive with mosaics, mirrors, and paintings portraying a girl playing a trumpet, a boy with a cello, and another girl playing a piano. From the center of the piano, there streamed an undulating ribbon decorated as a musical staff that moved first upward and then swirled down and around a small global earth. The notes on the staff were the notes to Hugo Teruel's song "Listen to the Children," written for the school and its students many years before.

Hidden within the larger patterns of the mural were small photo reproductions of actual students and classes at the school, which had been burned onto tiles and cemented into the mural. These photos served as recognition of the specific human history within the larger and more symbolic artistic representations. Among the many small photographic reproductions on the wall, there were several showing Rita Simó, both alone and with her students.

But Rita was also symbolically captured in the main art of the mosaic. Students of The People's Music School had helped design the mural. In their minds and the minds of all of Rita's friends, the little girl at the piano sending music to the world was Rita, a testament to the power and scope of what one person with a determined vision and a great deal of talent and energy could accomplish.

CHAPTER 97

The Rita Simó Scholarship at North Park University

Along with the bricolage project, plans for an another lasting tribute to Rita were progressing during the summer of 2011. Almost a year earlier, Bob Fiedler had begun meeting with representatives of the North Park University administration to explore a plan to create a scholarship in honor of Rita Simó.

By early February of 2011, the details had been worked out. The two organizations, in partnership, would offer a four-year scholarship, the "Rita Simó Scholarship," which would be given to a lower-income student from Central or South America to study at the college. Part of the agreement included an internship by the recipient with the YOURS Project. The first scholarship was awarded to a Brazilian student, Francisco Malespin, for the 2011-12 academic year.

Through the summer of 2011, discussions took place between representatives from the Ravinia Festival and The People's Music School regarding the creation of a longer term El Sistema partnership. However by late summer, negotiations between the two organizations had arrived at an impasse, leading to the amicable agreement that for both sides it would be best to continue El Sistema projects independently. The People's Music School would continue the program at Hibbard School, while the Ravinia Festival would plan for the creation of an El Sistema orchestra program at a school in which it had provided music instruction since 2008, Catalyst Circle Rock Charter School in the Austin neighborhood of Chicago. The Ravinia Fesstival's new El Sistema orchestra, to be called The Circle Rockets, was scheduled to begin in the fall of 2012.

Seasoned teachers from the YOURS Project were contracted to coach prospective teachers hired by Ravinia for their new program, and Javier Payano, a veteran teacher in the YOURS Project, was selected as the new program's director. In the meantime, the Ravinia Women's Board planned to continue to help fund the Hibbard orchestras for the near future, and Women's Board volunteers continued to welcome and encourage YOURS musicians at Hibbard School through the 2011-12 school year.

During this same time, there was growing uncertainty regarding leadership within the YOURS Project. For several years, it had been assumed that once Deborah dos Santos finished her education at North Park University, she would begin the process of acquiring a permanent visa and join the staff of The People's Music School as the director of the El Sistema projects. But Deborah had found herself in great demand throughout the Western Hemisphere as an advisor to new El Sistema nucleos. She was regularly spending as much time out of the country as she was in residence in the United States, which was negatively affecting her visa application. During her absences, everyone at TPMS very much appreciated the extra effort made by Milan Miskovic in competently filling an expanded role in the YOURS Project.

The end of summer brought a sad farewell to a longtime, devoted friend of The People's Music School. In August, Carter Hoyt retired after 35 years of teaching guitar and theory lessons at the school. Family health problems, coupled with the long commute from his home near the Wisconsin border, had made continuation of his teaching obligations very difficult.

CHAPTER 98

Meeting New Challenges in the YOURS Project

During the summer of 2011, it was announced that there would be only twenty-five openings for new students at The People's Music School for the upcoming year. As word got around about the limited number of spaces, the line of applicants began to form six days before the registration date of Saturday, August 27. On that day, the New York Times ran a story complete with photo about the school and the long registration lines, a story read across the country. Though no significant adverse situations occurred, it was now clear to Bob Fiedler and the Board that the current system of registration could not continue, and they began to discuss alternatives.

A thrilling opportunity for students of the YOURS Project came on September 9, when they were invited to join the hot new pop band Plain White T's and to perform with them at a concert at Daley Plaza in the center of the city. The outdoors concert attracted an audience of several thousand, who cheered the students as well as the pop band.

A few weeks before fall classes began, Bob received word that Monroe Elementary School had secured a special grant from the Logan Square Neighborhood Association, and they were hoping to be able to start an El Sistema orchestra as soon as it could be arranged. Since the ethnic and financial demographics of the area were similar to those of Hibbard School, Bob and the Board agreed that this could be a good location for a new El Sistema initiative.

A pilot orchestra program was begun at Monroe in November with the understanding that if all went well, the school could become the YOURS Project's second nucleo site. Sylvia Carlson was hired as the part-time director. To help the new group get off to a good start, students from the Hibbard orchestras went to Monroe Elementary School to perform and share their experiences with the children in the new orchestra.

In early October of 2011, word arrived that Deborah dos Santos' visa application had been denied. This was a deeply disappointing setback for the school, but Bob and the Board immediately set out to investigate what steps they might take in response.

As The People's Music School dealt with Deborah's visa denial, everyone was very grateful for major financial support received during the fall from several new sources. In October, the school learned that it had finished in first place in the Chicago Sun Time's Sunshine Project in the Arts/Culture category. By November, the Sun Times Foundation had announced that the school would receive the highest grant awarded that year, $45,000.

A few months later, the school learned that their grant from the Chicago Community Trust Smart Growth program would provide $40,000 for each of the next three years. All of these developments put the school on stable financial ground for the year ahead.

CHAPTER 99

Rita Simó: Latina of the Year

The final months of 2011 continued with a flurry of activity at The People's Music School. In addition to the developing program at Monroe Elementary School, new students were welcomed into the various Hibbard School orchestras. In November, The People's Music School was invited to participate in an eight-week exhibit at Expo 72 on East Randolph. Titled "Chicago Organizations Making a Difference," the exhibit was designed to showcase important creative initiatives within Chicago organizations and to encourage community and business support for them.

At 931 W. Eastwood, well-known professional musicians continued to perform on the school's concert stage. On November 23, Rachel Barton Pine gave a concert featuring all Latin composers, and on November 30, pianists Saori Chiba and Paul Dykstra performed six compositions for piano, four-hands, a performance partially funded by the Illinois Arts Council and the CityArts program of the Chicago Department of Cultural Affairs.

During Thanksgiving week, two students from the New England Conservatory El Sistema Fellows program paid a visit to The People's Music School. One, a young man from Mississippi named Albert Oppenheimer, was particularly inspired by what he saw.

Entering Hibbard School, Albert was immediately confronted by a wall of pictures of students from one of the grade levels at the school, each accompanied by a self-introductory paragraph. Some of the photos were only of the child. A few children held a baseball glove or a soccer ball. But an overwhelming number had been photographed holding music instruments, and the accompanying narratives spoke about their love of their instrument and of music.

To Albert, the message was clear. Here was an inner-city school in which the usual social and cultural dynamic had been dramatically shifted, shifted through El Sistema. He was deeply moved.

On December 10, The People's Music School was the beneficiary of the proceeds from the 9th Annual Holiday Show presented by members of the popular band Umphrey's McGee at the Park West on the corner of Clark Street and Armitage Avenue. In addition to the main show by the band, the People's Music School youth choir was invited to the stage to sing two songs, "Octopus's Garden" and "Christmas Time is Here."

November of 2011 brought an exciting and deeply significant new honor to Rita Simó. In recognition of her many accomplishments, the Chicago International Latino Cultural Center had named Rita its "Latina of the Year," and during the organization's Latino Music Festival, held in late November, she received special recognition for her many accomplishments. The high point of the festival was a November 20 concert by members of the Civic Orchestra of Chicago, conducted by Cliff Colnot, in Buntrock Hall at Symphony Center. The evening's program consisted of music by Latin composers Aristides Lianeza, Marcos Balter, and Carlos Chávez. Rita was the guest of honor for the evening.

At a post-concert reception, Rita received her award in front of a full capacity crowd of friends and admirers. Composer Elbio Bariliari, who presented the award, told the audience: "As a pianist, educator, and cultural activist, Rita Simó is a role model like no other in the Chicago musical scene."

CHAPTER 100

Looking for New Leadership in the YOURS Project

The year of 2012 began with new leadership for The People's Music School Board. After four years as president, Kate Evert retired and Chris Hennessy took over as president. Also, by January of 2012, the school was looking for new leadership for the YOURS Project. Bob had received word that Deborah dos Santos, frustrated by her visa issues and desiring to return to more familiar home ground, had accepted a position in Brazil. A search began for a new YOURS Project director. In the meantime, Milan Miskovic continued as director of the program at Hibbard School and Sylvia Carlson was named director of the program at Monroe Elementary School.

Though Bob Fiedler reached out in several directions in his search for a new YOURS Project director, he particularly focused on the current class of El Sistema Fellows at the New England Conservatory. In mid-January, Fellowship Director Erik Holmgren, who regularly notified the current class of job opportunities, announced the opening at the YOURS Project in Chicago. Three of the current ten El Sistema Fellows expressed interest, and all three were invited to Chicago for interviews. Albert Oppenheimer was one of the three.

The school's search for a new director coincided with a burgeoning worldwide awareness of the YOURS Project. A new book, *Changing Lives: Gustavo Dudamel, El Sistema and the Transformative Power of Music*, had just been published in January of 2012, and it was getting broad attention around the world. Contained within the book was a section describing the YOURS Project and its history.

Locally, PBS, WTTW-TV, once again approached the school about doing a profile, this time focused on the YOURS Project. Representatives of the local press and television channels were frequently in attendance at programs in which the YOURS orchestras performed.

The three El Sistema Fellows arrived for their interviews in February of 2012. Though he had been at the school the prior November, Albert Oppenheimer became disoriented as he approached the intersection of Wilson Avenue and Sheridan Road near his scheduled interview time. Approaching Sheridan Road, he encountered an older woman heading in the same direction, bundled up against the cold and munching on McDonald's French fries.

Figuring she looked like a person who must know the neighborhood fairly well, Albert asked her which way he should go in order to get to The People's Music School. She pointed to the intersection ahead and indicated the way he should turn. She then proceeded to engage him in friendly conversation for several minutes about the weather and events in Chicago. Eventually, commenting on his southern accent, she asked him why he would want to come to Chicago in the winter. As he explained his reason for being there and introduced himself, he felt it was only polite also to ask her name.

"Rita Simó," was the reply.

CHAPTER 101

Launching the National Alliance of El Sistema Inspired Programs (NAESIP)

Students from both The People's Music School and the YOURS Project continued performing in key venues around the city in early 2012. On February 12, the school's piano trio participated in the annual Chicago Consortium of Music Schools concert in Bradley Hall of the Cultural Center, and on Thursday, Feb. 23, members of the YOURS Project performed in the lobby of the Harris Theater prior to a performance by the New Millennium Orchestra.

On March 9, 2012, The People's Music School held its 36th anniversary celebration at an unusual venue, the stage of the Jay Pritzker Pavilion in Millennium Park, which had been closed off to the general public for the winter but was still heated. The evening's event was titled, "A Night of a Little Music," a playful turn on Mozart's *Eine Kleine Nachtmusik*. As a special treat, students from the school and the YOURS orchestras were invited to attend and to perform on the large stage on which many of them had seen major stars perform. Knowing they were performing in a space formerly occupied by their musical idols gave the students a great thrill.

Also in March, Bob Fiedler announced that Albert Oppenheimer had been hired as the new director for the YOURS Project and would begin working in June after completing the El Sistema Fellows program. From their first meeting, Bob felt that Alfred would be a natural fit for the YOURS Project.

At the same time, Bob reported that two new schools, Skinner North and Sumner Elementary, had contracted with The People's Music School for after-school music instruction programs. As a result, four public schools were now involved with TPMS in after-school music partnerships in addition to the two YOURS Project schools.

In the meantime, the El Sistema USA organization was in a state of transition. In the fall of 2011, the New England Conservatory had announced that it would no longer serve as the main coordinating center for national projects patterned after the El Sistema method, as it needed to redirect its resources to other priorities. The El Sistema Fellows Program at the conservatory would also be ending in a little over two more years.

At a fall meeting in Boston, representatives from various El Sistema projects from around the country agreed to pursue the formation of a new national organization to serve as an administrative and coordinating body for El Sistema projects within the United States. A series of group conference calls among leaders of some of the more established El Sistema projects resulted, and movement was made toward the creation of the new organization.

The need for such an organization and for continuing collaboration among U.S. El Sistema projects was obvious. From only three El Sistema programs in the United States in 2008 when the YOURS Project began, by the end of 2011, the number had grown to include nearly 50 projects operating as "El Sistema-inspired nucleos," so termed because of the varying degrees in which they employed the El Sistema methodology.

During the weekend of January 30 through February 1, seven representatives from The People's Music School and the YOURS Project attended an El Sistema symposium in Los Angeles. At the symposium, Bob Fiedler offered to host a convention in Chicago during the spring for the creation of a more detailed plan for the new El Sistema organization and the drafting of necessary incorporation documents. By March, a conference had been scheduled for the weekend of April 28, with the expectation that representatives from dozens of El Sistema-inspired groups across the country would attend. It quickly became referred to informally as the "drafting convention."

In the meantime, on Tuesday evening, April 17, Hibbard School welcomed an eminent youth orchestra from Versailles, France, L'orchestre du Collège Jean-Philippe Rameau, which gave a free public concert at the school as part of a weeklong visit that included concerts in Preston Bradley Hall of the Cultural Center and in the Ravinia Festival Bennett Gordon Hall. The orchestra was made up of students from schools around Paris and the Versailles region. Those who attended agreed that the concert and the exchange that followed provided an excellent cross-cultural experience for all involved.

The drafting convention for the new U.S. El Sistema organization began on Friday, April 27. Over the next few days, a great deal of progress was made toward the formation of the new alliance and the guidelines by which it would operate. The name decided upon for the new organization was: National Alliance of El Sistema Inspired Programs (NAESIP). As the facilitator of the symposium, Beth Babcock commented at the end of her summary of the weekend, "In Chicago we played and struggled, and we became even more convinced that this path was possible."

CHAPTER 102

Albert Oppenheimer, New YOURS Project Director

Through the spring of 2012, The People's Music School continued to receive frequent visits from representatives of organizations hoping to develop an El Sistema program. Many were from Midwest cities, but others came from states farther away and occasionally from other countries. In mid-May, visitors arrived from South Korea. All who came to observe the YOURS Project were impressed and inspired by what they saw happening in the Hibbard and Monroe orchestras and went back to their homes with new ideas and increased enthusiasm. As Abreu had hoped, the El Sistema torch was being passed from one nucleo to the next.

Though he made several short trips to Chicago in April and May to start getting acclimated to The People's Music School and the YOURS Project, Albert Oppenheimer officially took over the reins for the project in June of 2012. A native of Starkville, Mississippi, Albert had grown up surrounded by music. Both of his parents played in the local community orchestra.

Albert's first instrument was the French horn, but within a few years he had achieved reasonable mastery of several other instruments, as well. He also developed a strong interest in theater and in the ways that music compositions and theater can intertwine with powerful effect. When asked how he thinks of himself as a musician beyond his commitment to the El Sistema teaching method, his response is "as a composer, a postmodernist composer influenced by a wide range of styles."

A graduate of the New England Conservatory on both undergraduate and graduate levels, Albert was attending the school as it became involved with the El Sistema method of music instruction. He was immediately attracted to El Sistema's social change initiative coupled with its joy of music-making, and he applied to become an El Sistema Fellow.

On June 11, PBS, WTTW-TV, aired its ten-minute special broadcast on the YOURS Project as part of the Chicago Tonight program. Produced and narrated by Jay Shefsky, who was introduced by the program's host, Phil Ponce, the presentation followed the Hibbard YOURS orchestra during a concert. It also included interviews with several children from the YOURS Project, including violinists Sheila Esquivel and Eva Roman, cellist Giang Vu, and eight-year-old Jonathan Alday, who was mastering the art of conducting along with learning how to play the violin. All of the children spoke of how much they enjoyed playing their instrument and being part of the orchestra.

In addition to the enthusiasm of the students participating in the orchestra, the video showed the proud and attentive faces of parents and siblings in the audience, many of whom were having their first experience with music by classical composers including Dvorak, Rossini, and Beethoven. There was every good reason for them to be proud. The music was being played on a very high performance level.

Jay Shefsky's opening comment said it all, "When I go to an elementary school performance, I expect little more than to be charmed by the enthusiasm of the children. I don't expect to have my breath taken away."

CHAPTER 103

No More Lines: Registration by Lottery

Activities continued at a busy pace during the summer of 2012 at The People's Music School. On June 16, the school's jazz ensemble performed at a Chicago Park District event. On Friday, August 10, the Martin Quartet, composed of four siblings from the Martin family, gave a short program at Millennium Park before the evening's performance by the Grant Park Orchestra of Handel's *Creation*. The quartet, made up of violin, flute, trumpet, and piano, also performed later in the year at the Arts and Business Council's annual gala.

On July 29, the Ravinia Women's Board sponsored a "Festival Day" event for Hibbard and Catalyst Circle Rock El Sistema students, which, along with supper and an evening concert by the Chicago Symphony, included an instrument petting zoo. Children who had not yet begun their music study were encouraged to explore their options for an instrument to study, while those children already playing an instrument helped demonstrate them and answered questions.

In August, Mary Frances Lubahn came for an overnight visit with Rita. She arrived with Maria Zielinski, another former student of Rita's from Santa Clara. Though now semi-retired from operatic singing, Frances was still teaching at the University of Music and the Arts in Graz and doing a few minor opera roles at the Graz Opera House. Once again, Mary Frances gave a concert on the stage of The People's Music School.

In addition to his responsibilities with the summer YOURS Project activities, Albert Oppennheimer was also busy working with North Park University staff and teachers who had expressed interest in creating the first undergraduate degree program with an El Sistema emphasis in the United States. The Los Angeles Philharmonic and Longy Bard School of Music had recently created a master's degree El Sistema program and were glad to advise Albert and North Park on their effort.

Albert and Bob Fiedler were also faced with finding a replacement for Milan Miskovic, the director of the Hibbard School nucleo. Milan had announced that he planned to return to school fulltime in the fall to pursue a career as a Chicago public school teacher. Sylvia Carlson was given fulltime responsibilities for the orchestras at Hibbard.

For a number of years, the Board of The People's Music School had debated the best way of handling the problems caused by the first-come, first-served registration policy at the school. By summer of 2012, it had become clear that it was time to come up with a different system. All agreed, however, that the new system should preserve the spirit of fairness and openness that had always been Rita's primary goal. The only answer seemed to be the establishment of a lottery.

In early August, The People's Music School announced that sign-ups for the lottery would occur on Friday, August 10, from noon to 7 p.m. and on Saturday, August 11, from 9:00 a.m. to noon. Parents could come to the school only once during those times and could submit an application for only one child. Signups by phone or computer would not be accepted, and no name was to be submitted more than once. Only prospective students 18 years of age and under could take part in the lottery.

On the afternoon of August 11, names of the new students were drawn from a large, rotating drum by Rita Simó. While the drawing was not open to the public, it was videotaped for later viewing, so that everyone could be assured of the fairness of the procedure. Inside the lottery drum there were 137 names from which 70 new students were selected, bringing the total number of students in The People's Music School to 213.

At the same time, Albert shifted some YOURS Project resources from Hibbard School to allow for growth at Monroe Elementary School, where plans were moving forward to add a second orchestra. It was anticipated that the Monroe School orchestras would grow from 40 to 100 participants. With 170 students in the Hibbard orchestras, the total number of students benefitting from the YOURS Project would now be 270. Combining the numbers from the YOURS Project with the on-site program, The People's Music School was now providing in-depth free music education for 483 young students, most of them from lower-income families.

CHAPTER 104

Another Visit with José Abreu

During the fall of 2012, complications arose with the Monroe Elementary School location for the Logan Square YOURS Project, and it was temporarily moved to the Kosciusko Park Fieldhouse. However, that structure had little storage space for instruments. Several other schools in the area had expressed interest in serving as a base for the orchestras, so Bob and Albert began investigating those alternatives. Though these changes of venue caused some disruption, there was also a positive side to the transition. The Logan Square nucleo was beginning to draw students from several different area schools, thus broadening the reach within the community.

On October 25, the new Ravinia-sponsored Circle Rockets El Sistema orchestra was officially launched. Children from the YOURS Project were on hand to share their experiences and join in the celebration. For many of the children, it was a chance to renew friendships they had made earlier in the year at events shared by both schools. In addition to the summer festival visit sponsored by the Ravinia Women's Board for all the orchestras, Circle Rock students interested in music study had attended a Hibbard orchestra concert at the end of the prior school year, and soon afterwards, Hibbard YOURS students had traveled to Circle Rock to perform for students and their families.

Three El Sistema Fellows visited The People's Music School as part of their training during October and early November. Two of them, Rachel Hockenberry and Xóchitl Ysabela Tafoya, wrote extensive Facebook accounts of their visit. Xóchitl commented on how inter-supportive and unselfconscious the students were. She spoke of one situation in which a student who had a big solo in one piece was unable to attend a rehearsal. In response, the others in the section had eagerly taken turns sight-reading the solo, some with more success than others. But all who tried were encouraged and applauded for their attempts by their contemporaries.

In another example, Xóchitl spoke of the efforts one orchestra made to master the entries in a Vivaldi fugue, a difficult synchronization of counting and listening. When, after several unsuccessful attempts, they finally "nailed it," the resulting group euphoria was instantaneous and unanimous.

It was also in October that Program Director Aubree Weiley, announced that a student at the school had expressed interest in studying harp, and she was exploring that option for the following semester. At the same time, Aubree and Albert had begun creating a contemporary music study and composition program that they hoped could include students from both the Urban Academy and YOURS Project. While they had hoped to combine students from the two groups, they found this was impractical because of transportation difficulties for the YOURS Project students, so two separate programs were developed.

The year ended with several significant events for students in the YOURS Project. On Sunday, December 2, students from the YOURS orchestras performed privately for José Abreu at Symphony Center prior to a concert by the Simon Bolivar Orchestra. Abreu greeted the children warmly and presented each with a Venezuelan jacket. He also invited the students to sit in and play with the orchestra in Caracas if they were ever able to make the trip to Venezuela.

Then, on Wednesday, December 19, the Knox Youth Wind Ensemble from Australia visited Hibbard School, where they gave a concert and then played along with the YOURS students during a rehearsal. Once again, the coming together of two very different cultures was an enjoyable educational experience for all involved. At the end of the visit, the Australians said that they hoped the Hibbard musicians would be able to visit Australia some day.

As Bob Fiedler observed following the two invitations, "It's always wonderful to have dreams to ponder."

CHAPTER 105

Logan Square Orchestras at Ames Middle School

January of 2013 began with the news that the Logan Square orchestras had found a new home at Ames Middle School, about ten blocks south of Kosciusko Park. Now called YOURS Project Logan Square (YPLS), the project was currently drawing students from several area schools, including many who had been involved with the orchestras at Monroe Elementary School.

At the same time, Bob Fiedler announced that all of The People's Music School's other "fee-for-service" after-school programs were being discontinued. New funding from Mayor Emanuel's recently announced comprehensive cultural and arts education plan had resulted in the hiring of more music teachers and support staff within Chicago schools, including several of those who had been contracting for music instruction through The People's Music School. For the time being, at least, the financial and manpower resources of The People's Music School would be directed solely toward on-site and El Sistema efforts.

On January 14, Aubree Weiley escorted 90 students from the school to an open dress rehearsal of the Chicago Symphony Orchestra, as part of the opening of the CSO's Youth in Music Festival celebration. At the end of the final week of the Youth in Music Festival, on Saturday, February 2, musicians from the YOURS Project performed side-by-side with musicians from the Orchestra of the Americas and the Civic Orchestra in a concert program at Hibbard School. The students had been prepared for the concert earlier in the week following coaching sessions and sectionals with guest musicians from the visiting orchestras.

Sad news arrived at The People's Music School in early February. Former Executive Director, Mary Ellen McGarry, had died unexpectedly on February 2. Though she had struggled with illness and had resorted to using a cane and a portable oxygen tank, Mary Ellen had continued in her teaching position at Louisa May Alcott School up to the end.

In mid-February, Bob announced that Albert Oppenheimer had been elected to the newly formed Board of Directors of the National Alliance of El Sistema Inspired Programs (NAESIP). Soon after joining the board, Albert was named coordinator for the Midwest region of the organization.

Friday, April 19, was announced as "Day of the Canadians" at TPMS. Canadian pianist Marika Bournaki, star of the award-winning documentary "I am not a Rock Star," performed on the stage of The People's Music School while in town for a film festival. On the same day, a touring high school band from Quebec, Canada, performed at Hibbard School.

As 2013 progressed, The People's Music School continued to play a central role in the coordination of arts education efforts in Chicago. On April 20, the school hosted the first "Arts Assessment Swapmeet," organized by Chicago Arts Partnerships in Education (CAPE) to analyze and compare assessment instruments and strategies for music education programs.

CHAPTER 106

Two Days with TED

As a result of the many media stories about its two El Sistema nucleos, The People's Music School received periodic inquiries from various Chicago schools or park districts interested in starting an El Sistema program. Often the stumbling block was the site's inability to come up with adequate funding support or a suitable space. By spring of 2013, Albert Oppenheimer was thinking that since the Logan Square project was maturing nicely, it was time to give more serious thought to exploring possibilities for a third nucleo location.

When individuals from Evanston, Chicago's neighbor suburb to the north, approached Albert in the spring of 2013 with an interest in developing an El Sistema program, his first reaction was to assume that too few of the city's students were from low-income families. After educating himself further, however, he was convinced that Evanston had many areas where the demographics were quite suitable for an El Sistema program and talks continued.

In mid-May, The People's Music School received bittersweet news. Aubree Weiley learned that she had been admitted to the final class of El Sistema Fellows at the New England Conservatory. YOURS Project teacher Ayriole Frost had also been selected. Competition for the spots had been intense. Of the ten-member class, only six were from the United States. The other four were from Singapore, Tanzania, Germany, and South Africa, attesting to the growing worldwide interest in the El Sistema method.

While the school was proud that two of its own had been chosen for the final group of ten students, replacing them would be a challenge, especially in the case of Aubree, who had directed the educational programs at The People's Music School for five years as well as having been an employee for most of the preceding ten years. As a final farewell gift, a large framed composite photo of the school's musical groups was made and signed by all the students. It was presented to Aubree following the school's spring concert.

The 37th anniversary benefit celebration of The People's Music School was held on May 17, later in the year than usual, at The Grid on West Hubbard Street. For the children in the advanced orchestra of the Hibbard YOURS Project, however, a much more exciting event had occurred several weeks before, on May 3 and 4, when they gave two performances at the TEDxMidwest conference, participating in both the adult and youth days of the event.

Albert Oppenheimer had been selected as one of the speakers for the three-day conference, and his presentation on the El Sistema method and how it had transformed several Chicago communities included performances by the YOURS orchestra on the stage of the Harris Theater. The experience was a great awareness builder for all involved, both for the audience and for the students, who found themselves surrounded by world-recognized innovative thinkers from many fields, including business, science, technology, education, philanthropy, and art.

Albert was also a member of the Co-op, a new group that had evolved out of Chicago Ideas Week, an annual gathering of local leaders interested in stimulating new initiatives and creative thought, somewhat on the model of the TED organization. The Co-op was dedicated to eliminating barriers between community organizations and inspiring collaborative efforts.

At a spring gathering welcoming new members of the Co-op, Albert was mixing with the crowd when a young man noticed the word "music" on his name tag. When Albert mentioned that he was employed by The People's Music School, the man became quite animated. He identified himself as Sean Ackerman and told Albert that he had been a percussion student at the school. He was currently helping to form a Chicago chapter of Sponsor Change, an organization aiding young professionals in paying off student loans in exchange for volunteer service with nonprofit groups. Sean told Albert he had used The People's Music School as a model for Sponsor Change. He spoke of his wonderful memories of the school and its energetic leader.

"Is Rita still there?" he wanted to know.

CHAPTER 107

Natalie Butler Joins The People's Music School

On May 31, 2013, a concert took place featuring both the YOURS orchestras and The People's Music School New Music Ensemble, the contemporary music study and composition group that had been formed the prior October by Albert and Aubree and was now under the direction of Chicago composer Jenna Lyle. Following performances by the YOURS orchestras, students from the New Music Ensemble showcased their original compositions. The six students in the program then gave a world premiere performance of Jenna Lyle's *Spider Grass*, which had been written especially for the unique instruments of the group: violin, cello, two percussionists, and piano 4-hands.

Bob Fiedler was especially pleased to report at the May Board meeting that all on-site students had passed their end of semester final theory exams, the first time that had ever happened. In addition to a slightly longer school year and increased ensemble participation, Bob credited the school's continuing "up or out" model, now in effect for several years. Students who knew they could be replaced if they didn't meet sufficient improvement standards were clearly more motivated.

Late spring brought transition in the leadership of the YOURS nucleos. The new nucleo directors included: Carolyn Sybesma, Albany Park/Hibbard; Cara Sawyer, Logan Square; and Nicole Negrete, hired to aid in efforts to create a new nucleo in Evanston. In addition, Ben Bolter was hired as the artistic director of the YOURS Project, advising and coordinating all three programs, but especially aiding Carolyn at Hibbard School.

In early July, Natalie Butler was hired as the new director of The People's Music School Uptown Academy, the new name that had been given to the on-site program of The People's Music School. Her responsibilities included all the educational and program planning and activities at the West Eastwood location.

Natalie had taught in the Chicago Public Schools for over thirteen years, serving as a general music and band director at several schools, including the Walt Disney Magnet School and Bronzeville Scholastic Institute. She had worked closely with Chicago Arts Partnerships in Education (CAPE) on projects evaluating effective music teaching strategies, including the integration of technology into the music classroom. To become better acquainted with The People's Music School and the responsibilities she would need to assume, Natalie was able to send a few days working with Aubree Weiley before Aubree left for Boston.

The summer YOURS Project sessions proceeded well under the leadership of the new nucleo directors, who continued to receive comprehensive training from Albert Oppenheimer. On Friday, July 26, several ensembles from the summer YOURS orchestras performed in Millennium Park as part of the Grant Park Young Artists Showcase.

The school's focus on contemporary music and composition also continued in the summer, this time with students from the YOURS Project. As part of a final festival week of the YOURS summer session, composer Stephanie Ann Boyd was hired as composer-in-residence for a three-day workshop, during which she helped the students to explore and notate their musical ideas.

The children in the workshop collectively composed a piece titled "Eternal Golden Braid," and they were delighted when it was performed by the YOURS orchestra and recorded by Jason Carlock of Carlock Records during the final concert of the summer term on Wednesday, July 31. Several additional compositions were created by individual students in the workshop. One of them titled "Blue Cat" was performed by violin teacher Yonatan Grinberg at the concert.

The students were not the only ones who were delighted with the results of the workshop. "The three days I spent with The People's Music School YOURS Project were probably my favorite three days of the summer," commented Stephanie Ann Boyd.

CHAPTER 108

A Surprise Reunion in Utah

Rita and Tomás flew to Santo Domingo in mid-July of 2013 to visit brother Alfredo, who had been struggling with health problems. Near the end of her stay, Rita conducted a day of master classes at the Conservatorio Nacional, and she was delighted at the quality of playing and impressed with the high level of instruction the students were receiving. The teachers were delighted, too, when Rita's suggestions to the students reinforced many of their own recommendations to their pupils.

The fall 2013 registration was once again by lottery. Sign-ups for the lottery occurred on August 21 through noon August 23, and the drawing took place in the afternoon of August 23. As she had the year before, Rita Simó drew the names of the young people who would be invited to become students of The People's Music School Uptown Academy.

Since Rita's retirement as executive director of The People's Music School and Tomás' sale of his Spanish Speaking Bookstore, Rita and Tomás had taken a number of trips to areas they had not previously had the time to visit. Up until the fall of 2013, with the exception of Alaska, these trips had been to areas outside the United States, including Russia, Finland, Norway, Egypt, Argentina, Chile, Bolivia, and Brazil. Both felt it was now important to explore areas of the United States west of the Mississippi, and they made plans for an early September trip that would include visits to some of the beautiful U. S. national parks.

Rita's one worry was that she might have trouble with the altitude in some of the mountain areas. Once the trip was underway, however, she found that her concerns were groundless, and she was soon marveling at the great expanse and beauty of the country through which they passed. After exploring the Tetons and Yellowstone Park, Rita and Tomás traveled south through Salt Lake City to Bryce and Zion National Parks in southern Utah.

As they were standing outside the Zion National Park Visitor's Center, they were delighted to run into Chris Hodak, who had been employed at The People's Music School during the 1990s. Chris and her husband Larry were at the park to visit their daughter Eleanor, who was employed there as a park ranger. Rita was excited at the prospect of visiting with Eleanor, who had studied saxophone at The People's Music School and whom Rita had accompanied on several occasions.

"Where is Eleanor?" asked Rita. "I would love to visit with her."

Chris took Rita by the arm and ushered her into the Visitor's Center, where her daughter stood at the front counter. It would be hard to say who was more delighted at the unexpected meeting. Rita would love to have talked with Eleanor for a long time, but other visitors were entering the center, and teacher and student had to settle for a brief visit.

Several weeks later, back at The People's Music School, Rita shared her feeling of awe at the scenic beauty she had observed during the trip, but her most animated conversations were about the wonderful coincidence of reconnecting with Eleanor Hodak and her parents.

CHAPTER 109

A Memorable 35th Wedding Anniversary

Former students of The People's Music School were often writing letters or phoning Rita when they were in town. Now, with the growing popularity of Facebook, the school felt the need to have a presence on that online site. Facebook soon became a common point through which former students connected with the school.

On October 5, a posting came from former student Joaquin Ribon, now president of his own company in Florida, which expressed the sentiments of many: "I learned my first music notes on the piano 30 years ago at The People's Music School. Thanks, Rita. God Bless You!"

In mid-October 2013, Rita excitedly announced that she had just heard from another former student of The People's Music School, Alan Pierson, conductor since 2011 of the Brooklyn Philharmonic. Alan was scheduled to conduct the Northwestern University Contemporary Music Ensemble in Pick Staiger Concert Hall on Thursday, October 31, in a program including music by Schoenberg and John Adams.

After studying at TPMS, Alan had attended MIT and the Eastman School of Music. Founder of the contemporary music ensemble Alarm Will Sound, Alan had regularly collaborated with world-famous musicians including Dawn Upshaw, Yo Yo Ma, Osvaldo Golijov, and Steve Reich.

But he hadn't forgotten the teachers who had first instilled in him a love for music, and he remained deeply devoted to Rita and the school. He told Rita that he wanted to revisit the school while he was in town, and the date was set for Friday, November 1. His only playful request of her during their phone conversation was, "Just please don't ask me how much I have been practicing."

For Rita and Tomás, however, the most important date of the fall was October 21, the 35th anniversary of their wedding. That afternoon, Rita arrived at The People's Music School for a meeting more dressed up than usual. She and Tomás had tickets for Lyric Opera's *Otello* that evening, and Tomás had promised a special surprise dinner before the opera. The only puzzling thing to Rita was that he had told her to be sure to have a warm coat with her. While temperatures were cooler than they had been in recent weeks, they were still reasonably moderate for October.

When Tomás picked her up at the school, Rita noticed the big basket in the back seat from which delicious odors arose. Tomás proceeded to drive the two of them west from the school until they reached LaBagh Woods, the site of their wedding thirty-five years earlier. There, sitting in the gazebo-style shelter in the middle of the park, the two enjoyed their gourmet anniversary picnic, accompanied by a flood of memories.

CHAPTER 110

A Look to the Future:
Rebranding and Strategic Planning

Throughout the second half of 2013, Board and staff of The People's Music School were engaged in a major strategic planning process which addressed many facets of the school including mission, vision, and values clarification (Appendix VII); the setting of short and long term goals; and updated visual and naming elements for the school and its programs.

New, more ambitious development goals were established for both the operating fund and the reserves fund to aid the school in sustaining and further expanding its mission. To help with these goals, in November Randi Bergey was hired as the school's new director of development.

Randi arrived at The People's Music School with an impressive list of accomplishments. Her first career was as an elementary school teacher, following which she was a small business owner for six years. She then joined a larger retail company as a vice-president of sales and marketing. But she missed not being involved with her primary area of interest, education. For a number of years she worked in the area of alumni relations for several universities, including Kendall College, Northwestern University's Kellogg School of Management, and Marquette University.

Another of the Board's new goals was the establishment of a junior auxiliary of school supporters, and on October 24, a group of young professionals gathered at the Blackfin Ameripub to form a junior board for The People's Music School. During the evening, the group discussed ways in which they could help the school, and soon they began planning for their first benefit event, to take place the following spring.

A December 2014 newsletter officially announced the new names that the Board had created for the various programs under The People's Music School umbrella, as well as new identifying graphics for the school. The on-site school was now officially called The People's Music School Uptown Academy. The El Sistema orchestras as a group were now called The People's Music School Youth Orchestras. The advanced orchestra at Hibbard School continued to be called the YOURS orchestra.

The new logo that was unveiled depicted a treble clef sign with five beams fanning outward like the five lines of an ever-expanding musical score. When identified with the youth orchestras, the logo was a chartreuse green shade; when identified with the Uptown Academy, it was golden orange. The People's Music School in entirety was represented by a magenta logo.

The year ended on an exciting note when a feature story on the Hibbard School El Sistema orchestras was broadcast on the ABC, WLS-TV, "In Your Neighborhood" program. Amid the strains of Beethoven's *Egmont Overture*, performed by the students, journalist Karen Jordan spoke about the program and its effects not only on the students but also on their entire families.

Several students enthusiastically shared their thoughts and experiences with the orchestra, including violinists Mary Carmen Luna and Jonathan Alday. Parent Ana Solo spoke of the dedication of the teachers and of the joy exhibited by the children in the program, which "makes me want to participate and be a part of it."

CHAPTER 111

"I'll Never Forget That Green Color!"

The 38th anniversary of The People's Music School was celebrated on Thursday, February 20, 2014. An open house was held starting at noon that ran until 7:00 p.m. At several intervals, Rita led the group from the piano in rousing renditions of "Happy Birthday." Former students, teachers, and friends were encouraged to write birthday cards to the school and to include some of their special memories.

Christine Thompson, one of the people who had helped clean up the storefront beauty parlor in 1976 wrote: "Hard to believe it's been so many years -- seems like yesterday that the school first opened its doors. I remember painting the bathroom in the first school. I'll never forget that green color!"

In late February, five students from the Albany Park and Logan Square orchestras were among twenty-six young musicians invited to Los Angeles to take part in the "Take A Stand" symposium sponsored by the Los Angeles Philharmonic in cooperation with Bard College and its Longy School of Music. Over 400 musicians and social change advocates from all over the world gathered for the three-day symposium, which took place from February 20 through 22. Students traveling from Chicago included Adeline Alday, Alejandro Luna, and Karina Pinduisaca from Albany Park and Frank Alverez and Luis Mendez from Logan Square.

In addition to participating in some of the interactive teaching workshops at the symposium, they joined together in performance with members of the Simón Bolivar Symphony Orchestra. The Venezuelan orchestra had changed its name from Simón Bolivar Youth Orchestra a few years earlier, as some of its members had now passed the initial age span of eighteen to twenty-eight years.

In the April newsletter of TPMS, it was announced that Costa Rican violinist Andrea Benavides would be welcomed in the fall of 2014 as the second student to receive the Rita Simó scholarship at North Park

University. Though this would be the fourth year of the scholarship program, Andrea was the second recipient, as Francisco Malespin had been selected the recipient during the three previous years. In her home country, Andrea had been active with SiNEM, a music program for socially at-risk youth, and she looked forward to sharing her experiences with the YOURS Project students as well as learning new skills to take back with her to share with the people at SiNEM.

Also in late April, after a few initial setbacks, discussions were continuing with representatives from Evanston regarding the start of an Evanston El Sistema nucleo. Tentative funding had been arranged, and details of location and how students would be chosen for the program were being explored.

Just as the small seed that had been planted in the converted beauty shop in Uptown in 1976 had grown into a program which by now had brought music and expanded horizons to many thousands, so also the inspired vision of José Abreu, and the program he founded one year earlier in Venezuela had developed into a worldwide movement which was reaching a constantly expanding circle of young people with the gift of music and the hope for a better future.

EPILOGUE

And the Music Plays On

It is three o'clock on a Thursday afternoon in early May of 2014. Rita Simó is seated in the library of The People's Music School as she has been many times over the previous two and a half years, looking over notes and photographs, recalling events, and chuckling over certain memories. She knows an end must come to these scheduled sessions of reflection and "the project" must move into its final stage. In a few months, she will celebrate her 80 th birthday.

For many years, Rita has shared stories of her life with friends: humorous stories, poignant stories, stories of dreaming, stories of frustration, stories of celebration. When she was first approached with the idea of collecting these stories into a longer narrative of her life and the history of The People's Music School, she quickly dismissed the idea as unimportant.

"Why would anyone want to read about all of that?"

Most of the time Rita is right, but this time she was wrong. Her story is important. It is important for all of those who have ever worked with her, studied with her, and dreamed with her. And it is important for others who are dreaming and will dream in the future but are told their dreams are impossible.

The realization of Rita's dreams of a free music school are all around her, in the sights, the sounds, and even the smells, the smells that go with any building housing musical instruments.

People have often spoken to Rita about "her school." She is very quick to correct them. "It is not my school," she always replies. "It is the PEOPLE's school. It wouldn't exist without the dedication of all the people who have worked with me and made it possible."

She emphatically states that conviction once again. But then she hesitates, and appears to be in a reflective mood. Suddenly, she looks up with a wistful gleam in her eyes.

"On the other hand, the kids. They will always be my kids."

4417 N. SHERIDAN ROAD

4750 N. SHERIDAN ROAD

931 W. EASTWOOD

Rita Simo: List of Awards

February 1990	Chicago Tribune, Chicago's Most Beautiful Women
March 31, 1990	Boulevard Arts Center, President's Award
June 17, 1990	National Association of Music Merchants Award
July 1990	Helene Curtis, "People Who Make A Difference Award"
October 1991	Nordstrom Community Service Award
December 1991	Sidney R. Yates Arts Advocacy for the Arts Award, Illinois Arts Alliance
March 1992	City Brightener Award, Bright New City Committee
May 1992	Lake View Musical Society Award
April 1993	Dean's Arts & Humanitarian Services Award, Boston University, Boston, Massachusetts
May 3, 1993	Honorary Doctor of Humane Letters, Rosary College
June 1993	Sculpture Chicago's: 100 Women, Culture in Action
June 2, 1994	Honorary Doctor of Arts, Columbia College, Chicago
August 1994	Mercedes Benz Mentor Award
February 1995	Women in Philanthropy Award, Chicago Women in Philanthropy (CWIP) and Marshall Field & Company
June 4, 1995	Distinguished Achievement Award, The Longy School of Music, Bard College, Cambridge, Massachusetts
June 27, 1995	Athena Award, Uptown Chamber of Commerce
June 1996	100 Big Hearts for Young Heroes, La Rabida Hospital
September 1996	Chicago Latina Community Leader Award, American Friends Service Committee
May 10, 1997	Special Citation, The Friends of Literature
Sept. 24, 1997	Honorary Doctor of Humane Letters, St. Olaf College, Minnesota
April 25, 1998	Thomas Jefferson Award for Public Service, presented through the committee's local sponsor, NBC WMAQ-TV.
November 1998	Sor Juan Inés Medal, Mexican Fine Arts Center Museum
October 12, 2000	Outstanding Achievement in the Arts, Chicago YWCA
May 2001	Founder's Award, Lathrop Community Music Center
June 2001	Queen of Hearts of the Arts Award, Boulevard Arts Center
Summer 2001	Senior Citizen of the Year Award, Chicago Park District
September 2001	Hija Meritoria, San Francisco de Marcorís, Dominican Repub.
December 2001	Special Lifetime Achievement Award, Uptown Chicago Comm.
January 2002	2001 Chicagoan of the Year, New Centurians, Chicago Magazine
October 2002	Woman of Faith Award, Sisters of the Divine Savior, Milwaukee WI
November 2004	Neighborhood Excellence Initiative, Local Hero, Bank of America
April 19, 2005	Montblanc de la Culture Arts Patronage Award
May 12, 2006	Excellence Award, Dominican American Midwest Association
October 7, 2006	Performing Arts Award, Dominican American Natnl. Roundtable
Nov. 19, 2006	Musical Visionary Award, Continental Community Center
December 2007	Certificate of Appreciation, Jane Addams Senior Center
September 2008	Gem of Uptown Award, Uptown United and Business Partners
October 2010	Cook County Award of Excellence
Nov. 20, 2011	Latina of the Year Award, Chicago Int'l. Latino Cultural Center

APPENDIX

I

Boston Supporters of The People's Music School from its inception through many years:

Carole Bohn and husband, Robert Furman
John Corcoran
Richard Griffin and wife, Susan Keane
Margaret (Peggy) Hutaff
Ann Kelley
Laura LeBreton
Molly Lovelock
Diane Mahaney
Robert O'Shea
Robert Tipps
Alice Sapienze

II

Richard Young

Speech at the Groundbreaking at 931 W. Eastwood
September 30, 1993

All parents dream that their children may one day realize their full potential. As difficult as this is for *any* child to achieve, it is particularly hard for those kids who happen to have been born into less advantaged circumstances. America may be the country of greatest opportunity, where talent and hard work are most richly rewarded. But this is not yet the land of *equal* opportunity, where talent and hard work are always *equally* rewarded. This is not fair, especially to those children who must regularly face obstacles that other kids may never face in an entire lifetime. Conscience dictates that we find ways to help, so that *all* our children have a better chance of realizing their full potential.

The People's Music School does a remarkable job helping so many from this neighborhood. And there is simply no doubt that Rita Sino personifies the very highest standards of music education. But let's be frank: the People's Music School is not going to *remove* a single one of the obstacles that seriously jeopardize the futures of too many young people. But it can illuminate a path *around* some of these obstacles. It does so not just by offering free music lessons, but by stressing discipline and initiative, by encouraging excellence, and by demanding responsibility. It tells these young people that no one can ever expect you to do better than your best -- but that one should never be satisfied with any *less* than one's best.

I'm so grateful to all the outstanding professional musicians who have conducted master classes at the People's Music School. What is it that so strongly motivates them to work with these students? Certainly it's not money, for there is none for these master classes. Perhaps it's because each of us remembers someone special from *our* past -- someone who gave *us* an extraordinary amount of help and encouragement, someone to whom it was so important that we did our best. It's too late for us to thank many of these people. But it's not too late to do the next best thing: to pass along the favor to someone else -- to help *these* deserving students as we were helped when *we* were students.

There's another factor that explains the motivation of many of these professional musicians, though I suspect they may not fully appreciate its significance until the moment they are standing in front of the students. It relates to something President Clinton said in his inaugural address. He said, *"But for fate, we, the fortunate and the unfortunate, could have been each other."*

When I first told the students about the master classes, I said that the professional musicians coming here to work with them included some of the very best in the world. These are individuals who are often paid a lot of money to do what they do. But as generous as they may be, no one should assume that they are coming here for nothing. But there's no government program or private foundation underwriting these master classes. So who's going to pay? Since it's the students who directly benefit, it's only fair that *they* should pay. You can imagine the worried looks on the faces around me. Many were thinking, "how can I possibly pay?" But then I reminded them that it's sometimes possible to "pay" for things in other ways than with money. In this case, they must promise to do something similar for someone else one day. It may not be in the music field, for many of these students will successfully enter other professions. It might not be for ten or twenty years, and it might even take half a century. But when that day comes that each one of these students is finally in a position to pass along something of value to others, that's the day these master classes will be paid for.

I'm very comfortable with this arrangement. It's fair. Nobody is giving or getting something for nothing. Moreover it illustrates what America *can* be about. It's an arrangement that binds us all together with bonds of mutually-shared responsibility. Today, we are directly helping *these* children who attend the People's Music School. But in so doing, we are indirectly benefiting many others as well -- including, perhaps, our *own* children's children.

III

Nick Rabkin

(Excerpts from a column in *The Chicago Tribune* a few weeks after the groundbreaking for The People's Music School's new building, 1993)

Almost 200 years ago the leaders of the French Revolution transformed the king's palace into the world's first public art museum, the Louvre. After the storming of the Bastille, the Louvre is one of the outstanding symbols of French democracy. Its message was that the greatest creative achievements belonged to the king no more. They belonged to everyone.

Not many years later, great composers began to write music that was animated by the same impulses; music that carried the aspirations of freedom and democracy in its harmonies, colors and rhythms. Some of these composers found their inspiration in the lovely and haunting folk melodies of the people whose dreams of freedom were driving the movements for democracy across Europe. Their symphonic work, in turn, inspired those "folk" and kept their hopes alive.

Art has a profound relationship to democracy. Unfortunately it is too often associated with the privilege and wealth that so often divides our own imperfect democracy. Unfortunately, also, the arts system in this country has tended to see art as an object or product-a painting or sculpture, a sonata or performance. We tend to forget that art is also a relationship between artist and audience and a process that develops people's capacities to be creative. Art is humanity's historic pathway to creativity, the essential capacity that people have to understand things as they are and have been, and to imagine how they might be. Our material and social progress has been built upon that foundation. This is art's most profound but often attenuated contribution to democratic society.

Today in Chicago there are efforts underway that reflect the best of the relationship of the arts to democracy. A few weeks ago I attended a groundbreaking for a new home for The People's Music School, a community-based institution serving youngsters and adults in Uptown, one of the city's poorer neighborhoods, without charge. The People's Music School honors the profound democratic challenge of the arts by making music the possession of all, even the dispossessed. And it recognizes that the deepest value of music is in its making, a magical process that exercises and grows human creativity. The People's Music School has been true to these principles without great recognition or financial reward from arts patrons or critics.

It does not matter whether its students go on to careers in music, though the school has developed some prodigious talent. What does matter is that its students believe that they have the capacity to be creative, productive contributors to our society, and that despite all the obstacles they can grow that capacity. Music has taught them that.

Richard Young

Speech at the Inauguration of the New Building
931 W. Eastwood
November 1, 1995

The legendary violinist Jascha Heifetz once said, "There is no such thing as perfection. For once you attain a *certain standard*, only then do you realize that *it's just not good enough*."

We stood at this very spot a little more than two years ago for the groundbreaking ceremony. Though we couldn't allow our expectations to swell beyond modest proportions, we were brimming with confidence and pride as that first shovel-full of earth provided tangible proof that these expectations were about to be fulfilled. Having overcome so many obstacles, having accomplished more than even the most faithful could ever have reasonably prayed for, we celebrated our "work-in-progress" in a true spirit of community. But today, as we savor this remarkable achievement, we're faced with the sobering realization that there's still so much more to be done.

The fact is, this is a *beginning* - an uplifting beginning, a newsworthy beginning - but a beginning nonetheless. It is not a culmination, but rather an important commencement. Yet if this were a race, we wouldn't be content just to have made it to the starting line. In science, revolutionary advances can be immediately rendered obsolete as these very breakthroughs illuminate new and better solutions. Only after learning the answers to today's most challenging questions can one comprehend which questions to ask tomorrow. Perfection may be unattainable, but we move one step closer each time we recognize that our previous steps haven't yet brought us as close as possible.

Right now it is so tempting to revel in a spirit of lofty idealism and altruism, and to view this new building as an inspiring symbolic monument at the end of a long road. But not even the most compelling musicians are able to sustain inspiration indefinitely. Idealism is so easily overshadowed by reality, and the resonance of our heartfelt words will inevitably be reduced to a faint muted *pianissimo*. Therefore, we cannot afford to get too comfortable just yet.

We can point with pride to this fabulous facility, to an extraordinary director and a talented faculty, to a resourceful Board and a dedicated administrative staff, to a group of students of almost unlimited vitality and potential, to a direct connection with dozens of the best professional musicians in Chicago, to a program of master classes that is about as good as you will find anywhere in the world, and to a current level of public and private support that is overwhelming. But in order to fulfill its potential and remain an indispensable community asset, this school must always be the very best music school that it can be. And this is possible only so long as it continues to elevate, in Heifetz' words, it's *"certain standard."*

Provocative rhetoric can create the sparks that may eventually ignite glorious bonfires of achievement. But more important is how we back up our passionate words, how we give form to concept, how we deal with the dauntingly difficult daily nitty-gritty roll-up-your-sleeves kind of work that is necessary to help students like those at The People's Music School become better musicians. Slick rhetoric does not improve anyone's intonation. Idealism is powerless in developing better rhythm. Altruism is irrelevant when it comes to scales, arpeggios, etudes, vibrato, staccato, legato, rubato, or to Bach's cantatas, Mozart's operas, or Beethoven's late string quartets.

Here we have a *music school.* not just an inspiring symbol. What's offered here is neither recreation nor public assistance, nor some kind of elaborate daycare provided to the soothing background accompaniment of classical music. Though it can pay long-term *practical* dividends that reach far beyond the parameters of the performing arts, its primary mission is to concentrate now on bestowing the gift of music as effectively, as conscientiously, as indelibly, and as movingly as possible. In so doing, it instills discipline, it fosters initiative, it demands responsibility, it encourages excellence, all important tools for young development. But ultimately these qualities are simply by-products which result from focusing on musical excellence.

Let's enjoy today. We have earned it. Let us express our heartfelt gratitude to all those who helped make this dream a reality. But let's also heed the words of Jascha Heifetz. Let's be reminded that it is just not good enough to measure this day's remarkable achievement by yesterday's more modest expectations. It is just not good enough to assume that today's idealism will automatically solve tomorrow's problems. It is just not good enough to presume that the overwhelmingly generous support from the past will be sufficient to handle the daunting responsibilities of the future. It is just not good enough to be content with our progress so far, however remarkable that progress has been.

For only now, having attained this *certain standard* are we finally in a position to appreciate just how much more is possible and necessary. As long as The People's Music School remains committed to it's lofty ideals, but also continues to find ways to transform them into tangible results, it will succeed.

V

"Listen to the Children"
(from the operetta *Friends Without Words*)

Words and Music by Hugo Teruel

Listen to the children
And maybe tomorrow there won't be any more sorrow
In a land of peace, in a land of harmony and love.

Listen to us calling
On all our sisters and all our brothers
To stop the hate and change the fate of the world.

Come on everybody,
Come on everyone and lift your voices high
So we will never cry again.

Look into the children's eyes.
There's a song in us; it's trying to come out
And tell the people of a dream we had long ago.

Listen to the silent child.
Let's stand together; the future brings a new morning.
The birds will sing, the bells will ring, everywhere.

Come on everybody,
Come on everyone and lift your voices high
So we will never cry again.

There's still hope
If you want it, grab that note
And a melody will come right out. Just let it out.

Come on everybody,
Come on everyone and lift your voices high
So we can touch the sky.

Come on everybody,
Come on everyone and lift your voices high
So we will never cry again.

Listen to the Children

Words and music
by Hugo Teruel

(First of nine pages)

YOURS

VI

Explanation and History of El Sistema

Music has been proven to be an effective way to empower and transform children in at-risk environments. Given this understanding, the El Sistema method of music instruction was begun in the mid-1970s by José Antonio Abreu in Venezuela as a way of enriching the lives of children from poor neighborhoods through the creation of youth orchestras, or "orquestra escuelas." The amazing success of these orchestras in redirecting the lives of young people has come to the attention of music educators around the world, and the "El Sistema method" has become an inspiration for many musicians working with young people in low-income areas.

Unlike traditional music training, El Sistema begins not with the education of the individual but rather with the musical community, namely the orchestra. Individual music instruction follows later as students develop the desire to perfect their performance techniques. From the beginning, young people make music together, often in sections. In this way, they bond with each other through their common effort. Successes are always communal, as well as individual. In the process, cooperation and trust occur, qualities which then regularly transfer into other areas of life.

Students in El Sistema programs develop such a strong sense of commitment to one another that they voluntarily help others to "catch up." Peer teaching is central to El Sistema and benefits both parties. It is presumed that most students at some time in their experience will become a teacher. This responsibility is both encouraged and appreciated. It gives students self-confidence and makes them sensitive to the fact that they are part of something bigger than themselves.

Concerts of El Sistema youth orchestras may not follow traditionally expected models of protocol. They may involve impromptu choreography as students playfully change stands mid-concert, or perhaps the enthusiastic and spontaneous cheering of orchestra members for a fellow student who has just successfully navigated a difficult passage in the music. The goal is solidarity and optimum music-making, not traditional decorum.

As of 2014, there were approximately sixty El Sistema-inspired programs in the United States, and many, many others throughout the world. The numbers have been growing every year.

Each El Sistema location is called a "nucleo." Its name suggests a safe haven, a supportive environment full of joy and friendship, where students are encouraged to explore their potential. The nucleo functions as a second family. Indeed, it has become a first family for many young people who have had poor or no experience with "family."

THE PEOPLE'S MUSIC SCHOOL
May 2014

Administrative Staff

Bob Fiedler, Executive Director
Lilly Torres, Operations Manager
Natalie Butler, Uptown Academy Director
Randi Bergey, Director of Development
Renee Davis, Development Manager
Albert Oppenheimer, Youth Orchestras Director
Nicole Negrete, Program Director, Evanston
Cara Sawyer, Program Director, Logan Square
Carolyn Sybesma, Program Director, Albany Park
Juan Rivera, Building Maintenance

Board of Directors

Chris Hennessy, President
Mark Rhein, Vice President
Virginia Willcox, Secretary
Kate Evert, Treasurer
Rita Simó, Founder
Ellen Ahern
Steve Cooley
Erin Delaney
Joel Derstine
Tom Hebert
Barbara Jurgens
John Kiely
Jack Lowey
Sean Parnell
Amy Sheren

Uptown Academy Faculty

Anna Carlson, violin, viola
Stephane Collopy violin, viola
    and Junior String Ensemble
Julia Coronelli, harp
James Davis, trumpet
Greg Fundis, theory, percussion
Terrance Gray, violin
Anne Katzley, voice, theory
Yuem Kim, piano
Rebecca Kuo, cello
Jesse Langen, guitar, theory
    and saxophone
Monica Laytham, voice
Dominique Louis, jazz and
    percussion
Jaime McCool, piano
Ben McMunn, guitar
Melissa Morales, clarinet
Mio Nakamura, piano
Chris Neal, voice, theory
Scott Scharf, guitar, theory
Valerie Simosko, flute
Silvia Suarez, violin, viola
Steve Vázquez, guitar

Advisory Committee

Assir DaSilva, Retired, Exelon Corporation
Jan Feldman, Attorney, Perkins Coie LLC
Jeff Kelly, Partner, IBM Business Services
Ann Murray, Executive Director, International Music Foundation
Mary O'Connell, Mary O'Connell Communications

VII

The People's Music School
Vision, Mission, and Values Statements
2014

VISION

The People's Music School envisions a society where
all children have access to quality music education.
We believe music is transformative and empowers
the lives of youth, families, and communities.

MISSION

Our mission is to cultivate access to free, quality music
education. Through intensive instruction and
performance our students learn more than music.
They grow socially, emotionally, and intellectually,
and develop a foundation of responsibility, self-esteem
and purpose.

VALUES

Community: Parents, students, instructors, and
supporters work together creatively and harmoniously.

Hard Work: Discipline and focus guild each student's
path to achievement.

Passion and Joy: We nurture learning in a joyful
environment where music sparks motivation.

Opportunity: Music education is a key to
understanding one's potential.

ABOUT THE AUTHOR

A former New Trier High School English teacher, newspaper publishing company executive, and piano teacher, Cynthia Willis Pinkerton became acquainted with Rita Simó in the late 1980s when they collaborated in connection with visits by students of The People's Music School to concerts at the Ravinia Festival. This led to a special friendship and to the author's recruitment of a group of fellow musicians to help organize and document items in the library of the school's new building on W. Eastwood. One thing the library did not contain was a history of the school and its inspiring leader, an omission which needed to be corrected.

ACKNOWLEDGMENTS

Many individuals have played a major role in the life of Rita Simó and in the success of The People's Music School, and many of them have been of great help to me in the creation of this history. While it is impossible to name them all, I would like to give special thanks to Bob Fiedler, Paul Gates, Chris Hodak, Ann Kelley, Nalini Kotamraju, Ann Murray, Albert Oppenheimer, Lily Owyang, Bonny Rhodes, Lilly Torres, and Richard Young. Charles Lewis, a former student of the school, also deserves recognition as the photographer of many of the photos in this book. Most of all, I thank Rita's husband, Tomás Bissonnette, for providing photographs, helpful information, and encouragement.

A special thanks also to my husband and three sons whose interest and assistance with the project helped move it forward.

Cynthia Willis Pinkerton

Further notes

In writing this biography, circumstances put me in touch with some whose lives have been closely entwined with The People's Music School but not others who may have been equally involved. To those individuals whose names and stories should have been included or more completely told in this narrative, my apology. I encourage you to send your "Rita stories," by either email or postal mail, to The People's Music School.

This biography includes a large number of detailed facts about programs and events at The People's Music School. After wrestling with the problem of how many to include, I have decided to err on the side of inclusion, feeling that details uninteresting to some may bring to mind pleasurable or even inspiring moments for others as they relive their experiences with Rita and The People's Music School and picture themselves attending or involved in a particular performance or event. It is my sincere hope that many of the readers of this book will enjoy reliving their unique part of the history of The People's Music School.

CWP

Made in the USA
Lexington, KY
13 September 2014